Praise for W. Thomas Boyce's

The Orchid and the Dandelion

"[Boyce is] a wonderfully fine writer. His humanity and warmth inform his evidence-based insights, and his clear strong prose and poetic sensitivity make his stories compelling. . . . Our roles as adults are to understand keenly the nature of each child, and then to do our best to provide the nurturing responses they need along the way."

—*Psychology Today*

"Boyce's stellar research . . . will help parents and professionals develop greater sensitivity to the needs of orchid kids who are biologically challenged but surprisingly have much higher potential. A must-read for all parents, teachers, and psychologists."

—John M. Gottman, PhD, *New York Times* bestselling author of *Raising an Emotionally Intelligent Child*

"This book fills an important need. Tom Boyce's elegantly simple characterization of dandelion and orchid children belies the complexity and rigor of the research that informs it. His book shows parents why the same conditions that may be good for one of their children will not be best for the other."

—Nancy Adler, professor of psychiatry and medical psychology, University of California, San Francisco

"Tom Boyce is the foremost scholar in the world in the area of child growth and development. I have no doubt that his book will have a profound impact on readers everywhere."   —S. Leonard Syme, professor emeritus of epidemiology and community health, School of Public Health, University of California

W. Thomas Boyce, M.D.

The Orchid and the Dandelion

W. Thomas Boyce, MD, is the Lisa and John Pritzker Distinguished Professor of Developmental and Behavioral Health and chief of the division of Developmental Medicine at the University of California, San Francisco. He is also a member of the National Academy of Medicine and codirector of the Child & Brain Development program of the Canadian Institute for Advanced Research. He lives with his wife in Oakland, California.

The Orchid and the Dandelion

The Orchid
and the Dandelion

*Why Sensitive Children Face Challenges
and How All Can Thrive*

W. Thomas Boyce, M.D.

Vintage Books
A Division of Penguin Random House LLC
New York

The Library of Congress has cataloged the Knopf edition as follows:
Name: Boyce, W. Thomas, author.
Title: The orchid and the dandelion : why some children struggle and how all can thrive / W. Thomas Boyce MD.
Description: New York : Alfred A. Knopf, 2019. |
Includes bibliographical references and index.
Identifiers: LCCN 2017060895 (print) | LCCN 2018011333 (ebook)
Subjects: LCSH: Parenting. | Developmental psychology. | Child development. | BISAC: PSYCHOLOGY / Developmental / Child. | FAMILY & RELATIONSHIPS / Parenting / General.
Classification: LCC HQ755.8 (ebook) | LCC HQ755.8 .B694 2019 (print) | DDC 649/.1—dc23
LC record available at https://lccn.loc.gov/2017060895

Vintage Books Trade Paperback ISBN: 978-1-101-97021-8
eBook ISBN: 978-1-101-94657-2

For Jill, Andrew, and Amy

Contents

Introductory Note by Robert Coles

The following stories by a physician who aims to render the lives, the ups and downs, of his young patients summoned to my mind memories of my times spent as a medical student with the physician and writer William Carlos Williams. Dr. Williams often made home visits, and in so doing got to know where and how the children he met lived, spent their time, and, yes, pondered life's challenges, opportunities, travails. So it is with Dr. Boyce, who lets us lucky readers meet and learn about the lives of the youngsters he considers, treats as a physician, and then enables us also to do so. "Only connect," said the writer E. M. Forster, and in this volume we do—we find ourselves contemplating how it goes for a wide range of youngsters as they confront life's hurdles, and in so doing tell us through their doctor's knowing eyes, ears, mind, and heart so very much about human suffering, but also about the grit, and valor, and effort at endurance that so many assert, even as children, and beyond.

Robert Coles
Concord, Massachusetts
2017

Foreword by T. Berry Brazelton

This is an impressive and important book—a collection of ideas and research—that reveals the profound prenatal and perinatal factors that affect an infant's and child's later development. Dr. Boyce identifies a special group of children—"orchids"—who are outliers among groups of more typically developing children, or "dandelions." Orchid children are uniquely fragile, needing special nurturing to achieve their best. Dandelions are more rugged and likely to overcome any difficulty, but are often average or ordinary in outcomes.

Dr. Boyce outlines an argument and backs it up with convincing research showing that children vary greatly in their development due to the unique interactions between their genes and environments. These interactions start in utero, for the fetus is already influenced by stressors, nutrition, and the mother's emotions before birth. The mother and unborn child strive to adapt to these influences, as if preparing to deal with the same conditions after birth. Thus a fetus whose mother is under stress, eating poorly, or depressed before birth can become a newborn with high levels of stress hormones, excessive vigilance, and a diminished ability to attend easily to learning. On the other hand, babies whose mothers are not stressed or depressed, are looking forward to delivery, and are eating and sleeping well are exceptionally ready to learn, engage in effective relationships, and optimally develop. These infants will be better able to learn self-regulation (by, for example, sucking on a thumb or fingers to calm themselves down from an upset). A mother who immediately starts nurturing, holding, stroking, cuddling, nursing, and talking softly to her baby will pass on the ultimate ingredients for healthy, positive development.

These events become reflected in the baby's epigenome, leading, Boyce shows, to the eventual emergence of orchid or dandelion babies. All parents need to be given a chance to understand their babies' temperaments and individual differences right from the start. To facilitate this understanding, a pediatrician, neonatologist, or nurse practitioner can translate the baby's capacities and teach parents how a baby's behavior can serve as a useful language, helping them to become responsive and optimal parents. Such an understanding of the child and his or her behavior can magnify the caring and sensitivity of all parents.

I have been concerned in my own practice of pediatrics in Cambridge, Massachusetts, about loving parents who attempt to protect their infants and children from all stress of any kind. It is important for infants and children to develop early their own ways of handling stress and difficulty. Such self-regulating mechanisms must be acquired and practiced throughout early childhood, by both orchid and dandelion children, so that they are ready to cope with the adversity all children must eventually face.

This is a book that I hope all parents and professionals (doctors, nurses, early childhood specialists, teachers, and others) will read in order to help them understand how different children, like orchids and dandelions, develop and grow. It will add to their understanding of how best to nurture each child, especially those who most challenge conventional approaches to treating, teaching, and caring for children.

T. Berry Brazelton, MD
Barnstable, Massachusetts
2017

Introduction

What if the children about whom we worry most were actually those with the greatest promise? What if those youth whose lives are marked by turmoil and difficulty were plausibly heirs to the brightest, most creative futures? What if seemingly blighted and troubled childhoods could give way, under conditions of encouragement and support, to adulthoods bearing not simply normal lives and passable achievement, but deep, rich relationships and inspired accomplishment? What if even the very real burdens of a child's uncommon fragility could be reshaped, under responsive conditions, into the tangible advantages of human resilience? What if, in short, the apparent frailties and disarray of some young lives were redeemable—through the alchemy of nurturing families or communities and transformative care?

This book is the story of just such a surprising redemption. It is a narrative mined from a body of child development research and from a near lifetime of careful watching—by a once-young pediatrician who became, by blessing and luck, a father, a grandfather, and, in the end, a grizzled and well-marinated counselor of children and families. The story, at once scientific and personal, is offered as a gift of encouragement and hope for all those who teach, protect, care for, raise, or worry over children, as well as those who have struggled since childhood to understand the origin of their own affliction with human differences. If your life resembles my own to any degree, you have fretted incessantly over your children's well-being and future and have long pondered how their strivings and trials may stem in some manner from your own. You have likely thrilled at their triumphs and masteries, lived for their affections, taken pride in their accomplishments, and brooded over their troubles and sorrows.

When our daughter-in-law was pregnant with our first grandchild, my wife, Jill, and I were awakened one night out of the deepest of sleep by the sudden intrusive ringing of the bedside telephone and a call from our son, three thousand miles away in Brooklyn, New York. His young wife, nearing the end of her second trimester, had been unable to sleep because of a recurring sharp pain in her flank and pelvis. It hurt badly, and they were both alarmed, especially as rank novices in the business of babies and pregnancies.

Struggling to shake off sleep, Jill (a nurse) and I took a foggy but reasonably careful medical history of this pain, trying to discern with more precision its location, character, and possible cause. Chief among our tacit but mutual concerns was the fear that the pain signaled an early onset of labor and the possibility of a premature, thirty-two-week delivery, with all the attendant hazards to mother and child. As we heard about the pain in more detail, however, we became reasonably confident that it was a muscle strain, probably stemming from a tiny woman, with a belly of unaccustomed dimensions, turning too abruptly in bed. We reassured the young couple that the pain would likely go away on its own and that a heating pad and bed rest would hasten its resolution.

After we finished the call, I turned to Jill and exhaustedly remarked that, as truly wonderful as it had been for our children to have found their mates and launched their own families, it had the unforeseen effect of doubling the number of people over whom to worry and ruminate. Though we had intermittently fussed and stewed for nearly thirty years about the complexities of our own two children's ailments and scrapes, we now had three more—a daughter-in-law, a son-in-law, and a thirty-two-week-old grand-fetus—over whom we were also obliged to fret! Happily so, but still worried.

But these were largely mundane, relatively unremarkable concerns— the kind that are the normative land mines of ordinary parenthood: the two-year-old who lacerates her lip in a fall while trying to pee in the sink; the five-year-old who feels lonely and bereft in his kindergarten class-room; the middle schooler who misplaces, within a single year, five jack-ets and four book locker padlocks; the twelve-year-old who is bullied by "friends" who repeatedly force him into a trash can; the fifteen-year-old who issues open invitations for parties at her out-of-town parents' home, to their lasting annoyance and dismay. These are the banal offenses that nearly all parents have encountered, in one form and time or another, in the raising of their children. While sometimes laughable in retrospect, they are capable of generating in the moment itself considerable chagrin and distress.

But the pain of a parent whose son or daughter has gone seriously adrift—into drug abuse, delinquency, depression, or allegiances to de-structive friendships—is anxiety of an entirely different order. Watching as a child strays perilously off course and begins to sustain the feared, often indelible consequences of departure from a healthy life is the kind of parental apprehension that is almost physically sensed. It is the "pit in the stomach," the panicked, slightly nauseous desperation and dread that disallows sleep, becomes a preoccupation at work, and can erode even the strongest of marriages through miscommunication, acrimony, and disappointment. Watching a child slip away into the dark territory of serious psychological troubles, addiction, school failure, or criminality is an agony almost beyond description. Though never having sustained this level of worry as a parent, I have had a direct and indelibly memora-ble encounter with such anguish throughout much of my life—because of my sister, about whom more is to follow.

Among the most fervent ambitions of this book is to offer solace and hope to just such anguished "families": to the parents, teachers, siblings, and others who have lost their confidence in the retrievable promise of a child or children; and to those whose belief in a child's inherent goodness and potential has been shaken. For in the story of the figure of speech from which this book draws its enigmatic title—the metaphor of orchid and dandelion—lies a deep and often helpful truth about the origins of affliction and the redemption of individual lives. Most children—in our families, classrooms, or communities—are more or less like dande-lions; they prosper and thrive almost anywhere they are planted. Like dandelions, these are the majority of children whose well-being is all but assured by their constitutional hardiness and strength. There are others, however, who, more like orchids, can wither and fade when unattended by caring support, but who—also like orchids—can become creatures of rare beauty, complexity, and elegance when met with compassion and kindness.

While a conventional but arguably deficient wisdom has held that children are either "vulnerable" or "resilient" to the trials that the world presents them, what our research and that of others has increasingly revealed is that the vulnerability/resilience contrast is a false (or at least misleading) dualism. It is a flawed dichotomy that attributes weakness or strength—frailty or vigor—to individual subgroups of youth and obscures a deeper reality that children simply differ, like orchids and dandelions, in their susceptibilities and sensitivities to the conditions of life that surround and sustain them. Most of our children can, like dandelions, thrive in all but the harshest, most bestial circumstances, but a minority of others, like orchids, either blossom beautifully or wane disappointingly, depending upon how we tend and spare and care for them. This is the redemptive secret the story herein reveals: that those orchid children who founder and fail can as easily become those who enliven and thrive in singular ways.

But there are other reasons why you, as a reader, might want to explore the scientific story that this book tells. Perhaps you are a parent grappling with the disappointing realization that "one size does not fit all" in your efforts to parent effectively your remarkably diverse brood of kids. Maybe you have a child who is severely struggling in school or in life, despite your best intuition that he or she is a remarkable and promising young person. It might instead be that you are a schoolteacher groping for a better way to understand the disorienting menagerie of children you are charged with teaching (and managing!). Or perhaps you are yourself one for whom the metaphor of orchid and dandelion captures a personal reality you have always sensed but never spoken or understood.

In the coming pages, I will convey scientific findings and actionable advice relevant not just to the lives of orchids, but to dandelions as well. While less at risk than orchids, dandelions have their own unique set of physiological and psychological traits, and understanding these can impart greater measures of awareness, success, and contentment. And dandelions themselves still face the cruel vagaries of circumstance and chance. As we know from observing plants in nature, no matter how hearty or resistant a species may be, all are capable of withering at any point in their life span. So although this book takes as its point of departure the susceptibilities of children to their socioemotional worlds, our origins and sensibilities continue to shape us all the way into midlife and old age. This makes of human beings a not invulnerable species, but one with powerful, recurring opportunities for reclamation and renewal.

In the chapters ahead, it is my modest but serious intention to offer useful knowledge and assistance to a diverse spectrum of readers. We will explore the *early origins* of research relating stress and adversity to child development and mental health. We will see, in a frank admission of the sometimes accidental and serendipitous character of scientific discovery, how the first glimpses of powerful differences in neurobiological sensitivity to social contexts came about. I will describe what is known of the *developmental origins* of orchids and dandelions, why no two children are ever raised in the very same family, and how the field of *epigenetics* is revolutionizing our understanding of gene-environment cooperation in determining who we are and will become. I will summarize the evidence to date for all the ways in which differences between human orchids and dandelions are played out in the preservation of health and the genesis of chronic disease, in developmental attainments and educational achievements, and in positive responses to preventive interventions. I will consider what is known about loving, sustaining, and encouraging an orchid—whether your child, your student, your patient, or even yourself—and how the splendid potential of a human orchid can be unleashed in the social environments we devise and create. For orchid children, the world is sometimes a frightening and overwhelming place, but with loving and supportive help, they can, as we discovered to our great surprise, do as well as or thrive even more than their dandelion peers. In the end it is not vulnerability but *sensitivity* that defines the orchid, and when given the right support, that sensitivity can blossom into lives of great joy, success, and beauty.

As I map out the defining features of orchid lives, I will also reflect upon those of us more aligned with a dandelion's way of being and will take note of how essential, how vital such individuals are to what George Eliot referred to as "the growing good of the world." Though distinctive in several dimensions, dandelions have their own life struggles and challenges that will be important to understand and define. We will also discover that beneath the serviceable categories of "orchid" and "dandelion" lies the truer reality of a continuum, a spectrum of sensitivities to the world, along which we all have a place. In the end, it will be the remarkable complementarity of orchids and dandelions that we will want to sustain and remember: the usefulness, and often love, of the one for the other, the symmetry and mutuality of their symphonic roles in human discourse and history, and their coevolution as distinctive but equally cogent solutions to the deep dilemmas life calls forth.

Finally, and at a broader, more global scale, we live now in a time of resurgent disregard—perhaps unprecedented within our lifetimes—for the care and protection of the most susceptible and powerless of the world's people. In a growing number of nations around the world—perhaps most visibly and disturbingly in my own, the United States—the defenseless are bullied and mocked; the poor are blamed for their poverty; the homeless are scorned as slothful and inept; refugees from violence are turned away; the lowly are ignored; and the "least of these" are rejected and forgotten. There is a global and sadly accelerating turn from the plights and needs of our most marginalized, disenfranchised, and vulnerable people.

More illustrative of the broader concerns of this book, however, is the reality that it is the *children* of our societies who are the most sensitive and susceptible of all those who lack power, the most dependent among those who rely vitally upon grace and beneficence for survival. It is our children who are incapable of providing for themselves, who cannot stand alone without protection or help, who are most vulnerable to the failings and indiscretions of nations. Though orchid children are, as we will see in the pages to come, those especially responsive and tender to the manner in which we treat and protect our young, at the larger scale of human societies and populations, it is *all children* who are the orchids of the world.

The Orchid and the Dandelion

1

A Tale of Two Children

It is miraculous
that flower should rise
by flower
alike in loveliness—
as though mirrors
of some perfection
could never be
too often shown—
silence holds them—
in that space.

William Carlos Williams, "The Crimson Cyclamen"

This is the story of a redemption: a story of children who, like orchids and dandelions, differ dramatically in their sensitivities to environmental conditions; a story that has gradually but steadily emerged from twenty-five years of laboratory and field research; a story in which its author is deeply invested, both scientifically and personally, as one of the researchers from whose work the story issued, but also as one of the children for whom the story became painfully and compellingly real long before there was even a story to tell.

The story of the orchid and dandelion begins then with two red-headed children, of which I was one, born into a middle-class 1950s California family, a little more than two years apart in age, who experienced what seemed nearly twin, mirrored childhoods. Both children, parented with all of the love, hope, and buoyant expectations of the postwar generation, and each the other's best and truest playmate, were as indistinguishable in disposition and sensibility as any brother and sister can be. Yet at a pivotal time of upheaval and disarray in their family's collective life, the two children parted ways: one on a path of educational achievement, deepening friendships, long and committed marriage, and a life of almost shameful good fortune; the other on a trajectory of steadily escalating mental disorder, loneliness, and devolution into psychosis and despair.

My younger sister, Mary, was a freckle-faced, winsome little girl who was to one day mature into a young woman of stunning physical beauty. Cherubic as a child in both countenance and constitution, she charmed all who saw and knew her, with a quick, multiply dimpled smile, a coy reserve, and an acuity of thought you could see behind her young blue eyes. She had changed her name from Betty to Mary in mid-adolescence, in what could only have been an anguished attempt to press the reset button on her receding youth, by starting again with another name. Yet her decline into a life beset by suffering and incapacity masked an extraordinary array of often hidden but truly exceptional gifts. She had an artist's eye and an almost intuitive capacity for seeing and creating beautiful and engaging physical environments. In another life, she might have become a designer or a decorator of great renown, and even today many of her treasured paintings, chairs, tchotchkes, and baubles still adorn the homes of her brothers, daughter, nieces, and nephew.

But Mary's greatest, perhaps least visible asset was her immense intelligence, which became ever more apparent as she grew and studied, and which was ultimately rewarded by a baccalaureate degree from Stanford University and a graduate degree from Harvard. She was regarded by her professors not simply as a diligent and promising student, but as a gifted young scholar, full of uncommon insight and possessed of a luminous mind. She was surely the most intelligent, creative, and clever member of our family, her older brother a shadow of her astonishing acuity and vision. Clearly introverted and shy by inclination and temperament, by late childhood she had mastered the ability to win the attention and affection of other children and to engage in intimate and satisfying personal friendships. Many of her relationships in primary school were carried with her into adult life, despite the sad unwinding of her health that was soon to follow.

So the curly, red-haired infant girl that my parents brought home in my own third year of life became my first, best friend, the abiding, readily-at-hand playmate with whom I spent long hours in games, elaborate stories, and elegant fantasies. Seldom tiring of each other's company, we spun endless collaborative tales of make-believe adventure and intrigue and fed our dual fancies for magical, imaginary play. I marveled at her ingenuity when she managed, during one memorable naptime, to shove a whole small box of raisins up her nose one by one, a misadventure that brought a trip to the doctor's office. There she was magnificently emptied of scores of mucus-laden raisins with a long, shiny forceps that disappeared impossibly deep within a three-year-old pug nose. I became recurrently and loudly indignant at her penchant for carsickness on long car trips, when she reliably vomited on the seat between us, once on her brother himself, and once, most unforgivably, on his prized "Indian tent" (so named because he didn't know the words "teepee" or "wigwam"). I worried over her safety, once rushing to her aid at the beach when, tightly encircled with an inflatable life ring snug round her waist, she ended up an inverted buoy, butt and legs flailing in the air and a sputtering fount of seawater when righted. She and I were pals as much as sister and brother, an equal partnership of sublime, noisy play with no limits, few rules, and a mutual devotion to outrageous imagination. Though I couldn't have said it at the time, I really loved her, as much as a five-year-old can love his sister, and she loved me.

When our younger brother came along, nearly a decade after my sister's birth, we reveled together in the joys of joint big brotherhood and sisterhood and joined our parents in unabashed worship of this unheralded, carrot-topped infant. An archival 1957 Christmas card in our brother Jim's second month of life so captures this physical, encircling family endearment that it has been forever since referred to as "The Adoration of the Magi Card." Mary and I became even closer through our shared, sometimes competitive but always tandem joy at the advent of a new baby brother. As our minds and bodies began to change with the onset of puberty, we entered adolescence with as close and caring a relationship as siblings ever have—rich in history, suffused with love of family, and filled with a shared sensibility about the nature of the world and the character and purpose of our lives.

And then the bottom fell away. Our family moved five hundred miles north to the San Francisco Bay Area, where our dad would pursue a doctoral degree in education at Stanford, clearly by then a "mature student." In the months leading up to the decision to depart, he had become profoundly depressed, suffering in the language of that time a "nervous breakdown," which miserably fastened him to our living room couch for days at a time. It disallowed his work and sent him into a visible and unsettling oblivion of emotion, fierce tears, and uncertainty about his future. We nonetheless moved to the north, where all of the social, physical, and pedagogical environments we had known were gone. We were suddenly awash in a sea of newness, challenged and dismayed by unfamiliar social and geographical landscapes. The neighborhood in which we now played was unmapped and starkly foreign; the schools we attended were peopled with vast crowds of nameless kids; and even our family felt adrift and unanchored in these new, stormy waters.

Mary and I entered unfamiliar schools, and within a year or two had both encountered the even stranger, enemy territory of middle school. Our mom, preoccupied with the exigencies of caring for an infant child, did her best to soften the blow of how our young worlds had turned upside down, but her own support, our dad, was immersed in a deepening vortex of graduate studies, classes, and student obligations. Our parents' marriage, perennially troubled by discord and disagreement—over family budgets, child discipline, conflicting wills, and imagined slights—took an ominous turn toward more physical, serious struggles. Two beloved grandparents and two uncles died; we moved a second time to a new home closer to the Stanford campus; and our dad, having completed his degree, took a new and even more challenging and consuming job.

None of these closely clustered events in the life of a young family about to enter the 1960s were uniquely onerous or even remarkable for their severity or perniciousness. Indeed, many families routinely sustain disruptions and stressors of equal or greater magnitude and scope, and some have endured unspeakable adversities that only their most fortunate members survive. But the aggregation of these multiple, if mundane events proved gravely traumatic for my sister. Following our family's second residential move and her enrollment in the local middle school, she developed a serious, systemic physical illness that was distressingly unidentifiable for several months. Her recurrent fevers, whole-body rashes that would come and go, and swelling of her spleen and lymph nodes were at first suggestive of leukemia or lymphoma, leading to a series of hospitalizations and painful, invasive tests. But ultimately, as her joints began to hurt and swell, the illness became recognizable as Still's disease, an unusually severe presentation of juvenile rheumatoid arthritis. Our parents took Mary out of school, and she spent an entire year at bed rest, treated with aspirin, steroids, and alternating heat and cold to loosen and quiet her angry joints. As her big brother, I watched, bewildered and uneasy, as my sister's life unraveled in a bedroom at the end of the hall. Though she continued to have recurrent arthritis throughout the remainder of her life, by year's end she had sufficiently recovered to return to normal life.

Sadly, however, normal life did not return to her. Rather, in the aftermath of her chronic rheumatologic illness, Mary began showing signs of something awry in her mind. She stopped eating and lost weight, withdrew from her friends, and was eventually diagnosed with anorexia nervosa, an eating disorder that disproportionately affects adolescent girls. She returned over and over to the hospital for therapy and imposed nutrition, was enrolled in a series of boarding schools that her psychiatrists thought possibly therapeutic, but continued to descend into a maelstrom of depression, insomnia, withdrawal from social contacts, and increasingly unusual behavior and thought. By the end of high school, she carried a suspected devastating diagnosis of schizophrenia— arguably the worst medical news that parents can ever hear, possibly exceeded only by that of a child's death.

Nonetheless, Mary's intrinsic brilliance carried her forward into a promising, if precarious, undergraduate admission to Stanford, where despite recurrent struggles with her mental health, she continued to excel in anomalously spectacular ways. Looking back, her four years at college framed a promising landscape of ascending academic success beside a horizon of steepening descent into a troubled and anguished mind. Following graduation and a brief, uncompleted period of study at a law school in San Francisco, she was admitted to the master's of theology program at the Harvard Divinity School. There, she hoped to study personal religious experiences and their commonalities and convergences with psychiatric symptoms. However, her own psychotic symptoms—principally hearing hostile, venomous voices and experiencing periods of catatonia, when she was unable to move or talk—led to even greater impairment. She was admitted several times to a local psychiatric facility, engaged in a series of sexually promiscuous one-night stands, and eventually became pregnant. The pregnancy culminated in a difficult, prolonged labor, and her daughter, a sweet, now thirty-nine-year-old woman with special needs, was born with birth asphyxia and a seizure disorder. Despite the clear challenges of raising a disabled child while contending with her own serious and disturbing handicaps, Mary was a caring and responsive mother who reared her daughter in an atmosphere of love and attentiveness. Mary's mental disorder continued, however, to inflict havoc and desperation upon her life, and her adulthood became an increasingly implausible assembly of fragmented ruins, held together, however marginally, by her family's tenacity and her own resolute unwillingness to surrender.

The Nonrandom Apportioning of Illness and Misfortune

Why do some children struggle and others succeed? Why are some people's lives filled with rank misfortune and others with satisfaction and happiness? Why do some people get sick and die young, while their peers live into healthy older age? Is it simply chance and luck, or are there early patterns of development revealing lawful pathways into bounty or calamity? Why did my sister's life consign her to growing desperation and an enduring, slow-moving catastrophe, while mine led to unanticipated and often undue successes? These were the questions that fired my imagination, inspired my education as a young pediatrician, and eventually drove my quest to understand the vivid divergences in child development and pediatric health that shape the adults we become and the lives we lead.

We now know from the science of epidemiology—the study of disease and health within human populations—that there are indeed reliable and highly uneven patterns of illness and well-being. The graph below illustrates the single most well-replicated finding in all of health services research, a fact that has fundamentally driven how we think about the challenges of population health science. Fifteen to 20 percent of children—about one child in five—experience the majority of all the physical and psychological illnesses found within a population of children over time.

The same one in five is responsible for over half of the health care consumed and the majority of health care dollars spent. Further, the same disproportion in illness experience is found in adult populations, and there is evidence that children with unbalanced rates of ill health become similarly afflicted adults. The same children who bear inordi-

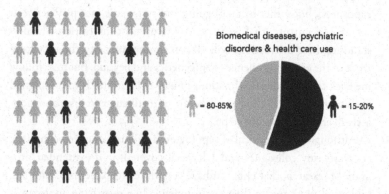

The single most well-replicated finding in child health services research: that 15 to 20 percent of children—about one in five—from any population sustain well over half of the illnesses and mental disorders population-wide and are responsible for the majority of the population's use of health services.

nate burdens of disease in childhood become adults who also disproportionately suffer. Remarkably, all of this appears equally true for children
around the world: from rich and poor nations, in both socialist and cap-
italist societies, on every continent of both the East and the West, from
both Northern and Southern Hemispheres. The public health importance of these observations is clear: if we could understand and address
the disease inequity of this small minority of children, we might stand
a chance of eliminating over half of the biomedical and psychiatric illnesses within the population and could dramatically reduce costly needs
for health care and hospitalization. In other words, we might be able to
create more balanced societies, filled with happier, healthier people. We
might foster the emergence of stronger families with less physical and
psychological hardship and sustain parents and children with futures of
greater hope and optimism.

Children's ill health and later adult morbidity are thus highly non-
random in distribution. Instead of being spread evenly and more "fairly"
over the entire childhood population, illness is irregularly apportioned
to just an afflicted few, like my sister and so many others. Because of this,
there are systematic and broad differences in the rates of illness among
subgroups of children, and this dramatic irregularity appears driven neither purely by nature (i.e., genetics) nor by nurture (i.e., experiences and
exposures), but rather by an ongoing and systematic interplay between
nature and nurture: that is, by gene-environment interactions. Understanding these interactions will take us in due course to the very fore-
front of the emerging science of epigenetics and beyond. But first, follow
me back to our earliest intimations of *why* child health is so misaligned
within groups of children and *who* the unfortunate and disproportionately ill children turn out to be.*

Although I am skeptical of typologies of children or overly simplistic
contrasts, my colleagues and I have discovered, in an extended program of research, that children have very different patterns of internal,
biological responses to their environments. In a shorthand approxima-

---

* For those readers less encumbered with the arcana of biomedical terms, like "morbidity,"
"gene-environment interaction," and "epigenetics," there is a glossary on pages 247–48.

tion of what we will later see that the science shows, we can usefully suggest that these responses fall into two distinctive categories. Some children, like *dandelions,* show a remarkable capacity for thriving in almost every environmental circumstance they encounter. Dandelion flowers can seemingly grow and flourish anywhere their seeds happen to land—from fertile mountain meadows to the cracks in urban sidewalks. Other children, like *orchids,* are exquisitely sensitive to their environments, making them especially vulnerable under conditions of adversity but unusually vital, creative, and successful within supportive, nurturing environments.

The provenance of these metaphors—of orchid and dandelion children—was my short interaction, nearly twenty years ago, with an old Swedish man who attended a lecture I gave at Stanford University. After I had finished my talk, a wizened, Yoda-like older man with bushy eyebrows and a twisted, rootlike cane came slowly down an aisle to the front of the lecture hall, pointed and jabbed his dreadful cane at me, and said, "You're talking about *maskrosbarn!*" I responded that I had no idea I was talking about maskrosbarn, nor had I any idea what a maskrosbarn was. Maskrosbarn, he explained, is an idiomatic Swedish expression that translates to "dandelion child" in English. The Swedes use the term to refer to those children who, like dandelions, can thrive wherever they find themselves—a kind of limitless "blossom where you are planted" capacity. Prompted by this charming and evocative figure of speech, I then coined a Swedish neologism—*orkidebarn,* or "orchid child"—to denote those children who, like orchids, are highly susceptible to the character of their environments and can blossom into magnificent organisms when carefully nurtured, but can wither and decline when neglected or harmed.

Orchid children, who are more sensitive and biologically reactive to their circumstances, in both the laboratory and the world, are the sources of much of our collective anguish, grief, and worry, as parents, teachers, and health care workers. These children—and their adult counterparts, who are the friends and colleagues about whom we often worry—when not properly understood and supported can create great pain, sorrow, and disappointment for families, schools, and societies.

Stories of Orchids and Dandelions

Two stories of children are nicely representative of the challenges that orchid children face. The first involved a ten-year-old boy (call him Joe) from a distant county who was sent for hospitalization by his family doctor, to be evaluated for a possible gastric ulcer. As his attending pediatrician, I was among the first to hear his story and examine his troubled belly. His pain was crampy and severe, and lay directly over his stomach in the left upper quadrant of his abdomen. He had no other symptoms and specifically denied any change or blood in his stool, any vomiting, or any alteration of the pain before or following a meal. His diagnostic workup, including X-rays, tests for blood in his stool or urine, and blood measures of inflammation or anemia, was entirely unremarkable.

Thinking that these must be episodes of psychosomatic pain brought on by difficulties in the family, I launched a full-bore search for the family or school dysfunction that was surely a root contributor to young Joe's disabling pain. All was well at school, and though Joe frequently stayed home as a consequence of his pain, there was no history to suggest experiences of social or academic stress in his school life. He had good friends, was a talented student with good grades, and got along well with his teacher. I then interviewed Joe at length, on multiple occasions, about how life was going at home, about his parents' relationship, about any possible abuse from one or both of his parents, about any worries or troubles that his family had. The result was a definitive *zero:* no history of anything unusual or suspicious in his report.

So I then turned to the parents—both of them present and attentive during the entire hospitalization. Was there any worry or concern on Joe's part about either of the parents? How was their marital relationship? Any exposures to violence or conflict? Did they have any hunches about the origin of their son's pain? Nothing. The parents, in perhaps three or four serial interviews, turned up not a single psychological or relational issue that we could deem implicated in the genesis of Joe's pain. So we started him, despite absolutely no evidence for a gastric or duodenal ulcer, on an acid-blocking medication, and his pain promptly began to subside. After several days in the hospital and with Joe's pain receding, we discharged the boy back home to the care of his primary care physician.

That was all I heard of Joe or his family until three months later, when I got a call from the district attorney's office in their home county. Did I have any reason to suspect violence or maltreatment from Joe's dad? Because "last night after supper" his mom had gone to the bedroom, retrieved a hidden handgun, and put a bullet through her husband's forehead, precisely between his eyes. Months later, a jury acquitted the mother, ruling justifiable homicide stemming from the father's chronic, relentless psychological and physical abuse of mother and child. The mom had finally reached a point of no return, when her only recourse, it seemed to her at the time, was to put an end to the husband who had tormented her and her son, Joe, for years. I had missed this crucial piece of family history by virtue of never interviewing the parents separately, only at the same time. There were no visible stigmata of child abuse on physical examination, and Joe and his mom, terrified by the retribution that would surely follow a revelation of abuse, had been unable, with the dad constantly present, to provide me with that essential detail of their family's plight. In retrospect, it was almost certainly the case that Joe was a classic orchid child—awash in the overwhelming terror of his mom's and his own endangerment, psychologically undefended from the feelings the abuse produced, and unconsciously displacing the pain into its only safe and acceptable form, a bodily complaint. Joe's story also stands as a reminder of how we all live, one way or another, on the brink of great misfortune, caught between the uneasy safety of dissembling nature and the awful truth of a real and dangerous world.

A second story of what it is to be an orchid child lies in the portrayal of two young boys in the artistry of an unforgettable photograph and a timeless book. Importantly, both "pictures" also begin to hint at another dimension of orchid children—their hidden strengths and uncommon sensibilities. One, whose image (see next page) was captured on an afternoon in 1988 by photographer Paul D'Amato, appeared on the cover of *DoubleTake* magazine. A perhaps ten-year-old child stands in a

Photographer Paul D'Amato's visual portrayal of what is surely a young orchid boy (foreground) with a group of other boys in a vacant lot in Portland, Maine.

rumpled blue shirt with his arms crossed, unassailable, looking outward from a chaotic, vaguely aggressive pack of feral prepubertal boys. For me, the photograph has always been a near-perfect physical rendition of an orchid child and the social environments with which such children sometimes contend. The child stands calmly, sentient and open, both vulnerable and strong, at the margins of an angry, splintered society of peers. The picture seems to convey a kind of paradoxical co-occurrence of the boy's stolid, indifferent marginality to the group and a brimming cauldron of emotion, combining loneliness, vulnerability, reserve, and resilience.

It is the same sort of chimeric image that William Golding framed in words rather than pixels in his classic coming-of-age, innocence-lost novel, *Lord of the Flies.* In it, we encounter one of the child protagonists, Simon, who finds himself lost on an island, in a time of war, with an increasingly malevolent corps of British schoolboys whose airplane has been shot down over uncharted enemy territory. The boys gradually become conscious of a collective dread, of a shadowy "beast" concealed just beyond margins of their sensate awareness. Simon, surely an orchid child marooned in an alien world, is variously described in these ways:

He was a skinny, vivid little boy, with a glance coming up from under a hut of straight hair that hung down. . . .

Simon felt a perilous necessity to speak, but to speak in assembly was a terrible thing to him. . . .

"Maybe," he said hesitantly, "maybe there is a beast." . . . The assembly cried out savagely and Ralph stood up in amazement. "You, Simon? You believe in this?" "I don't know," said Simon. His heartbeats were choking him. . . . Simon became inarticulate in his efforts to express mankind's essential illness.

While both D'Amato's blue-shirted boy and Golding's Simon are iconic embodiments of the vulnerability of orchid children, both are also portraits of such children's remarkable and often unrevealed strengths. These are the children whose tender, courageous presence we so need in our communities and societies. They can be, as family therapist Salvador Minuchin taught, the "identified patient" who is sacrificed for a dysfunctional and abusive family. In other words, their tender responsivity causes them to absorb emotionally and physiologically the cost of their deleterious circumstances. As we saw with Joe and his family, identified patients—often, though not universally children—become, within the context of enmeshed and impaired family systems, a kind of metaphorical "Christ figure" who "dies" for the family, bearing its burden of suffering and pain as a means of ensuring survival and the immutability of its sad but compulsory dysfunction. But an orchid child can also be a source of insight, creative thought, and human virtue. What my colleagues and I have discovered, over the course of twenty-five years of research, is that the same extraordinary, biologically embedded sensitivities that render such children so unduly susceptible to the hazards and adversities of life make them also more receptive to the gifts and promises of life. Therein lies an intriguing and life-giving secret: that *orchids are not broken dandelions* but a different, more subtle kind of flower. Within the struggles and frailties of orchids lies an unimagined strength and redemptive beauty.

Orchids—both orchid children and the adults they become—often weather, in families, schools, and life, threats of which others are only marginally aware. Like their namesake flowers, they are both endowed and burdened with an exquisite sensitivity to the inhabited, living world, and, also like the orchid, have both frailties that can threaten their existence and health, as well as hidden capacities for lives of beauty, honesty, and notable achievement. Make no mistake, however, that such *internal* sensitivity to the world could supplant or override the *external* threats and hazards we know from long experience—those toxic exposures to poverty and stress, war and violence, racism and subordination, toxin and pathogen. The strength and health of both orchids and dandelions are jeopardized by these and many others of the world's menaces, and childhood poverty remains the single most powerful determinant of ill health for the entire human life span. But orchids' *differential susceptibility*—that is, their special sensitivities—to such threats systematically surpasses that of dandelions.

It is neither the inequalities of environmental exposures nor the susceptibilities of genetic differences that alone create the profound imbalances between dandelions and orchids, in illness, disorder, and life's misfortunes. Rather, such imbalances are the interactive products of environments and genes operating together—an emerging scientific reality to which we will return in earnest in a later chapter. While both environments and genes play an important role in the emergence of orchid and dandelion children, we now know that their interactions, at the molecular and cellular levels, calibrate a fundamental, decisive aspect of such children's biology: how reactive and sensitive they are to the environments in which they grow and develop.

Though my *scientific* interest in the remarkably distinctive trajectories of children's development and health was driven by statistics and data, my *personal* investment in the science had its deepest roots in the astonishing divergences of life course between my sister, Mary, and me. For two lives that had had such common points of origin and such parallel early paths, they led to sadly different ends. I was the dandelion and she the orchid.

So it is a tale of two children—the deeply intertwined histories of a future pediatrician and his sister, Mary—that forms readers' gateway into a new science, describing and to some extent now explaining how children from a single family can have such divergent life paths.

Although her delicate sensitivity held within it the possibility of distinction and accomplishment well beyond my own, she was overcome by the tragedies and sadnesses of life, which prevented that promise from fully blooming. Confronted by the realities of family discord, disappointment, loss, and death, my sister stumbled upon rocky ground to which her dandelion brother was largely impervious. And just as the dandelion can take no rightful personal credit for the resilience it musters in the face of such realities, so Mary bore no private responsibility for the disarray into which her sad life finally descended. Reared at a different time or in a different family, she might have become a gifted preacher, a celebrated theologian, or the leader of a redemptive spiritual movement touching thousands of lives. She might have led a magnificent life, full of joy and celebration, replete with acts of great kindness and ideas of great moment. And had she found her way, through some miracle of protection, to that redeemed and abundant trajectory of life, no one would have guessed that the possibility of calamity lay so close on the other side.

2

The Noise and the Music

A screaming pregnant woman, in a single-engine plane, flying through a snowstorm, under the control of a World War II bush pilot. This was no holiday at the sea. It was testing every fiber of my dandelion roots and the last sticky drop of their sap. The year was 1978, I was a thirty-two-year-old novice pediatrician, and I had no idea how this day would end.

Two hours earlier, at 5:00 a.m., I had been wrenched from uneasy sleep by a call from the Crownpoint Indian Health Service (IHS) hospital on the arid, forgotten eastern edge of the Navajo Nation's tribal land. The only pediatrician for fifty to a hundred miles in any direction, I was responsible for all the serious medical emergencies involving children, born or unborn. Walking the half-block distance between the government-issued home in which Jill and I lived, at the base of a scrubby New Mexico mesa, and the thirty-bed hospital, I went directly into the labor and delivery "suite." It consisted of a single room with a table and stirrups, and an official photograph of Jimmy Carter gazing presidentially down upon all obstetrical proceedings and always looking a little embarrassed about being there. Here, I was confronted with a tiny, two-inch preemie foot emerging, like a daffodil in spring, from the vagina of a twenty-something Native American mom, who'd had no prenatal visits and two previous children. According to her pregnancy dates, she was at thirty-two weeks' gestation, but she looked bigger than she should have at that pregnancy stage. So we took her to an imaging room and there discovered the presence of not one baby but two pree-mie twins.

The Crownpoint hospital was not, especially forty years ago, where you wanted to deliver high-risk, premature twins, one with his left foot already delivered and wiggling. So I grabbed the phone with my list of surrounding, though remote, tertiary care medical centers with neonatal intensive care units (NICUs), calling each in nervous, quick succession and in ascending order of distance. Every hospital NICU—in Albu-querque, Gallup, Phoenix, and Tucson—was full to overflowing with newborns who had already arrived, each in need of special neonatal care. Finally, as a last attempt, I called the University of Colorado Children's Hospital and was powerfully relieved to learn that they could indeed accept my tiny, as-yet-unborn Navajo twins.

I woke up another young local doc, the one with the keenest obstet-ric skills within our small roster of IHS physicians, and asked him to meet me at the Crownpoint "Airport," a nearby stretch of arid dirt, scraped clean of sage and tumbleweed, and leveled as much as a tiny Bobcat backhoe could manage. The roster consisted of five trained but greenhorn physicians, all wet behind the ears and up to their necks in their first real medical practices beyond assorted residencies of varying length and specialty. Taken together, we were a ragtag assembly of new-ness, inexperience, and fear, held together by the camaraderie of young doctors alone in the American third world. Gil, my sleepy but willing colleague on this early morning mission, arrived at the airport, followed by an elderly aviator, named something like "Ole Bob," who was the local bush pilot, with an airplane of comparable vintage. We loaded the young mom (let's call her Serena as a testimony to her astonishing placidity amid all that was to follow) onto a gurney behind the pilot, with Gil poised at the business end and I beside Serena, manning the single infant bag-and-mask resuscitation equipment and small bottle of oxygen. We took off into an enormous, high desert sky streaked with the brilliant colors of a New Mexico sunrise. So far, so good.

As we climbed to maybe ten thousand feet, it looked like everything was going to work out. Gil was monitoring the position of the babies in Serena's birth canal, I was ready to handle newborn resuscitation should an unanticipated delivery occur before landing, and Ole Bob was heading us north toward the snowcapped Rocky Mountains, with periodic sweaty glances over his shoulder at the scene playing out in the rear of his airplane. But as we approached the New Mexico–Colorado border, we hit a snowstorm of magnificent proportions. The sky grew ominously black above us, the view ahead obscured into grainy white opacity, and the air below became a barely translucent window onto a vast sea of white mountains and featureless plains. The airplane began to shake like a squirrel in a dog's mouth, plummeting and ascending two to three hundred feet in vertiginous falls and leaps, and clearly challenging Ole Bob's already unsteady, not-quite-Parkinsonian control. Serena, surely frightened by the prospect of delivering her twins in turbulent midair, into the hands of rookie physicians, started into serious labor and began to push. Gil, unexpectedly overcome by violent motion sickness, retched and vomited, turning the cabin of the plane into a rocking, catapulting washing machine filled with floating vomit, amniotic fluid, and urine. Ole Bob was discouraged but steadfast in his piloting of the Maytag.

Then, the first boy twin, whose foot had been the tiny, pink harbinger of this day's adventure, descended fully into the world and Gil's waiting, tremulous hands. Gil clamped and cut the baby's cord, cleared his airway with a red rubber suction syringe, and handed a taut, shrieking Navajo papoose to me. I wrapped the little fellow in a newborn "space blanket" to keep him warm, held him on my lap, between my legs, face up, with his head north toward me, and began to deliver oxygen and ventilation via the bag and mask. For a poor Native American kid, conceived on a lonely reservation, untouched by prenatal care, and launched into a snowy, cold world high above the New Mexico plains, he wasn't doing badly; in fact, I was amazed at his self-evident vitality—he wanted to live! Minutes later, the second baby, following his brother's lead, made a similarly noisy, skidding, and dramatic entrance. In our subsequent debriefings, we realized that Twin A had been delivered over New Mexico, while Twin B was a naturally born citizen of Colorado—identical twin boys, born in different states, traveling at 90 miles per hour into the upper atmosphere of a major snowstorm. Similarly wrapped in foil, like little pigs in blankets, both boys now lay on my lap, each one getting alternating fifteen-second bursts of lung inflation and extra oxygen.

As we neared the Denver airport, air traffic control—presumably in response to Ole Bob's dithered recounting of what was happening in his tiny, sputtering plane—began rerouting and delaying major aircraft on approach, clearing the way for two tiny, sputtering newborn infants to land. We coasted to a stop near the Denver terminal and were there met by the more-than-welcome sight of the Children's Hospital ambulance and newborn transport team. The two small boys, each weighing no more than three pounds, were whisked away in warm, cozy incubators, along with their bewildered but smiling mom. In the weeks that followed, my periodic calls to the Denver hospital revealed that both twins were having relatively benign hospital courses, had started to grow, and would be discharged in about six weeks to the care of their welcoming and already abundant family.

Later, as I reflected on the circumstances of those twins' birth in a setting of astonishing adversity and threat, and on their hardiness and vigor in contending with those early perils, I remember thinking that their survival depended upon so much more than the presence of doctors and the availability of medical care. True, they may well not have survived in the absence of the NICU that finally cared for them with skill and vigilance, but their nesting into a loving, three-generation Navajo family was likely of equal or greater importance. As I was to learn in the years to come, this intuition, which stayed with me well beyond the most eventful plane ride of my life, would become reflected not just in the research path I would soon choose to follow, but in the startling findings to which that path would one day lead.

Two Kinds of Charts

Western medicine gets "into the body" through a panoply of routes and paths. Vaccines are injected, medicines are swallowed, scalpels open the dark recesses of bodies, X-rays penetrate tissues, producing shadowed images of organs and bones, and knowledge of disease and health is delivered into our minds and psyches by the language of physicians, nurses, brochures, the internet, and educational programs. But how do the circumstances of life, the vicissitudes of birth into advantage or disadvantage, the stresses of life and the protection of human care and community—how do these ineffable conditions of life get into the body to affect the health and well-being of a human creature? Vaccines and pills you can hold in your hands, but adversities and relationships? What are we to make of a tangible, physical body that can be undermined or sustained, in structure and in function, by forces so vaporous as adversities and relationships? It was not simply intensive neonatal care that allowed those Navajo twins to survive and thrive, but how could we scientifically account for or explain the very real, biological effects of immaterial experiences in the lives of a Navajo family and community?

The great South African epidemiologist John Cassel—one of the two father figures of the social epidemiology field (the other being Dr. Leonard Syme, professor emeritus at the University of California, Berkeley, about whom more will eventually be said)—had played a transformative role in my professional development and in the decision Jill and I made to move to Crownpoint, in the heartland of the Navajo people. John had emerged from many years of practicing medicine among the ten-thousand-member Zulu tribe in Natal province with many of the same questions that had preoccupied me and some of the answers I had yet to learn. Why are social conditions so powerfully predictive of disease and longevity? What renders the people of one village so dramatically healthier than those of another? How do the social, economic, and psychological circumstances of a person become biologically embedded, changing the risks of heart disease, schizophrenia, and tuberculosis? Cassel didn't know *how* such circumstances were transmuted into human biology, but he was certain that they were.

John had graduated from medical school at the University of the Witwatersrand and eventually took a job with a multidisciplinary health care team staffing the Pholela Community Health Centre in the Zulu tribal reserve of South Africa. This center, founded in 1942 by Dr. Sidney Kark, was a remarkable and prescient organization, where white and black health workers lived and worked side by side, doctors became committed beyond their medical care to the provision of sanitation, food availability, and adequate housing, and an international movement toward "community-oriented primary care" was born. Through his own investment and practice in this indigenous setting, John became increasingly aware of aboriginal beliefs about the origins of health and disease—beliefs that were striking departures from the tenets of the Western medicine in which he had been educated and steeped. The Zulu shamans, alongside whom John often worked, averred that the forces of social context were far more deeply implicated in disorders of health than he might once have believed. The shamans often prescribed structural changes in families, reaffirmations of tribal support, treatment with local herbs, or the meting out of overdue punishment as remedies for specific symptoms and illnesses.

Through his growing understanding of these alternative views of disease causes and treatments, John became more and more convinced that the highly constrained versions of pathogenesis (how diseases develop) in which he had been schooled were only partially valid and that broader cultural and social factors must underlie the observable patterns of disease within human populations. Then, as the South African parliament became dominated by the National Party and apartheid became law in the early 1950s, his life there grew increasingly untenable. The Pholela Centre was eventually shut down by the government as an "illegal activity," and John moved his young family to the United States, where he first studied epidemiology and eventually chaired the Department of Epidemiology at the fledgling School of Public Health of the University of North Carolina. And it was at that institution, following my residency training in pediatrics, that I encountered John in a pivotal and life-changing moment of good fortune.

One lesson that pediatric residency had taught me, among many others, was that in the years long before electronic medical records, children's medical charts came in two sizes: very thin and very thick. The medical histories of most children and youth over the first two decades of life were routinely captured in a crisp handwritten document about the size and condition of a newly delivered average magazine. You knew what you were in for, however, when a patient's chart was a ponderous tome, inches thick, dog-eared, sometimes arriving in several volumes, and with a strained metal clip at the top holding a cacophony of information in some pretense of order and chronology. These were the unfortunate children with recurrent infections or multiple injuries, with long-term chronic diseases—the children that populated that 15 to 20 percent so unfairly burdened with the early morbidities of life. And what many of them shared in common—not all, but many—were the varied misfortunes of poverty, exposure to violence, abusive parents, insufficient food, family chaos, and neighborhood disarray.

Early in my life as a pediatrician-researcher, I decided that the most compelling and challenging questions in the science of child health were those surrounding how exposures to adversity and social stressors were transmuted into the biological processes and events that led in some to biomedical disease and disorders of mental health. They were the questions that Cassel brought from the ghettos and reserves of apartheid South Africa, and as I listened to his stories of life in the velds, in the early years of my training, his questions became my own. They seemed the kinds of questions and issues on which a life might be legitimately, even usefully spent. Even then I had begun to sense how the poignant tales of adversity, poverty, and despair that patients or their families often told bore a fundamental connection to the hardships, however slight in comparison, that my own family had endured.

All pediatricians (and family physicians, too, for that matter), especially in winter, orchestrate vast choruses of sniffling, red-eyed, pus-nosed kids, racked with fever, cough, hacking, and wheezes. It is, each year, a kind of Mormon Tabernacle Choir of packed sinuses, purulent tonsils, and voiceless misery. So it was no astonishing surprise that my first real study as a shiny, newly minted pediatrician-scientist, was focused on respiratory illnesses—that is, the colds, flu, bronchitis, sinusitis, sore throats, and such that are the mucus-imbued home territories of childhood. Here were diseases as common to children as taxes to adults, and right down the road in Chapel Hill was an ongoing, world-class study of respiratory disease in young children, under the aegis and direction of the UNC Frank Porter Graham Child Development Institute. The causes of these illnesses, according to pediatric wisdom then, and to some extent even now, were viruses and bacteria, pure and simple, with a smattering of fungi thrown in to make it interesting.

In other words, respiratory illnesses were caused by bugs, end of story. Apart from the truly disabled immune systems of children with diseases like leukemia or congenital immune deficiencies or those being treated with powerful immunosuppressive medications, little consideration was given to what differences in susceptibility or vulnerability to infection might lie hidden within the masses of otherwise healthy, unafflicted kids. Almost no research at all had considered why some children were frequently ill with colds and coughs and others almost never. In the medical community, there was precious little interest in host resistance to (or defenses against) infectious agents within the great majority of children and adults who were free of recurrent infection and had normal immune function. As far as anyone knew, there was *no variation at all* in the capacities of well children to ward off or at least rapidly recover from respiratory infections; what variability there might be was all exposure and bad luck.

Yet clearly there *were* such differences, even among the children of a single family. Parents were (and still are) always telling their children's doctors that one of the siblings was reliably and persistently sicker than any of the others. Within a classroom of kindergartners, the teacher always knows that some children are dependably more susceptible to the bugs *de la semaine* than their peers and playmates. Some kids are just always more often absent due to illness compared to the rest, from their schools or teams, their churches or clubs. And as we have already seen, a small subgroup of children sustains over half the infectious illnesses within the population to which it belongs.

Even in that long-past era of my own research debut, some scientists and observers were exceptions to the general inattentiveness to these differences in susceptibility. René Dubos, the famed American microbiologist and public intellectual, had described how host (i.e., the person), pathogen (the cause of the sickness, usually bacteria or viruses), and environment were engaged in a triadic ecological process, in which health or disease depended upon the balance of host resistance, the virulence of a disease agent, and environmental circumstances, like diet and air pollution. John Cassel himself had written a famous paper in which he observed that "a remarkably similar set of social circumstances characterizes people who develop tuberculosis and schizophrenia, become alcoholics, are victims of multiple accidents, or commit suicide." Common to each of these, he argued, was a marginal position in society. Thus a few visionaries had begun to understand that the constitutional or innate ability of the person exposed to a virus to mount an immunological defense played an important added role in the outcome of the exposure, beyond that of the virus itself. Whether the person got sick or stayed well depended upon a crucial balance between pathogen virulence and host protection.

Even more provocative, a handful of scientists had begun to suspect that host resistance to infectious agents might not just be affected by diet, radiation, medications, or toxins—all aspects of the physical environment—but might actually be influenced as well by features of the *socioemotional environment*. In other words, social relationships and their attendant emotions could affect physical health.

Now here was a truly outrageous idea! How in the world could forces as diaphanous and ill-defined as "stress" or "social isolation" or "loneliness" move into the physical body and change a person's capacity for resisting infection through immune processes? This was genuinely weird stuff—in the same fantastical league, perhaps, as acupuncture, intercessory prayer (praying for other people), or medical hypnosis. But the legitimacy of each of these has been affirmed to one degree or another in the interim years, and there were now respectable researchers who were examining stress, immunity, and illness as legitimate topics of study in both animals and human subjects. Following in the tradition of Walter Cannon's early studies of how stress perturbs physiological homeostasis (balance or well-being), investigators such as Lawrence Hinkle, Hans Selye, and Harold Wolff had all begun to systematically investigate linkages between "stressful life events" and both acute and chronic illnesses, and between both physical disease and mental disorders. There were also those, like Robert Ader, who were using powerful experimental studies to examine and document how psychological stress could undermine human and animal immune competence, leaving the host measurably more vulnerable to viral and bacterial agents of disease. There thus appeared to be accumulating legitimate scientific evidence, mostly in studies of adults, that stress and adversity in some manner affected individuals' liabilities to acute and chronic diseases.

Against this backdrop of scandalously new ideas about the causes of human illness, my colleagues and I proposed a study to the quite traditional infectious disease specialists running the respiratory studies at the UNC Child Development Institute: a project examining the possible role of family stressors as risk factors for respiratory illnesses in preschool children. To the great credit of those pediatric subspecialists in 1975, the project was approved. So we began—with great enthusiasm and little idea of where we were headed.

We intensively studied fifty-eight preschool-age Chapel Hill children—mostly African American and uniformly poor—by interviewing their parents to assess recent stressful "life changes," such as divorces, grandparent deaths, or financial troubles, and by frequently examining each child for clinical and laboratory evidence of respiratory infections. Vivid memories remain of the many conversations I had with children's families in their musty, hot North Carolina living rooms, where the only air-conditioning was handheld fans and the sipping of sweet southern tea. When children's infections occurred, we cultured the child's nose for bacteria and viruses and carefully estimated the severity of the illness using a checklist of symptoms and physical signs. We found and reported, in a 1977 paper in *Pediatrics,* that family-reported stressors were strongly predictive of both the average severity and average duration of respiratory illnesses over the one-year period of study. Using an inventory of "family routines," which we theorized might counterbalance the effects of stressful change, we also showed that the relations among family stressors, illness severity, and illness duration were blunted or tempered by the family's adherence to strong, reliable routines. That is, the effect of stressful *changes* on illness characteristics was notably diminished among children whose families had predictable, *unchanging* aspects of their day-to-day routines.

This first, memorable and heady introduction to doing empirical science and to the testing of novel and compelling new hypotheses left a permanent mark on my identity and imagination. Although my long-held intention had been to enter a somewhat traditional life of pediatric practice, in a rural, underserved setting (an intention that my then new bride heartily shared), I was suddenly finding myself swept away by an unmistakable tidal current—moving inexorably in the direction of academic medicine, of knowledge creation, rather than simply knowledge use, and of a life immersed in this nascent science of how children's social and emotional experiences might affect their physical bodies. In the years since, recalling that moment when my career seemed to gather its own momentum, independent of me, I have often reflected with my students and trainees how my motto had become, "Your life is none of your business."

Early Studies and the Problem of "Noise"

So I was launched helter-skelter into a previously unimagined life in medicine, borne there by the storied vision of a South African epidemiologist, by the glimmerings of a new science of mind-body medicine, and by an early, enthralling encounter with a study of my own, with my own results. From there, I began to attempt what all young investigators are obliged to try: a replication of my prior findings to be sure the results were not a one-time fluke.

In the early venues of my work—on the Navajo reservation and in my first university faculty position—I returned many times to a search for that same signal of stress effects on the physical health of children. These studies involved many and varied groups of children: from Navajo boarding school students in the outposts of the high New Mexico desert to bright-eyed preschoolers in the Tucson barrios, from the urbane kindergartners of leafy San Francisco neighborhoods to the streetwise kids of Berkeley. Sometimes the stressors and adversities were sampled less from the lives of families than from the collective experiences of neighborhoods and communities. Sometimes the challenges were the incursions of a natural catastrophe, like a major earthquake that damaged homes, started fires, and frightened children. Other times, the studies focused on the normative, almost mundane challenges of beginning primary school for the first time, meeting new kids, getting to know a new kindergarten teacher. There were replications, to be sure, of the respiratory illness findings, but there were also extensions into stress effects on accidental injuries, on immune system responses to vaccines, and on behavioral and psychological problems.

Remarkably, a set of clear, thematic findings emerged across all of these early studies. In each one, there were statistically significant linkages between aspects of stress or challenge and the broad array of illnesses, injuries, and disturbances of mental health. But there was a problem. Although the statistical significance of these findings affirmed that they were unlikely to have been due simply to chance or error, they were always, without exception, only modest in magnitude. The identified associations never accounted for more than about 10 percent of the variation in illness outcomes, whereas stronger, more solidly causal relations might have accounted for 30 to 50 percent. I now faced an entire suite of such studies, each bearing replicable findings of childhood adversity predicting multiple effects on illness, but never with the kind of explanatory power for which my colleagues or I had hoped.

An actual plotting of the data points from these early studies revealed two inseparable stories. On the one hand, the data showed an overall linear trend for children's experiences of adversity and stress to predict developmental and health outcomes. For example, in one analysis, children's behavior problem severity scores became greater as family stressors increased. On the other hand, the data points themselves showed how scattered and varied that association actually was. There were anomalous children, for example, with quite high family stress scores who showed very low behavior severity scores, and there were also those with minimal stressors but remarkably severe behavior problems. So even though the data, taken as a whole, revealed a reliable, statistically significant connection between stress and problem behaviors, there was also a tremendous degree of "noise"—or random, unexplained variation—in the actual specifics of that connection. For a given level of family stress, it was hard to say for sure what the behavior problem severity score would be for an individual child, because so many of the actual data points lay so far from the line linking stress to behavior.

My collaborators and I tried hard for several years to clean the noise from these stress-health associations, in order to understand better and more carefully the true nature of the connections we could see were there. We searched for better and more valid questionnaires and scales with which to measure the stress and adversity in children's lives. We tried asking children instead of their parents about their stressors, and both parents rather than just one of them. Sometimes we asked teachers instead of either parents or children. When these approaches produced much the same kinds of findings, we developed our own measurement instruments, with items from our own repertoires of questions. We sampled neighborhood stress, like crime and violence, instead of that based only within families. We spent colossal efforts building the most careful and robust measures of illness incidence, severity, and recovery time, rates of accidental injuries, differences in injury severity, and subclinical mental health problems.

No matter what we tried, our findings were always the same: significant but modest associations between early stress exposures and rates of illness, injuries, and behavioral disturbances. Such findings were never enough for a breakthrough in the science of childhood stress and adversity, not even close to revolutionizing a field.

So, mired in frustration and exhaustion, we began finally to ask a new question, of an altogether different sort. We began to ask ourselves whether the "noise" that we had tried so valiantly and persistently to purge from our results might not really be the "music." What if the problem were not the data, but rather the way we were looking at the data? Maybe the doggedly persistent variability we found ourselves unable to remove, in one study after another, was actually the very phenomenon to which we should have been attending all along. Maybe the fact that the consequences of children's exposures to stressors were so tenaciously disparate was really the heart of the matter—the key to the door we had been trying so hard to open.

Even at that time, there was anecdotal recognition, both public and scientific, that some children—termed "resilient children"—were uncommonly capable of persisting and thriving, even in the face of dire adversity. There were reports, for example, of children outliving and overcoming the savagery of the Nazi camps in World War II, and more contemporary observations that a subgroup of especially hardy kids from poor communities found their way out of poverty and racial oppression to become respected professionals and highly successful entrepreneurs. There was also a less well documented, more vague belief that at the other end of the spectrum, there were especially "vulnerable" children, whose capacities for resisting hardship were compromised and whose defenselessness could impair their health and development under conditions of adversity.

Thus, even before the systematic and elegant studies of resilience by Norman Garmezy and Ann Masten at the University of Minnesota, there was an appreciation for how individual dissimilarities—in temperament, personality, or constitution—could result in highly varied consequences from exposures to stress, calamity, and ill luck. A certain background level of noise seemed somehow part of the natural fabric of human responses to the hardships life presented. Importantly, that spectrum of resistance and survival was regarded as varying between the two poles of *resilience* and *vulnerability*, between a sturdy, empowering capacity for resistance to misfortune and a powerless inability to meet and overcome even modest challenges. The two ends of this resilience/vulnerability scale were—and still are—further imbued with a kind of moral tenor, in which resilience is deemed heroic and triumphant, while vulnerability is seen as somehow sadly craven. These two dimensions of public and scientific conventional wisdom—the defining endpoints of resilience and vulnerability and their vaguely principled moral coloring—would come to figure prominently in our emerging work, which would eventually dispute both.

The tendency to view variation in the outcomes of adversity as in some way tinged with honor or with shame was at least partly a consequence of an assumption that the origin of such variation lay within character or will. But equally plausible, it seemed to my colleagues and me at the time, was a deeper, more fundamental source, within the basic, involuntary biology of the human stress response. What if the health consequences of adversity were diverse because children's internal, unseen biological reactions to such adversity were themselves dramatically different? What if children's inherent *stress reactivity* was what had been driving the remarkable variation in the health effects of environmental adversities all along? Previous studies, primarily in adults, had certainly shown that individual differences in stress reactivity were associated with a variety of mental and physical disorders, including psychopathology, coronary heart disease, and traumatic injuries. What if the very flaw we sought to expunge—that is, the noisiness of the link between stress and illness—was actually the most interesting and revelatory aspect of our data? We had begun to learn a far more global and telling scientific lesson: that the natural world is always more elegant, more complex, more radiant than our most cherished hypotheses and assumptions.

The "Music" of Individual Variation

If variation in stress reactivity were the actual, critical element of the stress-illness story, then elucidating that variation must lie, at least in part, within the neurobiology by which reactivity happens. So we had to look more closely at the two principal neurobiological stress response systems in the mammalian brain. The first of these—for simplicity, let's call it the *cortisol system*—is based within the hypothalamus at the very center of the brain. If you draw a line between your ears and run another directly back from the space between your eyes, where the two lines meet is where your hypothalamus lives: a central crossroads so critical to communication between brain regions that it is sometimes referred to as the "Casablanca" of the brain. Just as Casablanca served as a central commercial and cultural crossroads in the ancient Mediterranean and Atlantic world, the hypothalamus operates as a point of convergence and interaction for many of the brain's principal neural circuits. Two nuclei of the hypothalamus contain hormone-producing cells that lead down into the pituitary gland, which hangs on a stalk from the hypothalamus. The pituitary, in turn, produces a long-distance hormone (adrenocorticotropic hormone, or ACTH) that enters the bloodstream and travels to the adrenal glands, which sit atop each of the kidneys. ACTH causes the adrenals to release cortisol—a powerful hormone, like a shot glass full of stress chemicals—that is released by stressful experiences and has profound effects on the body, including the cardiovascular and immune systems. Together, the hypothalamus and the pituitary and adrenal glands are referred to as the hypothalamic-pituitary-adrenocortical (HPA) axis.

The second stress response system—for simplicity, we'll call it the *fight-or-flight system*—is based in a tiny center in the brain stem that is also activated under conditions of stress. That center contains neurons that extend up into the hypothalamus, igniting the fight-or-flight responses of the autonomic nervous system (ANS), which produces the sweaty palms, dilated pupils, increased heart rate, and tremulousness that most people are familiar with in acutely stressful circumstances. The cortisol and fight-or-flight stress response systems do not activate and function altogether independently or even in parallel, but rather engage in extensive crosstalk, where activation in one system tends to resonate into activation of the other. Both systems have powerful monitoring and regulatory effects on multiple bodily processes, including sugar and insulin levels in the blood, blood pressure, heart rate, and other cardiovascular functions, and the balancing of immunological responses to bacteria, viruses, and foreign substances, such as pollens or vaccines. Children who are acutely or chronically responding to stressful environments tend to have higher blood sugar and an increased risk for Type II diabetes, higher blood pressure, greater risk for coronary and cerebrovascular disease, and shifts in immune functioning toward either immune suppression or inflammatory responses.

All of these physiological stress responses, accumulated over time in the human body, result in a systematic shift toward long-term disease risk in multiple categories. Neuroscientist Bruce McEwen has suggested that the body's perennial efforts to maintain physiological balance begin to create a chronic wear and tear on biological systems, resulting in a condition of *allostatic load*. Allostasis is the process of achieving biological stability, or *homeostasis,* through physiological or behavioral changes; allostatic load is then the biological cost of maintaining that stability. Imagine two elephants sitting on either end of a children's teeter-totter. Although a kind of precarious balance is maintained, there is a terrific level of strain on the board that holds them, and the teeter-totter can eventually even snap. Thus even where a kind of physiological steady state is possible for years, the underlying process of stress exposure can be one of gradual, cumulative disease risk over time.

We had come to a fork in the path of our research. Because we were now interested in the possible differences *between* children in the magnitude of their stress reactivity, we needed to devise a way of measuring that reactivity under rigorously standardized conditions. Even if wireless monitoring equipment had been available in those early years (and it wasn't), assessing blood pressure or heart rate in school or at home might have revealed differences, but we wouldn't have known whether they were attributable to biological disparities in individual children's reactivity levels or to the inherent stressfulness of the specific school or home. We needed carefully controlled laboratory conditions and a set of yardsticks by which both of the stress response systems could be simultaneously indexed. Further, the challenging conditions in which we put the children had to be carefully calibrated—stressful enough to precipitate reactivity, but not so stressful that kids would cry or run away.

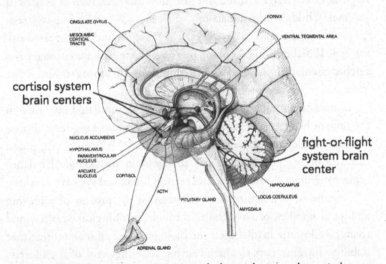

The two principal stress response systems in the human brain are the cortisol system and the fight-or-flight system. The cortisol system involves communication among nuclei in the hypothalamus, the pituitary gland, and the adrenal glands, which are positioned over each kidney. The fight-or-flight system (or autonomic nervous system, ANS) is activated by a nucleus in the brain stem and has two distinctive branches: the sympathetic branch, which serves as an accelerator of fight-or-flight reactivity; and the parasympathetic branch, which opposes the sympathetic arm, serving as a brake on the system. The fight-or-flight system ignites many of the familiar physiologic stress responses: a dry mouth, tremulousness, an increased heart rate, and a nervous gastrointestinal tract.

My colleague Abbey Alkon and I set about identifying a collection of mildly stressful tasks that could elicit just the right level of cortisol and fight-or-flight system responses. At first, we tried stressors that had been used in adult studies of cardiovascular reactivity,* like the cold pressor test, which requires the subject to immerse a hand in a bucket of ice water for one minute. When we first tested this task with a five-year-old boy, he stuck his hand in the water, made a sour face, said, "That hurts!" and walked briskly out of the lab—proving thereby: (a) the wisdom of children, and (b) the idiocy of scientists. To test stress reactivity in a child, we had to find a set of "Goldilocks" tasks—those that were not too harsh, not too mild, but just right. To find this sweet spot, we needed tasks that were adjustable in intensity, appropriate to the whole range of three- to eight-year-old children (the middle childhood group on which we were principally focused), and "ecologically valid," that is, challenges that children actually encounter in their day-to-day lives. We decided on several of these, in different categories of challenge:

- An interview with a previously unknown adult (a research assistant) who asked about the child's family, birthday, playmates at school, favorite foods, and last birthday party (i.e., a *psychosocial* challenge; see the photograph on the next page);
- A drop of lemon juice on the tongue (a *physical,* sensory challenge);
- Viewing an emotional video clip from a movie (an *emotional* challenge); and
- Reciting a three- to eight-digit sequence of numbers read to the child by the examiner (a *cognitive* or thinking challenge).

*Here, and often throughout, I have used the plural pronoun "we" to represent the remarkable conclave of students, trainees, and volunteers who become the abundant, talented eyes, arms, and legs of any university program of research. They are the public faces of every project, the manual labor that moves the vehicle of science, and many times the sources of valuable insights into the phenomena under study. Though they are often anonymous in both publications and the public crediting of scientific contributions, the truth is that almost nothing would be accomplished or successful without their gifts to and investments in the enterprise of research.

For some special studies, we also used:

- Setting off a fire alarm at the end of the reactivity protocol, alleg-edly the result of steam from a kettle for making hot chocolate (i.e., an *unexpected, arousing* challenge), and promptly thereafter reassuring the child that no fire was actually happening.

Immediately before and after these challenging tasks, the research assistant read the child a calming, age-appropriate story to obtain rest-ing measures that could be compared to those taken during the tasks. For reactivity scores, we used measures that were responsive in both the cortisol and fight-or-flight systems, as well as some that were specific to each. Examples of the former were blood pressure and heart rate, which are affected by both systems, and examples of the latter were salivary cor-tisol (the levels of the stress hormone cortisol in spit, closely comparable to levels in the blood) and impedance cardiography, which measures heart rate variability (an index of parasympathetic ANS function) and the precise timing of cardiac pumping cycle events (a measure of sympa-thetic ANS activation).

A child being tested by a previously unknown adult in a stress reactivity protocol. Cortisol and fight-or-flight system responses were monitored while the child completed a diverse series of mildly stressful challenges.

Salivary samples for cortisol measurement were simple to collect, since every child on the planet is secretly yearning to spit, at any moment, on demand, and under any circumstance—a barely suppressed enthusiasm for expectoration, almost certainly a result of parents' universal admonition, "Don't *spit*!" In none of our studies, among hundreds and hundreds of children, have we ever yet encountered a three- to eight-year-old child who did not relish the provision of a saliva sample, in great, foamy, and often noisy abundance.

The cardiovascular measures of fight-or-flight, autonomic function were something of a different story, requiring the collection of electrophysiological data from the heart, over several continuous minutes. We did this by attaching electrodes, electrolyte gel, and wires to the child's chest, front and back, and to an ankle, allowing millisecond-to-millisecond measurement of the timing of electrical events in the heart as it pumps blood into the lungs and body. The application of all this equipment, the testing of the system, and the management of some children's natural anxiety during the setup procedures can itself take ten to fifteen minutes. Seven- and eight-year-olds can be cajoled and enthralled with stories of how astronauts are similarly wired up for spaceflights. Three- and four-year-olds, on the other hand, are not as easily engaged in valorous space travel fantasies and must be more slowly brought along using soft, soothing words, a slow pace of action, and continuous reassurance. Even at this stage of the reactivity protocol, however, a watchful observer could begin to see the behavioral and emotional differences between young children in their responses to a strange experience. These differences, as we will see, became even more vividly apparent at the level of the stress physiology that all the laboratory procedures were designed to evoke and reveal.

As researchers are sometimes prone to do, Abbey and I first tested all of these procedures and measures in our own children, who at the time were in precisely the same age group as the children we were planning to test. My then six-year-old daughter Amy thus kindly volunteered to be a guinea pig in her dad's stress reactivity experiments—an accession for which she was handsomely rewarded with treasure and prizes. She proved to be among the more reactive children tested in our laboratory.

Though never floridly orchidish, she abhorred "wrinkles" in the socks inside her shoes, hated the scratchiness of wool sweaters against her skin, and showed great sensitivity to the emotional color and intonation of choral music. These sensitivities, we would eventually come to learn, were among the behavioral and sensory signatures of other children (whom we would one day call orchids) with more extreme neurobiological responses to the laboratory stressors. These more extreme, sometimes high-risk children—some of whom became my patients in due course—also had special, often problematic sensitivities to naturally occurring challenges in life outside the lab and a predisposition to be overpowered by intense or overwhelming social settings. I thus found myself studying the developmental and health consequences of this exaggerated reactivity to stress—a physiological territory that my own beloved daughter inhabited.

During this "messing-around" phase of developing our laboratory reactivity protocol, we had experimented voluminously and for long months with different tasks, different measures of cardiovascular response, and different varieties and ages of children. Once satisfied that we had just the right set of tasks and a reliable set of measures, and that all of these worked with children of different ages and different temperaments, we began to systematically survey the landscape of stress reactivity among hundreds of young children. Although we began with studies of three- to eight-year-old children, Abbey went on to demonstrate and codify the same basic findings in younger children, even among infants in the first year of life. Essentially, what we have consistently found is that measures of neurobiological reactivity to laboratory challenges vary enormously within populations of children and that their variation follows a standard normal (bell-shaped) distribution, in which many children occupy the middle ground and smaller numbers create the extremes on either side.

The graph on the facing page shows a representative sample of values for fight-or-flight and/or cortisol measures of reactivity. It shows that stress responses have a smooth, continuous spread of reactivity values, with the orchid children in the top 15 to 20 percent of such values and the dandelions in the bottom 80 to 85 percent. Orchid children show quantitatively, but not categorically, greater stress responses than their dandelion counterparts. In other words, orchids and dandelions occupied the same continuous distribution, rather than completely separate ones. Not shown, but perhaps interesting, was our finding that boys and girls were equally represented among dandelions and orchids and at all levels of the reactivity continuum. Most important, there is a large, uninterrupted spectrum of reactivity values within groups of children.

Our first observation, then, as we began using our newly crafted stress reactivity protocol, was the great distances that lay between children in their measurable levels of reactivity to standardized laboratory challenges. Although many children occupied the center of the reactivity distribution, there were a reliable few—usually about one in five—who showed startlingly higher levels of fight-or-flight and cortisol system responses to our multiple experimental tasks. Similarly, there were about the same number of children who showed remarkably low reactivity, occupying the other tail of the distribution. Was this extensive variability in neurobiological responses to lab tasks the "music" we were hoping to find? Was this differential reactivity the factor that might

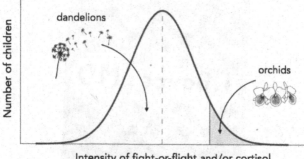

Distribution of fight-or-flight and/or cortisol reactivity to standardized laboratory challenges in children. The graph shows that stress reactivity is continuously distributed, over an entire spectrum of values, with orchid children occupying the top or high-reactivity portion of the continuum and dandelion children the lower 80 to 85 percent.

explain the reliable "noisiness" in our previously identified associations between environmental stress and impairments of health and development? Could unseen internal biological responses to standard challenges explain why some children foundered in conditions of poverty and adversity, while others seemed anomalously to thrive?

A year and a half after Gil and I shepherded those Navajo twin newborns into the world, ten thousand feet aloft of the New Mexico–Colorado border, I had left the reservation and the Indian Health Service behind and was beginning my first authentic university faculty job at the University of Arizona in Tucson. One afternoon, a mysterious package arrived with a return address lying somewhere to the north, in the distant, sprawling, and prickly wilderness of the New Mexico high desert. Inside, with no note needed, was a lovely Navajo rug, rendered in traditional style by the twins' grandmother and with my name, "T. Boyce, MD," woven into the design. I reflected that day, and in many

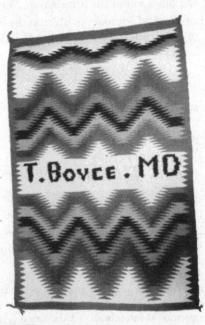

The personalized, hand-woven rug sent to me by the grandmother of the Navajo twins.

days to come, on the gratitude we all deeply feel for family, for the little ones who enter unheralded into our lives in often surprising ways and at unforeseen moments in time, and on how their modes of entry and their reactions and replies to the world are so magnificently and stunningly unique. Though my own delivery into the world of academic medicine was yet fresh and new, I was about to discover a completely unanticipated reality that would forever change my understanding of childhood adversity, my views on what biological responses to such adversity actually signify, and my assumptions regarding the benefits of resilience and the misfortune of vulnerability.

3

Lemon Juice, Fire Alarms, and an Unanticipated Discovery

In one of our first studies exploring the music amid the noise in adversity's effects on health and behavior, a shy little girl—let's call her Molly—became a harbinger of discoveries yet to come. Molly, who had just completed our stress reactivity protocol, which tested her neurobiological responses to a set of standard laboratory challenges, was now faced with a well-engineered dilemma. She had been brought into a room with two tables placed on either side of the child-sized chair on which she now sat, facing a kindly young female research assistant. The young woman explained to Molly that they would be doing some talking and playing, with the toys that sat atop the table to her left—a motley, unenticing array of old, faded, broken toys that looked like relics of a Salvation Army Christmas long past. On the other table, to the research assistant's right, lay a spectacular assembly of brand-new, shiny toys, like a window display at FAO Schwarz compared to its dismal counterpart. The research assistant said she had forgotten something in another room that she needed to retrieve and would step out for just a few minutes; in the meantime, she said, Molly could play with the toys on the former (dismal) table, though the ones on the latter table were someone else's (shiny) toys and could not be touched until the research assistant had gotten permission.

She then exited the room, and Molly was left to contend with this agonizing moral quandary: Which toys to play with? All the while, her behavior was being covertly videotaped from the other side of a one-way mirror. In the immediately prior stress reactivity procedures, she had proven herself to be a highly reactive child, showing a remarkable level of stress system activation to virtually all challenges—answering an interviewer's questions, tasting lemon juice, watching a sad movie, and memorizing several series of numbers. As we watched undetected through the one-way mirror, Molly mustered every conceivable strategy within her five-year-old repertoire to inhibit her overpowering urge to play with the new, shiny but forbidden toys. Her small round face became a lucid window onto the torment of her perplexity about what to do. She attempted to distract herself momentarily with the deteriorating relics on the authorized table of toys, but quickly abandoned the tactic as hopeless. She tried averting her gaze from the enticing new toys, holding her hand up to the side of her face so that the toys were screened from view. She sat on her hands and wiggled; she got up and circled the perimeter of the room; she bit her fingernails and twirled her hair; she made faces at herself in the mirror. Finally, in a fit of desperation, she began a long, animated monologue, admonishing herself to obey the research assistant's instructions, to ignore temptation's charms, to act as the adults would want her to act. For ten excruciating minutes she warded off desire, until the research assistant returned and told her she could now play with any of the toys, which she did with delectation and delight.

In contrast to this extraordinary restraint, the "delay of gratification" revealed by most other children, placed in the same behavioral dilemma, could have been measured in seconds: almost the moment the door closed upon the research assistant's departure, most other children were all over those new toys, engaged in an ecstatic festival of unapologetic, unfettered play. It was nearly always the highly reactive, biologically activated children who showed a seemingly limitless capacity for resisting temptation, delaying gratification, and self-regulating their impulses to transgress a boundary clearly set by the adult authority figure. Why was this, and what could it add to our research?

The Sickest or the Healthiest

Even as we explored, very early in our research, the *behavioral* signatures of children with highly reactive responses to laboratory stressors, we had begun to witness a conspicuous discontinuity between them and our other study kids. It was almost as if our new stress reactivity protocol was acting as a prism does with light, separating out children occupying different visible "bands" of neurobiological response and revealing those with an exceptional, exaggerated reactivity to our modest challenges.

With the protocol now in hand, we began to use it as a tool to render visible what was otherwise hidden and unseen, and to employ the lab reactivity measure within broader epidemiologic studies of children's everyday lives. In contrast to our laboratory-based protocol, these larger studies assessed naturally occurring social environments, where real-life stressors rather than laboratory surrogates were linkable to measurable differences in children's health, disease, and development. Because our goal was an illumination of how such differences in stress response operate in unselected, real-world settings, we chose from the beginning to study groups of children in *communities or schools,* rather than pediatric patients in clinics or hospitals. The latter are clearly important to study and learn from as well, especially when searching for the etiologies of specific diseases and disorders. But we wanted to understand the implications of actual stressors and differences in reactivity as they occur and function in normative, generally healthy populations of children. We wanted to study prevalent adversities in unexceptional environments, and their influences on common forms of illness, injury, and dysfunction in the lives of typically developing children. So we went out looking for representative groups of children in ordinary, representative neighborhood environments.

That is how much of our work became centered within preschool, kindergarten, and early primary school settings, where legions of children assemble every fall in great, multilayered billows of energy, Brownian motion, infectious pathogens, and an abundant, bright-eyed readiness to learn. Among the truest, unsung heroes of any contemporary society (as we will learn in greater detail in a later chapter) are the teachers who somehow manage to turn chaos into structure, wrest learning and discovery from the jaws of pandemonium, and forge a kind of micro-civilization out of the Dark Ages and noisy cacophonies of early child-hood social relationships. There is no research laboratory quite like a kindergarten or preschool classroom.

Thus our first two studies examined children's infectious illnesses in relation to stress exposures, reactivity, and health. One took place in the Marilyn Reed Lucia Child Care Study Center preschool of the University of California, San Francisco (UCSF), and the other with a group of kindergartners enrolled in San Francisco neighborhood schools. In the first of these, we tested three- to five-year-old children of UCSF faculty and staff in a little windowless closet at the back of the center, adminis-tered interviews and questionnaires in which parents reported on family stressors and difficulties, and assessed the rate and severity of respira-tory illnesses (colds, ear infections, asthmatic episodes, pneumonia, and so on) using weekly examinations of the children by a pediatric nurse practitioner. The stress interviews and questionnaires asked parents about stressful events in the lives of parents and children (such as the death of a loved one, maltreatment by other children at school, residen-tial moves, parental divorce, or wetting your pants at school), as well as more chronic, persistent adversities, such as family financial problems or exposures to violence, marital discord, or parental depression.

For the second, kindergarten-based study, we brought children to our lab at UCSF one to two weeks before and after they started primary school for the first time. Entering kindergarten is a major adaptive and developmental challenge for five-year-olds, because of the confluence of new, exciting, but sometimes demanding and stressful social relation-ships with twenty or thirty previously unknown peers. The start of kin-dergarten also marks an escalation of teachers' behavioral expectations in school, the advent of actual early academic learning, and exposures to a multiplicity of new respiratory and other pathogens. It's a big deal for little bodies and five-year-old minds—a kind of perfect storm of social uncertainties, challenging expectations, and virulent exposures to bugs and disease.

A week or two before and after kindergarten began, we obtained small samples of blood to measure changes in immune system function resulting from activation of the cortisol and fight-or-flight stress reactivity systems. Illness rates were derived from biweekly parent-completed checklists of respiratory symptoms in their children. We had hypothesized and anticipated that kids showing high fight-or-flight responses, strong cortisol reactivity in the lab, or resulting changes in immune function would have substantially more frequent and severe illnesses when they were from families with higher levels of stress, adversity, and turmoil. As such, our expectation was that the worst respiratory illnesses would be found among those children with the *combination* of high stress-related reactivity and high naturally occurring family environmental stressors. (The graph on the facing page shows the merged results for both studies.) As predicted, the sickest children were those whose heightened stress reactivity compounded the stress effects of their more aversive family settings. Their inordinately high rates and severities of respiratory illness were accountable to a *confluence* between an internal biological sensitivity and an external burden of familial environmental stressors.

What we had *not* hypothesized, and what took us entirely by wide-eyed, head-scratching surprise, was the finding that equally high-reactivity children living in very low-stress (and thus more predictable, coherent, and supportive) families had the very *lowest* rates of respiratory illness of all the children in the study—lower even than the low-reactivity children in low-stress families! Their illness incidence was not merely lower compared to their counterparts from more stressful homes, but the lowest of any of the children we studied. *The highly stress-reactive kids were either the sickest or the healthiest, contingent upon the socioemotional tenor of their families.*

Flummoxed at first by these convergent data from two different studies, we cast about for possible explanations and asked how a single kind of child could have *both* the highest and lowest rates of disease. I will remember forever a cool fall afternoon in 1993 at UCSF when three of us—Abbey, our research assistant Jan Genevro, and I—almost physically wrestled with this conundrum, filling a blackboard with drawings and figures, scribbling out logical arguments, vigorously debating candi-

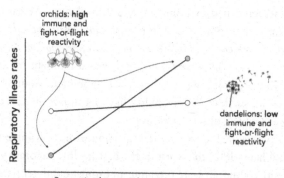

Graph showing children's respiratory illness rates as related to social environmental adversities and stress reactivity status. The orchid children, with high levels of reactivity in the fight-or-flight system or the immune system, had either the highest or the lowest rates of respiratory illness, depending upon their levels of exposure to stress. The dandelion children, with average or low levels of reactivity, had only modest levels of illness under both low- and high-stress circumstances.

date explanations. At issue were two entirely distinct interpretations of our findings.

On the one hand, it made eminent sense that kids who were so biologically reactive to artificial stressors in the lab would have more illnesses under real-world, nonlaboratory conditions of great adversity and stress. The latter would be just a predictable—though at that point unrecognized—consequence of the former. On the other hand, we had an almost clinical intuition that these highly reactive children, in supportive rearing environments, might be even healthier than their peers, by virtue of their reactivity—their responsiveness—to the goodness and nurturance of those settings. In a moment that might be best compared to how depth perception results from the same image seen from the differing points of view of two eyes, we arrived abruptly at a stunning explanation. It was not "either/or," but "both/and," because the children in question had about them an exquisite sensitivity to the character and nature of both aversive and supportive surrounding social environments.

They foundered in bad environments and thrived in good environments for the same remarkable reason: *they were more open, more permeable, more tender to the powerful influences, both bad and good, of the contexts in which they were living and growing.* It was a moment of epiphany that every investigator longs and hopes for—a sudden, vision-changing insight that reconciles an impossibility, like a harmonic musical cadence resolving a troubled, dissonant chord.

So our provisional answer to the question of how a single kind of child could have either the worst or the best health outcomes was that highly reactive children were revealing an exquisite differential susceptibility, or *special sensitivity to the character of their social environments,* both stressful and supportive. In a 1995 report in the journal *Psychosomatic Medicine,* we wrote:

> We further—and more speculatively—propose that exaggerated psychobiologic reactivity may reflect a relative deficit in self-regulatory capacity, which results in a heightened sensitivity to the character of the social world. Highly reactive individuals may therefore show either exceptional vulnerability or exceptional resilience, depending on the level of stress and adversity that characterizes the ambient social environment.

Perhaps, we tentatively suggested, the core feature of a high-reactivity child is not vulnerability, but rather an unusual susceptibility to social conditions of whatever character or valence. These highly sensitive, orchid-like children bore far more of the health and developmental burdens of stressful, adverse environments, but when reared in supportive, nurturing settings, they disproportionately prospered and thrived.

The Biology of Shyness

One of the earliest and most persistent questions that parents and colleagues have asked about these sensitive, orchid children was whether there were other, more visible markers of such children—that is, behavioral or other *phenotypic* characteristics that might reliably signal their underlying reactivity. A phenotype refers to the set of observable, visible characteristics—eye color, height, personality, and behavior—that describe an individual person or organism. The answer to the question of whether an orchid child's behavioral phenotype could be identified appears to be a qualified yes.

Jerome Kagan, a professor of developmental psychology at Harvard, spent much of his career studying what he called "the biology of shyness." He began with the observation that even newborn infants show clear and dramatic differences in temperamental dimensions, temperament referring to those aspects of early personality that characterize young children's enduring, cross-context behavior. According to the early work of Alexander Thomas and Stella Chess in the New York Longitudinal Study of the 1950s, even early in life, infants show systematic differences in such behavioral dimensions as activity level, regularity of sleeping and eating patterns, adaptability, intensity of emotion, mood, distractibility, persistence and attention span, and sensory sensitivity. Building on this work, Kagan studied infants and children who according to their parents, caretakers, and teachers were systematically inclined toward low adaptability, introversion, sensory sensitivity, and withdrawal from novel or challenging situations. Focusing on the "shyest of the shy," he documented these children's tendencies to be reactive in the fight-or-flight system, showing sharp heart rate accelerations under conditions of threat, novelty, and challenge. He also documented an unusual sensitivity to sensory stimuli, such as the taste of lemon juice, in his very shy kids. Thus, working in the opposite direction from our own later studies—that is, moving from behavior (extreme shyness) toward neurobiological response patterns (heart rate reactivity)—Kagan established clear linkages between shy temperament and bodily responses to stressors.

Similarly, Jay Belsky, professor of human ecology at the University of California, Davis, examined differential susceptibility to negative parenting among young children reported or observed to have "difficult" temperaments—that is, those high in the negative emotionality dimensions of early personality. Negative emotionality is some infants' proclivity to experience and express distress, emotional lability, restlessness, and attentional difficulties, especially during challenging circumstances, such as a separation from their mothers. Using parent questionnaires and observations of children's emotions expressed in their faces, voices, and behaviors, Belsky identified infants and toddlers with a constellation of early negative emotions and then studied their subsequent liability to externalizing (for instance, oppositional, aggressive, or defiant) and internalizing (depressive or anxious) behavior problems. Parenting behavior was also rated, using in-home observations of anger, hostility, and intrusiveness in parents' interactions with their children. What Belsky found was that negatively emotional infants had neither systematically lower nor higher levels of later behavior problems, except when they were being reared by parents who themselves displayed emotional negativity. Infants with temperamental negativity had higher ratings of both internalizing and externalizing problems when being reared in households with negative parenting. His interpretation of this and later findings was that infants with temperamental negative emotionality showed differential susceptibility to rearing influence.

Taken together, the studies of Kagan and Belsky suggested that although the connections are loose and not always reliable, there are linkages between the extreme neurobiological reactivity that defined the orchid child in our early work and the temperamental characteristics of shyness, negative emotionality, and a predisposition to withdraw from novel or challenging conditions. Does this mean that all orchid children are shy and withdrawn? Not at all. Does it mean that shy children are universally reactive biologically to stressors? No, it doesn't. What it does seem to suggest is that highly sensitive, differentially susceptible orchid children are more often, but not always, prone to shyness, sensory sensitivity, fearfulness of novel situations, and the development of problematic behavior under adversity.

Butterfly Wings and Fitness

We thus arrived at a tentative explanation—really more of a workable account—for this phenomenon in which orchid children, with a common neurobiological reactivity to laboratory challenges, sustained either the worst or best health outcomes and the least or most adaptive developmental endpoints. We began to think of such children as "thin-skinned" or excessively "permeable" to the environment, or "canaries in the mineshaft"—all metaphors that, along with their designation as orchid children, seemed to helpfully convey this central feature of an inordinate sensitivity to the character of the social world: their siblings and families, their schoolrooms and social groups, their neighborhoods and communities. But an enormous and steadily growing harvest of questions remained to be pondered and answered:

- Could these highly reactive, orchid children be the same ones who show such exorbitant rates of illness, injury, and behavior disorders in health services research (see pages 9–10)?
- If so, what might be the public health implications of the revelation of orchid children? How might societies effectively address this disproportionate burden of disorder that such children carry?
- From where and for what reason would this complex phenotype have arisen in human species? Does it occur only in human children?
- What happens to orchid children over time? Do they become more or less reactive? Do they falter in school and in achievement?
- How early and by what means might we detect the high-reactivity phenotype? At birth? In gestation?
- Is high reactivity genetic or environmental in origin?

About this time, in 1999, as luck and providence may have had it, I spent several days as a visiting professor at Vanderbilt University in Nashville, Tennessee, where I met and began an extended dialogue with Bruce Ellis, a bright, fiery, and talented young evolutionary psychologist. Bruce likely was (and remains) himself an orchid child. Initially shy and hesitant in his interactions, he would quickly reveal to those who listened carefully a prodigious intelligence, a deep allegiance to the scientific process, and a passionate belief in evolutionary theory regarding the origins of the natural world. In the early days of his graduate education in psychology, Bruce had become dismayed and disappointed by a general incoherence that he discerned in the conceptual grounding of contemporary psychology. He wanted to know not just how human behavior might be best categorized and described, but where it came from, why certain behavioral patterns persisted in human populations, and how to account for behavioral aberration and the emergence of psychopathology over the course of early development. In one of his graduate seminars, Bruce had discovered the writings of Charles Darwin and what he soon came to regard as lucid and consistent answers to many of his questions about the roots of human behavior. He was even then on a path to becoming an evolutionary psychologist, steeped in the laws of natural selection, and one of developmental psychology's most imaginative and prolific theoreticians.

The summer following my Vanderbilt visit, Bruce Ellis arranged to spend a number of weeks in our Berkeley lab, and he and I began to brood together upon a theoretical framework that might account for the emergence and conservation of highly sensitive, differentially susceptible human children over millennia of evolutionary time. The summer collaboration whetted our appetites for what eventually became a four-month writing project together in Christchurch, New Zealand, where Bruce had by then accepted his first faculty position and where I spent a short sabbatical visit. In long and mutually instructive conversations, we traced the perimeter of a fully articulated evolutionary theory of special sensitivity, made predictive hypotheses based on that theoretical orientation, and conducted confirmatory analyses of previously collected data. The core tenets of that fledgling theory were presented in two 2005 papers in the journal *Development and Psychopathology*.

First, we alleged, some children have highly reactive phenotypes that are forms of enhanced, neurobiologically derived sensitivity to the social contexts in which their lives are nested. Evolutionary theory contends that all such naturally occurring phenotypic variation derives initially from random changes in genetic DNA, called mutations. A *genotype* refers to the specific, highly individual molecular sequence of DNA that is present in each of our cells—a compendium of genetic code that is inherited from our parents—half from our moms and half from our dads. This genetic code is changed under normal circumstances only by mutations—that is, frequent, permanent but subtle changes in DNA sequence that are brought about by exposure to chemical toxins, radiation, or random DNA copying errors that can occur during cell division. We believe that mutations resulting in highly reactive special-sensitivity phenotypes have been favored by natural selection over the millennia of human evolution due to their enhancement of reproductive fitness and survival chances in both maximally untroubled and maximally stressful environments.

Thus in stressful, high-threat settings, such as those imaginable within the ancient environments of hominid (near-human) troops, special-sensitivity phenotypes would have been protective to both individuals and social groups by virtue of such phenotypes' enhanced vigilance to danger and threat. Sensitive individuals would have been evolutionarily conserved by natural selection as a means of fostering survival in conditions of peril. Yet in other, presumably long prehistorical periods of relative peace and safety, special sensitivity to context would have also been conserved due to its capacity for rendering sensitive children more open and receptive to all the personal and health benefits of such environments. Since the core feature of high-reactivity children is their sensitivity, rather than vulnerability, they would have also been disproportionately able to absorb and benefit from the positive, protective social conditions during such stable, tranquil prehistoric epochs.

The result would have been a natural selection that would favor special sensitivity to the environment in both very high- and very low-stress conditions, in the former as a purveyor of vigilance to threat and in the latter as a source of greater permeability or openness to the benefits of safe, quiescent conditions. So we proposed that the expected relation between early exposure to psychosocial stress and adversity and the general level of biological reactivity found in the population would be a U-shaped curve. For reasons of both openness to protective, low-stress conditions and vigilance to endangering, high-stress settings, highly reactive individuals would be favored at each extremity of environmental stress and adversity. The curious persistence of high reactivity, which we know creates liability to mental and physical illness, within the pool of human populations would thus be attributable to its protective advantages at the extremes of early exposures to adversity.

A legitimate question is how all of this might happen during development. The ability of a developing fetus or infant to sense and anticipate the potential harmfulness or protectiveness of the conditions into which it is born implies a capacity for adjusting or calibrating stress response systems to match the early environment. Pause for a moment to admire the wonder of such a process—an unborn baby sensing and biologically preparing for a world into which it has not yet even been born! This is what evolutionary biologists call a *conditional adaptation:* an evolved mechanism that monitors specific features of the childhood environment as a basis for adjusting biological development to adaptively match those features. We know that such conditional adaptations occur in animals. Caterpillars, for example, develop completely different body types depending upon what there is to eat in the first three days of life. Kittens respond to early weaning by engaging in more object play, but not social play, compared to normal controls—a behavioral calibration that may foster adaptation to environments where food is scarce. Buckeye butterflies develop completely different wing patterns and coloration depending upon the length of daylight as they are emerging from their pupal stage of development.

Perhaps the best-known example of a conditional adaptation in humans is how mental disorders in mothers are linked to earlier puberty in their daughters and how this adjustment in the timing of maturation is attributable to tumultuous family relationships and often the absence of a father. According to evolutionary theory, children (and perhaps especially girls) whose early experiences in their families lead them to see others as untrustworthy, relationships as opportunistic or self-serving, or resources as scarce and unpredictable will develop a reproductive "strategy" and patterns of behavior that serve to accelerate puberty, decrease their age at first sexual intercourse, and orient them toward shorter-term rather than longer-term relationships. Thus children who sense family disarray in the first few months or years of life may unconsciously hasten reproductive development as a biological tactic for earlier dissemination of their genes.

Similarly, and especially important in the development of orchid and dandelion children, the malleability of the stress response systems, along with their context-driven calibration, suggests that these systems may also undergo conditional adaptations, in which higher reactivity is allowed to emerge in both very low- and very high-stress early environments. In both conditions, survival and reproductive "fitness" may be enhanced by adjusting stress responses—and thus special environmental sensitivity—to relatively high levels of reactivity. Jay Belsky has correspondingly suggested that parents "hedge their bets" against an uncertain future by producing different types of offspring. More fixed, less accommodating children would achieve better reproductive success in ecological niches that match their genetic predisposition, while more flexible or malleable children would fit and thrive in a wider range of niches, depending upon the rearing conditions encountered in early life.

Thus, within the evolutionary framework that Bruce Ellis so usefully brought to this work, we were able to suggest an account for the seemingly paradoxical emergence and persistence of these risky, high-reactivity phenotypes within human populations, to generate hypotheses about how early stress and reactivity prevalence should be related if conditional adaptations occur and the account were true, and to produce early evidence that confirmed the existence and shape of those relations.

Monkeys and Malevolence

An opportunity to test these ideas within a true evolutionary context came along in an unexpected way. In a happy serendipity a number of years ago, Steve Suomi and I found ourselves presenting our work in the common forum of a scientific meeting on early development. Steve is a primatologist and comparative ethologist who studies the behavioral development of rhesus macaque monkeys of the species *Macaca mulatta*. He was originally trained as a biopsychologist at Stanford by Seymour Levine and later at the University of Wisconsin by Harry Harlow, the psychologist who conducted the widely known wire mother experiments with young monkeys. Steve's research has produced fundamental new insights into how early development occurs, how individual differences in stress reactivity arise, and how the early social environment influences the calibration of such differences.

At the scientific meeting in which our individual research programs first converged, Steve presented evidence that a highly reactive phenotype of young macaques surfaces in a small subset of individuals within natural environments and that a higher proportion of these reactive individuals occurs when groups of young monkeys are raised together, without the influence of their natal troop (see photographs opposite). I presented startlingly parallel data showing how a high-reactivity profile occurs in about 15 to 20 percent of young humans, how one child in five has disproportionately higher rates of infections and injuries in stressful early environments, but how unusually low rates of such morbidities are seen in more supportive, predictable, and nurturant conditions. Steve and I also discovered that we had met and spent a day together in the 1960s, when we were both freshmen at Stanford University. Neither of us had seen or spoken to the other during the intervening thirty years!

Hoping to capitalize on this providential reunion and the remarkable intersection of our work over the previous three decades, we planned a sabbatical visit when I could work for an extended period of time in his National Institutes of Health (NIH) primate laboratory in the countryside northwest of the Bethesda, Maryland, NIH campus. During that sabbatical year, Steve and I happened upon an interesting and revealing natural experiment. A thirty- to forty-animal troop of macaques lives at the primate center in a protected six-acre natural habitat consisting of a grassy, tree-lined reserve equipped with climbing structures, a variety of toys, and a large swimming pond with a small island and bridge. It is, in short, a kind of summer camp for monkeys that becomes an ice-sliding playground during the coldest winter months. The enclosure also had a small cinderblock building to which the troop could escape during thunderstorms, rain, or snow, and this building had come to the end of its useful life, compelling a period of new construction on the habitat grounds.

During the year prior to my sabbatical visit, all of the troop's monkeys had been temporarily confined to the original cinderblock build-

Two different behavioral and biological phenotypes of rhesus macaque infants. The young monkeys on the right, like 80 to 85 percent of their peers, will actively and aggressively explore their environment, vigorously engaging challenge and novelty. By contrast, about 15 to 20 percent of young rhesus monkeys, like that on the left, will show early evidence of fearfulness, withdrawal from novelty, and exaggerated biological responses to challenge and stress.

ing to keep them protected and safe while the extensive construction project took place within the larger habitat. The period of rebuilding was projected to last one to two months, but as with so many such projects, it stretched into six months, during which the animals had access to few amenities apart from food, a woodchip floor, and a corrugated tin roof—no pond, no trees, no toys, and no running! The confinement had proved very stressful, and the primate center veterinarians, who checked on the animals at regular intervals, reported a substantial increase in violence between the monkeys, traumatic injuries, and unexpected illnesses. Indeed, three monkeys died during the confinement: one from an acceleration of a preexisting degenerative neurological disease; one via a postpartum hemorrhage; and one at the hands of the other troop members—a so-called mobbing in which a targeted animal was violently pummeled to death by its peers.

Now, it happened that all of these animals had been characterized prior to the period of confinement as high or low in behavioral and biological reactivity to stress. Recall that, as with human children, about one in five macaque infants is described as highly reactive to challenge, fearful of novel conditions, and prone to exaggerated biological responses to threat or provocation—a vivid description of an orchid monkey! (See the fearful young monkey on the left in the previous photographs.) Plus, we had all of the veterinary records for each monkey, before, during, and after the stressful six-month confinement period. We were thus able to look back at the number and severity of violent injuries that had occurred during each of these periods.

We found that there had been a fivefold increase in both the number and severity of violent injuries during the six-month period of confinement. The graph below shows that almost all of the acceleration in injury incidence and severity was attributable to attacks on high-reactivity, orchid-like animals, echoing human bullying (which we will explore later in relation to orchid children). The incidence in the majority, low-reactivity monkeys increased only slightly during confinement, not even close to the level seen in the high-reactivity individuals. The high-reactivity monkeys were being selectively and violently injured at the hands of their troop mates.

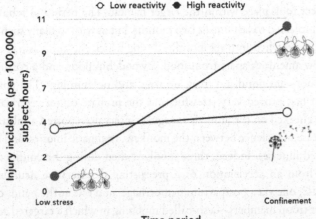

Graph showing injury rates in a troop of rhesus macaques in relation to a period of stressful confinement. Animals exhibiting high reactivity (orchid monkeys) had the highest rates of violent injuries during the period of confinement but the lowest rates during the year preceding. Those with low reactivity (dandelion monkeys) showed moderate injury rates in both low-stress and confinement periods.

But the graph tells another story as well. Just as we had seen in highly reactive human children, their primate counterparts had not only the highest number of injuries during the stressful period, but also the lowest number in the low-stress periods that preceded and followed the troop confinement. Somehow, these highly sensitive, orchid-like young monkeys had managed to effectively avoid attacks during the quiet, low-adversity conditions in the natural habitat, but had sustained enormously disproportionate rates of violent injuries—many of them very severe—during a highly stressful but unavoidable incarceration. Our orchidish evolutionary forebears—these context-sensitive young monkeys—bore a striking resemblance to their hominid descendants: powerfully intuitive, prodigiously reactive to novelty and threat, and subject to massive oscillations of fortune and health.

From shy little Molly, who had literally talked herself out of playing with the shiny but prohibited toys, to Steve Suomi's reactive macaques, who hid from confrontation until hiding was all but impossible, a consistent and compelling evolutionary story had begun to emerge. A small subset of both species has been conserved by natural selection to impart vigilance and sensibility to the social conditions of life. These sentient, reactive, and especially permeable young anomalies carry a kind of binary predilection: both the decided advantages of receptivity when conditions are protective and right, and the often treacherous liabilities of vulnerability when they are wrong. In environments of placidity and quiet, they are the exemplars of health and exceptional wellness, but when malevolence and enmity prevail, they can endure a form of scapegoated perdition that William Golding portrayed in his small boy, Simon.

As vivid and irresistible as this account had now gradually become, it was just the beginning, as there was so much more to learn, about both orchids and dandelions, their origins and their potentials. Would our early findings still hold in the light of later, larger and methodologically stronger studies? What other measurable signs of special sensitivity might there be? Could it be detected beyond the walls of the Boyce laboratory? How would it fare within the broader sea of research, analyses, and thoughts of other scientists?

4

An Orchestration of Orchids and Dandelions

Out of the cacophony of individual variation in the health effects of adversity and in children's biological responses to our stressful laboratory challenges, we had detected a distant whisper of music and song. But might there be an even larger, more orchestral shape to which our findings might conform? Sooner than we might have imagined, the melody rising unexpectedly out of the early years of our work began to swell into new science and new discovery. There was an even larger symphony to which we were being called to listen.

Fresh results confirming the idea that certain children are unusually susceptible to the nature of their social, interpersonal environments continued to emerge, not only from my research group's ongoing work, but also from that of other labs and other investigators around the world. A team of scientists in London began to reveal the differential susceptibility of certain infant temperaments as they adapted to postnatal life in families of different strengths and liabilities. Investigators at the University of Pittsburgh started work confirming the pace of puberty finding and showed that a genetic variant in the estrogen receptor gene (which produces the cell surface protein that recognizes and responds to the sex hormone estrogen) produces later menarche (first menstruation) among girls with strong family environments but substantially earlier menarches in those with conflictive, less supportive family relationships. In

Jerusalem, another group similarly reported that a genetic variant in the dopamine receptor gene (which makes a response protein for the neurotransmitter, or chemical messenger, dopamine) results in high levels of positive social behavior among three-year-olds with highly supportive moms but a deficit in such behavior in children raised by punitive, unsupportive moms.

Taken together, these results began to produce a symphonic convergence defining a new field of study and a new way of understanding the uses, liabilities, and virtues of variation in human sensitivity. The science that undergirds this new knowledge is testimony to the collaborative spirit of fellow researchers, to the collegiality that is vital to the research enterprise, and to the potency and efficacy of the scientific process itself. Science is never the only accessible path to truth, but the truths it has uncovered about the remarkable variation in children's openness to the social world have begun to transform our vision of human commonalities and differences.

Lend Me Your Ears

In the fall of 1993, when Yasser Arafat and Yitzhak Rabin were shaking hands over a (temporary) Bill Clinton peace accord, when Benazir Bhutto was becoming the prime minister of Pakistan for the second time, and when NASA was preparing to launch a space shuttle mission to repair the optical flaw in the Hubble Space Telescope, my colleague Steve Suomi and I were further pondering the vulnerabilities of monkeys. There was an early, deep snow in the Maryland countryside, and the Canadian geese that normally linger until the ice is well upon them had refiled their flight plans and made an early departure for the beaches of Sinaloa and the broad, cathedraled plazas of the Mexican state of Chihuahua. In the NIH's ramshackle primate village, where fifteen hundred resident monkeys were nested within five hundred acres of now white rural farmland, it was coming on winter, and the veterinarians were restless about a new flu season bearing inexorably down upon their small, furry charges with tails. Having begun to understand the remarkable range of physical and psychological susceptibilities among both human children and young rhesus macaques, Steve and I were considering new questions: Might highly reactive, orchid-like young monkeys be more vulnerable to influenza and other viral infections during a seasonal epidemic than their hardier dandelion peers? Would the one young macaque in five that we knew was more sensitive to its social environment show higher or inordinately lower rates of flu, depending upon the animal's rearing conditions? And might the local monkeys teach us why orchid children are sometimes more vulnerable to infection, or even help us find ways to keep them healthier and infection-free?

In monkeys, as in their human equivalents, looking for infections requires physical examinations of noses and throats, ears, lungs, and skin—all the places where winter viruses tend to congregate and flourish. But there was an interesting and challenging problem in doing these exams. Young macaques, in keeping with at least some of their young human cousins, don't accommodate easily or hospitably to being physically assessed by a pediatrician. I had tried long and hard to do an exam like I might have done in a pediatric clinic, using an assistant to "bear hug" an unruly monkey in a circumferential embrace while I attempted to sneak a listen or a look in the constantly shifting and wiggling spaces between human and monkey body parts. But when approached with a stethoscope and mask, monkeys bite, scratch, scream, screech, defecate, and flee, with a malice and maniacal willfulness unrivaled by any human two-year-old. Monkeys won't hold still while you're looking in their eyes or ears, they ignore all requests for deep breaths or samples of urine, and they vigorously refuse to stick out their tongues and say, "Aaaah." A group of monkeys is as difficult to examine as a posse of hyenas on the run.

Happily, it turned out that as part of the regular routine of the primate center, all the animals in a given colony and social group were briefly sedated on a rotating quarterly schedule, so that veterinary care could be provided painlessly and any needed samples could be obtained without coercion, conflict, or discomfort. So it happened that this sedation routine produced quite frequently a mound of limp, angelically sleepy and drooling monkeys, ready and blissfully willing to be examined in detail and without any later memories of the ordeal. When this procedure occurred, I could carry out on each motionless macaque a careful and exhaustive physical exam, much like those I have done with thousands of (conscious) child patients. I was delighted. I peered into the monkeys' eyes and ears, looked top to bottom for skin rashes and lesions, and listened to their hearts and lungs—just as I would have done with a batch of kindergartners. I opened their mouths without fear of a bite and recorded the condition of their teeth, tongues, tonsils, and throats. It was like a round of preseason football physicals with a squad of unconscious monkey athletes.

Another essential component of these exams, especially given our then-current focus on infection, was the detection of fever. To measure the animals' core body temperatures, we used an infrared ear thermometer, exactly like the ones now almost always used in doctors' offices and hospitals (and that can be bought at a local Walgreens). These thermometers, unlike the old mercury tubes that we put in babies' mouths or bottoms, measure eardrum temperatures using a micro-thermometer that literally computes the amount of heat emanating from the eardrum. For the purposes of accuracy and replicability, I decided to take a temperature reading from both ears rather than just one. And even though we were measuring ear temperatures on both sides of the head rather than in the body's midline, as we would have with an oral or rectal thermometer, we had every expectation that the two readings would be close to identical.

But they were decidedly *not* identical! In most of the animals, the left eardrum temperature was just slightly warmer than the right, by roughly half a degree centigrade (or one degree Fahrenheit)—a statistical difference not likely to be due to random chance. The average monkey had a left eardrum temperature of about 37.5°C (99.5°F) but a right eardrum temperature of about 37.0°C (98.6°F). It was a reliable *asymmetry:* a systematic, recurring difference in eardrum warmth measured on the left and right sides. Although in group after unconscious group we kept finding the same, slightly warmer left ears, we also discovered that about one monkey in five had a *right* eardrum that was slightly warmer than the left—just the opposite of the asymmetry we had found in all the other animals. Was there a pattern in this asymmetry, a hidden physiological melody perhaps worth listening to and transcribing? Once again we had stumbled upon that 80/20 divide—four monkeys with warmer left ears for each one with a warmer right ear, echoing the same proportional breakdown present in that most important finding in health services research. But what could it mean? Probably nothing, we thought, since we believed the finding was surely flawed. Why would monkeys have reliably different ear temperatures on the two sides of their heads?

Assuming these asymmetrical ear temperatures were physiologically impossible, we set out to correct our obviously flawed measurement techniques. I tried alternating which side was measured first. Maybe, I thought, if the right side was always first, the left would be warmer, because it would have been in the "downhill" position, closer to the exam table, where warm blood might have pooled by gravity. Next, I tried switching the thermometers that I used, thinking maybe one was faulty or inaccurate. Then I did two measurements on each side, rather than just one, conjecturing that perhaps the asymmetry was simply a measurement error, correctable by increasing the number of data points. Finally, I tried placing myself in just one carefully standardized physical position as I measured the temperatures, speculating that perhaps I had been switching my stance as I moved from one ear to the other, creating slightly different angles in the thermal "pictures" recorded by the infrared thermometer on the two sides of the head. None of these corrections changed a thing. No matter how diligently and carefully I measured monkey ear temperatures, the same predominantly warmer left-sided laterality kept showing up. And it was true of males and females, young and old, caged and free-ranging monkeys.

We had landed on terra incognita. As far as we knew, core body temperatures had seldom been carefully and reliably measured on both sides of the body, in either humans or monkeys. It was a finding never previously recorded in any species, and we had no idea what it meant. Even more intriguing, when we began to compare left-to-right temperature differences in relation to the behavior, temperament, and stress reactivity characteristics of individual monkeys, we saw that the smaller number of animals with the higher right-sided temperatures (the one in five) were also those with previously observed behavioral patterns of poorly adaptive, negative emotional responses to novel or challenging conditions. These right-side-warmer monkeys had shown us less exploratory activity and greater cortisol system activation, for example, when temporarily separated from their moms or their usual social groups. They were orchid monkeys, and they seemed to have mysteriously warmer right eardrums! Why?

As strange as this seemed at the time, our results were reminiscent of observations that had been made by Jerome Kagan, the previously mentioned Harvard psychologist, in his earlier studies of extremely shy, behaviorally inhibited young children. Kagan had noted that when responding to unfamiliar events, such children showed two, possibly related, physiological changes. First, they had greater brain wave (electroencephalographic, or EEG) activation of the right prefrontal cortex—the part of the brain just behind the right side of the forehead, which is involved in emotion regulation, impulse control, and planning. And second, they showed a cooling of the skin on the forehead, due to diminished blood flow, with the right side cooling more than the left. In other words, Kagan had begun to link certain enduring temperament-related behaviors, like shyness, to certain types of asymmetrical activity in the brain and midline shifts in body temperature. This was a powerful discovery, because it offered a physical explanation for why, in part, humans are the way they are. Understanding our brain-based personalities might unveil some of the mysteries of why we do what we do and how we can better understand ourselves and others.

As we considered Kagan's findings in his shy kids in relation to ours with orchid monkeys, the constellation of findings finally began to form a coherent and enticing picture. Although at first glance the human brain looks anatomically symmetrical, it is actually both structurally and functionally asymmetrical. We know, for example, that the brain is slightly larger on the left side than on the right and that there are differences in the functional roles of the left versus right cerebral hemispheres—the gray, convoluted surfaces of the brain that control speech, thought, emotions, reading, writing, and learning. For reasons that we don't entirely yet understand, these two sides of the brain have evolved to diverge in certain aspects of both form and function. The right prefrontal cortex, for example, is more attuned than the left to emotion regulation, to understanding "wholes" rather than "parts," and to the importance of contextual and relational aspects of experience. People with clinical depression also show unusually greater activation of the right prefrontal cortex than the left. This "lopsidedness" isn't so odd, mechanically, if you think about it. The left sides of car engines, for example, aren't mirror images of the right sides, just as the top three strings of a guitar aren't a reflection of the bottom three strings. In the case of the human brain, the issue is what new insights about behavior this asymmetry could reveal to us.

Blood flow to either side of the brain is controlled in part by the autonomic, fight-or-flight system on the same side, and when flow to one side of the brain is enhanced, flow to other parts of the head on the same side is proportionally diminished. It's a question of where to devote limited resources. Activation of the right prefrontal cortex, which requires more blood flow to deliver oxygen to the ramped-up neurons, is accompanied by decreasing flow to the skin, which results in a cooling of the right forehead. And since blood supply to the brain on each side is via the same arteries that supply the eardrum, any increase in blood flow to the right prefrontal cortex results in a parallel increase in flow to the right eardrum. Thus right prefrontal activation produces a slight rise in right ear temperatures, and a corresponding decrease in the skin temperature of the right forehead. To better understand these coupled dynamics of EEG activation, forehead temperature, and eardrum temperature, spend a minute with the picture on the facing page.

With these observations considered together, we had a cogent, if tentative, explanation for why the more negatively emotional, reactive and sensitive monkeys had a slightly warmer right ear. Their greater, orchid-like sensitivity was linked to a stronger activation of their right prefrontal cortex, the brain region directly involved in negative emotionality and shy behavior. The right prefrontal activation recruited, in turn, greater blood flow to the right side of the brain, and because the eardrum is supplied by the same system of arteries, the right ear was also asymmetrically warmed. We began to see a warmer right eardrum as a marker or a signal of the reactive, orchid phenotype, at least in rhesus monkeys. And the reason that the orchid monkey ears were hotter on their right side was because their brains were doing more work on that side to keep their thoughts and behaviors stable and under control—no simple task.

The next logical step was to try repeating the study in groups of human children. For this project, we amassed more than 450 four- to eight-year-old kids from four separate projects, in four different cities: two samples of children from my own laboratory, recruited in San Francisco and Berkeley; one sample from the long-term study of child development led by Marilyn Essex at the University of Wisconsin (the Wisconsin Study of Families and Work, or WSFW); and a fourth group of children studied by Jerome Kagan himself at Harvard. Again, eardrum temperatures were carefully and repeatedly recorded in both ears using infrared thermometers. Although each study used slightly different measures of temperament and child behavior, all of them offered a way of distinguishing children with biological and behavioral patterns suggestive of orchid phenotypes.

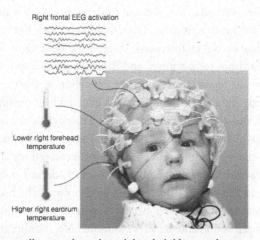

Right frontal EEG activation

Lower right forehead
temperature

Higher right earorum
temperature

This picture illustrates how shy, inhibited children, with more negative emotionality, show a combination of three concurrent physiological differences: (a) a pattern of greater activation in EEG tracings taken from the right, compared to the left, prefrontal cortex; (b) higher right eardrum temperatures; and (c) cooler temperatures in the skin of the right forehead.

As illustrated in the preceding picture of the little girl wearing the EEG cap, when we examined such patterns and ear temperatures in this large, combined group of children, clear patterns began to emerge. First, differences in temperature between the left and right ears were arrayed in a smooth, bell-shaped distribution, with some children having warmer left eardrums, some warmer rights, and many in between. Warmer left ears were associated with more risk-taking, socially competent, and emotionally positive behaviors, whereas warmer right ears were related to problematic, emotionally negative behaviors. These observations, in several hundred young children, paralleled our discovery of temperature asymmetries in the eardrums of rhesus monkeys. Sensitivity to difficult social contexts, liability to negative emotion, and susceptibility to depression were all correlated with greater right-sided brain activation and warmer temperatures in the right ear.

Kagan's older work had shown that this same kind of child has a cooler right forehead, and all of these temperature differentials were likely attributable to the changes in blood flow to a more activated right prefrontal cortex. In contrast, children with warmer left ears were somewhat less sensitive to the social world, had a predisposition to positive emotion, and showed relative resistance to depression—all features linked to greater left brain activation. Thus, orchid children, like their nonhuman primate orchid counterparts, showed the same right > left asymmetry in eardrum temperatures, and their dandelion opposites revealed left > right ear temperatures, just like dandelion monkeys. We had set out to study flu and colds in monkeys but had become unexpectedly distracted, and ultimately enlightened, by a more curious and revelatory discovery, which appeared true in both monkeys and children.

So did these findings mean that if I had measured my then twelve-year-old daughter's ear temperatures (which of course I could not help but do) and the right eardrum was found hotter (which of course it was), she was an orchid even in her ears and brain and was thus relegated to a life of depression and negative emotions? No, it didn't at all. Recall, as described in chapter 2, how examining relations between family stress and behavior problem severity scores showed a general statistical connection, but with plenty of exceptions to that rule. Some kids, for example, had very high family stress scores but almost no behavior problems at all, and others had low stress scores but many troubling behaviors. Similarly, though my twelve-year-old girl with the hot right ear was more likely to have an orchid's susceptibility to the effects of her social environment, eardrum temperature asymmetry is no more a ticket to the downside of an orchid's sensitivity than red hair is a binding certification of Scottish ancestry. It's simply a correlation, not a fait accompli or a pre-ordained outcome. But who would have thought that looking for fevers on a wintry monkey farm in the Maryland countryside would produce such a strange, simple, and unexpected marker of a child's sensitivity to the world? And where else might this finding now take us? Such a strong correlation opened up an opportunity to learn more about orchids and dandelions, even as it illuminated more clearly the distinctive strengths and weaknesses of both.

First Grade in the Heartland

This tendency to experience and show negative emotions that we documented in groups of orchid monkeys and young children suggested the possibility that highly reactive, orchid children might be more susceptible not only to injuries and colds, but to disorders of psychological and behavioral health as well. This freighted our research with a more ponderous significance. We were quite possibly sniffing around the edges of new knowledge, not just of minor perturbations in physical health, but of mental health as well, and how these two aspects of health combine to shape a life.

During my enlightening sojourn to the federal monkey ranch, I had become a member, along with a dozen or so valued colleagues, of the MacArthur Foundation's Research Network on Psychopathology and Development. Through that network, I became more closely allied with the Wisconsin Study of Families and Work and its lead scientist, Marilyn Essex, a sociologist in the Department of Psychiatry at the University of Wisconsin. She and her colleagues had begun a study in 1990 of 570 pregnant women, their partners, and their second-trimester fetuses,

soon to become their newly born children. Though the study was originally conceived as research on maternity leave and women's transitions
back to work, Marilyn realized that, carried forward in time, the project could become one of the rarest of research prizes: a longitudinal
(done over a period of time), prospective (looking forward) study of a
whole cohort of kids, enrolled before birth, and potentially document-
ing developmental change and stability over many years. The enrolled
women averaged twenty-nine years of age, were mostly white and in
mid-pregnancy, and 95 percent of the time were married to their baby's
father (this was, after all, the Wisconsin heartland). Through careful
and frequent collection of data on social environments and relationships, stressors and adversity, child development, and mental and physical health from fetal life through high school graduation, the WSFW
became a wonderful source of insight into the development of orchid
and dandelion children.

As my research group's findings on laboratory stress reactivity were
emerging, the Wisconsin cohort of young children was graduating from
kindergarten, about to enter first grade, and were readying themselves
for a first serious encounter with "real school." Because of the evidence
we had compiled—that stress reactivity seemed to reflect a special biological sensitivity to social conditions—Marilyn and I decided that
measuring reactivity in a subgroup of her children was a crucial and
pressing addition to the WSFW. But once again, it was not as easy as
we imagined it might be.

With help from the MacArthur Research Network, during a fast-
moving summer of 1998, we embarked on an effort to assess fight-or-
flight and cortisol reactivity in the Wisconsin children during the
summer before they entered first grade. Because it wasn't practical or
feasible to bring the kids from their homes in rural Wisconsin to a
university-based laboratory, we decided to bring the laboratory to them,
specifically to their neighborhoods and driveways. This was accomplished by cramming a fully equipped child-sized psychophysiology lab
into the confines of a gray soccer-mom Chevy van. What had almost
certainly served in its past life as transportation for some swarm of Wisconsin siblings and their dogs was now to become a sophisticated, state-
of-the-art stress lab.

The challenge was like an immense Rubik's Cube puzzle—fitting video and TV monitors, physiological measurement equipment, sample vials, a refrigerator, all our testing materials, a table and three chairs, two research assistants, and a six-year-old kid into a space the size of an average kitchen pantry. We tried every possible configuration: all seats taken out/all seats left in; testing area in the far back/testing area in the front or middle; doors open/doors closed. Finally, after a week of work, our combined research staff emerged grinning, smug and triumphant. As the following photographs show, the child and research assistant were situated in the largest space, immediately behind the driver and passenger seats. In the back, behind the last row of seats, another research assistant sat monitoring readings from the equipment, recording notes in a time log, controlling the presentation of video clips for the child, and creating a registry of responses.

We soon found, however, that three people in a closed van, with multiple pieces of active electronic equipment, surrounded by the hot, wet, cicada-laden Wisconsin summer, produced life-threatening interior temperatures. To counter this added complication, we bought and installed an industrial air conditioner in the passenger space in front. All of this equipment was connected by a heavy-duty power cord to an outlet in the family's garage. With everything in place, we had a mobile full-service child lab that lit up like the Griswolds' house at Christmas and was capable of evoking and measuring stress system reactivity, collecting and storing samples of spit, recording child behavior, and keeping a first grader and two research assistants reasonably comfortable, if moderately cramped.

That summer, we pulled into the driveways of 120 Wisconsin families and returned from each with a full array of stress reactivity and other measures. Along the way, we saw vivid reminders of the great differences in children's ordinary lives, surviving, sometimes thriving, always striving to accommodate themselves to the challenging and unexceptional worlds they called home. There were families and children who were thrilled to have a research lab parked in their driveways and whose curious neighbors buzzed around the edges, wondering what the Engbergs were up to now. There were kids who hid in their bedrooms and closets and others who greeted us with joyful leaps and hugs. There were

Summer on the road in Wisconsin, 1998: our child psychophysiology laboratory transplanted into a 1995 Chevrolet van.

moments of trepidation, as six-year-olds were reassured by parents and staff that climbing into a van with three only vaguely familiar adults was safe to do in this circumstance, even if to be strictly avoided in others. And there were occasions of celebratory triumph, as kids emerged from the van as heroes, to the accolades of their buddies lurking on the front lawn.

The measures of biological reactivity we garnered from these home visits could then be used in studies of emerging mental health problems—both concurrently, during the children's upcoming first-grade year, and prospectively, as they later entered puberty and adolescence, the period when psychological disorders become far more visible and identifiable, sometimes tragically. In the concurrent work, we found that, compared to children with no early signs of incipient mental disorders, first graders with internalizing symptoms—those of depression or anxiety—showed clear patterns of excessively high reactivity within the fight-or-flight system. On the other hand, the dandelion-like kids—those 80 percent with more normative reactivity—showed no appreciable mental health symptoms at all. Here was new, added evidence from young Wisconsin schoolchildren that highly reactive, orchid kids had a predisposition to the mental health symptoms of depression and anxiety, while the dandelions, with modest, average reactivity, had few if any psychological or behavioral problems. These findings, in a whole new sample of children, from an entirely different part of the country, offered an exciting validation of our original results.

But what would happen as these Wisconsin first graders grew and ripened into vulnerable adolescents, required to navigate challenges and negotiate the shifting social environments and relationships of high school and beyond? Would their reactivity levels in the summer before first grade still predict differences in mental health several years later? And as they entered the emotional briar patches of puberty, would there be differences between orchids and dandelions as striking as those we had already seen and reported?

As the same youth entered seventh grade, at thirteen years of age, their mental health symptoms were again assessed. And instead of correlating reactivity measures collected in the summer study with concurrent mental health, we were now attempting to *predict* mental health in early adolescence from measures of reactivity and stress collected six years earlier, during the summer before first grade. Scientists much prefer such longitudinal analyses, because they are less liable to the false conclusions that can sometimes be drawn from cross-sectional data and are far more likely to uncover linkages that are actually causal. For predictors, we used appraisals of teacher-child conflict by the children's first-grade teachers and the level of biological and behavioral reactivity obtained from the van-lab visits during their first-grade summer. For targeted outcomes, we used the combined reports of children's mental health symptoms in seventh grade from mothers, teachers, and the young people themselves.

Results showed the now familiar pattern of a special sensitivity: orchid children with high fight-or-flight reactivity and behavioral inhibition showed either the highest or the lowest levels of future mental health symptoms, depending on how things went with their first-grade teacher. Reactive first graders with lots of teacher conflicts had concerningly high levels of mental health symptoms even six years later, while equally reactive kids with few teacher conflicts showed exceptionally low rates of such symptoms. In contrast, the dandelion children who weren't sensitive or shy were barely affected by teacher conflicts, if at all. Here was an even more powerful demonstration of differential susceptibility: not only did measures of biological and behavioral reactivity predict mental health symptoms in the present, but they time-traveled and were also related to symptoms six years later, beyond the onset of puberty.

Two memorable Wisconsin kids are nicely emblematic of these powerful prospective connections between early classroom environments and psychiatric symptoms bridging first and seventh grade. One was a shy little orchid boy who in the summer of 1998 had to be coaxed not only into the van-lab in the driveway but out of his home just behind. He was a slight, towheaded six-year-old with his two upper front teeth already gone and a shy grin through which a small truck could have driven unimpeded. His restless anxiety about our team's impending visit had evidently begun the day before, well in advance of our actual arrival. He hid through much of the opening pleasantries behind his mother's skirt and produced a first saliva sample so suffused with cortisol you could almost see the hormone in the spit, like vinegar in a puddle of oil. In the van, he displayed his orchid biology in florid form, with ready fight-or-flight responses to every category of challenge we presented. Despite the boy's industrial-strength reactivity to stressors and his self-evident anxieties about beginning the first grade a few weeks later, he seemed to thrive brilliantly in school, had a series of teachers that every parent dreams of, and by seventh grade was a robust, reasonably confident middle schooler with no particular mental health symptoms at all.

A second child—this one a dark-eyed dandelion girl—was in so many ways a defining opposite of the boy: she greeted us at the door with aplomb and excitement, eagerly explored the van and its contents, and talked nonstop about her summer activities and her fever-pitched anticipations of first grade. She produced copious saliva samples that were nearly devoid of cortisol and displayed in the van a fight-or-flight system nearly inert to the modest stressors to which we subjected her. Not surprisingly, she flew through the first seven grades of public school like a swallow, notwithstanding some conflicts with teachers along the way and a first-grade year marked by a particularly difficult teacher-child relationship. She remained throughout the very picture of childhood mental health and well-being. Here then were illustrative examples of both an orchid child in a positive, encouraging school environment, radiantly succeeding and prospering, in part *because of* his relative open-ness and sensitivity to the world of school, and a dandelion girl whose comparative indifference to her sometimes troubled classroom setting allowed a middle childhood unimpaired by psychological concerns.

Onward to Puberty

As we watched these Wisconsin children edge toward adolescence, we wondered as well whether puberty itself (as suggested in chapter 3) might involve adaptations to the quality and dependability of these youths' social worlds. Might the parental relationships of these orchids and dandelions, the closer equivalent to the earth in which both kinds of flowers grow, have an equally potent effect? If so, we might also see differential susceptibility effects of parenting on the timing and pace (or rapidity) of pubertal maturation. As noted in chapter 3, pediatricians needn't look far to see how kids, especially girls, from chaotic, highly stressed families often enter puberty at an earlier age and then mature at an accelerated, often too rapid pace. Again, the evolutionary account for this quickened maturation is that survival and reproductive success may be boosted in children from tenuous family circumstances by becoming ready to reproduce at an earlier age and potentially leaving that family of origin. Think of a sensitive young woman, born to two alcoholic and combative parents, who moves too quickly into reproductive readiness in an unconscious, evolutionarily conserved mechanism for boosting her chances for offspring and a genetic legacy.

The WSFW cohort once again offered a perfect longitudinal study in which to test such a prediction. The timing of pubertal onset and the pace of sexual maturation are also clinically important because ear-lier, faster puberties have been linked to younger ages at sexual debut (beginning sexual activity), which in turn is related to the risk of teen pregnancy and the acquisition of sexually transmitted diseases such as gonorrhea, syphilis, and HIV.

The Tanner scale is a five-staged estimate of physical pubertal develop-ment in children and adolescents, based on the progressive maturation of primary and secondary sexual characteristics, such as breast budding, pubic hair, and testicular and genital size and configuration. We all start off rated as Tanner 1s, with squeaky voices, no breasts, no extra hair, and no genital changes, but we all end up sooner or later as Tanner 5s, with a full complement of visible sexual characteristics and not uncommonly an unwelcome harvest of pimples, abject longings, and oversized feet. But how we get from one stage to the next turns out to matter substantially in our reproductive health risks. Best in terms of long-term health outcomes is entering puberty later and progressing more slowly; worst is an early pubertal onset and a more rapid pace of acquiring secondary sexual characteristics. For reasons that are only partially understood, the age of puberty onset for both sexes has been dramatically declining over the past century, resulting in earlier menarche for girls and earlier and increased sexual activity in boys.

Using stress reactivity data from the summer van-lab study of 1998, along with parent-report and observational measures of parental supportiveness during the preschool period, we examined trajectories of pubertal development over six years. These trajectories were based on Tanner staging that came from the serial reports of parents and youth, where descriptions and line drawings depicted the development of secondary sexual characteristics. The low-reactivity, dandelion kids with supportive or less supportive parents had two average, linear paths of puberty, which were statistically indistinguishable. The high-reactivity, orchid children, on the other hand, showed either a dramatically accelerated pubertal change among those with less supportive parents or a delayed onset of puberty until 12.5 years among those with highly supportive parents.

Here again, the orchid children had either the earliest, fastest, and most perilous puberties (linkable to those outcomes, like adolescent pregnancy, that we would like to prevent) or the most delayed, slowest, and safest puberties (with far more salubrious outcomes, like delays in sexual debut). Which trajectory of maturation the orchid children followed depended specifically upon the level of parental support and encouragement in their homes. The dandelion children showed a linear, midlevel course of puberty, irrespective of their parental support. What is remarkable about these results is the implication that the effects of orchid children's special biological sensitivity extends not only to future health outcomes, but to *nonclinical, developmental risk factors* as well. Being an orchid child implicates the quality of their close social environments in both the advent of disease and the acquisition of risk, such as that imposed by early puberty.

Fire Alarms, Noise, and Igor Stravinsky

These studies of "associations"—that is, the measurable connection between two variables like reactivity and the pace of puberty—are sometimes liable to spurious conclusions. It might be readily shown, for example, that gambling and cancer are statistically related, so that people who gamble might be plausibly expected to have higher rates of certain malignancies. But if such an association were indeed found, before outlawing casinos as part of a "war on cancer," we would be smart to consider the possibility that both gambling and cancer are linked to a third variable, like smoking, alcohol consumption, or other "confounders" that can create illusory connections. Thus what might appear to be a meaningful association—gambling predicting or perhaps even causing cancer—would really only be the trivial result of each factor's underlying connection to the third element of smoking or alcohol. The same could be said of the provable association between the number of ministers in a town and the count of its telephone poles. Although the two numbers would probably be highly correlated, it is only because of their mutual associations with a confounding factor, the size of a town's population.

Because of this confounding problem, scientists often turn to *experimental* studies as a way of searching for genuine causal relations. A true experiment is a study where participants are randomly assigned to at least two different conditions, usually a treatment group and a control group that gets either no treatment or a modified, less effective treatment. An example would be a clinical trial where patients are allocated at random to receive either a promising new drug or a placebo. Doing this random assignment helps remove (or "control for") the effects of confounding variables, since both groups are likely to end up with the same average levels of confounders, like smoking, alcohol use, or population size. So we think of experiments as a kind of gold standard for evidence revealing a meaningful causal linkage between two variables—a way, as it were, to fight cancer with more efficient and less fallible methods than closing casinos. And in fact, all of the evidence for special, orchid sensitivity that we had gathered thus far had been nonexperimental, observational, and potentially circumstantial.

To build a more convincing argument, one of the former postdoctoral fellows in my Berkeley lab decided that the differential susceptibility theory needed to be put to a truly experimental test. So she brought four- to six-year-old children into the lab and had them complete our standard stress protocol for measuring fight-or-flight and cortisol reactivity. At the end of the protocol, however, she added a new element. She told the children that because they had done so well during the protocol, she would now make them a cup of hot chocolate as a reward for their efforts and successful completion of the test. With that, she turned on an electric teakettle filled with water and prepared the ingredients for making hot chocolate on the table in front of the child. She assembled a bag of chocolate powder, some marshmallows, and a packet of sweet, colorful sprinkles. As she expected, the children began copiously salivating, their eyes widened into little brown and blue moons, and they began bouncing on their chairs in expectation of a familiar sweet indulgence.

Then, as the kettle began to steam and whistle, a research assistant in the next room, watching through a one-way mirror, activated a loud, shrill fire alarm, which remained sounding for a period of twenty long seconds. The child was promptly reassured that there was in fact no fire, but the postdoc then went through a scripted series of specific actions—turning off the kettle, moving it away from the alarm, fanning the steam away, placing it on the table—in a putative effort to identify and eliminate the reason for the alarm. She reassured the child that in all likelihood it was the steam from the kettle that had set off the alarm, then continued preparing the hot chocolate in another, carefully sequenced set of actions. The water was poured into the cups; the chocolate stirred in; and the marshmallows and sprinkles finally added on top. The child and the postdoc then enjoyed a welcome cup of hot chocolate together, and the child returned to his or her parents with exciting stories to tell.

But we the scientists, of course, were searching for another, hidden story. In the two weeks that followed the reactivity and fire alarm procedures, two additional elements of the study were put in place. First, each child's fight-or-flight and cortisol reactivity scores were computed using the data collected during the protocol, and children were identified as either low or high in stress reactivity. All the children in each of these two groups were then invited back to the lab for a second visit, during which they were asked a series of very specific questions about what they remembered from the visit two weeks before. The questions were both open-ended (for example, "Tell me everything about what happened the last time you came to our laboratory") and direct ("Did you get to put whipped cream in your cup?"), and were delivered by an interviewer the child had never previously met.

The experimental part of the study was that the children in each of the two, dandelion and orchid, groups were randomly assigned to one of two interview conditions. In one condition (we'll call it the "nice interviewer"), the person interacting with the child couldn't have been more pleasant: she affirmed the child, talked kindly and encouragingly, and went out of her way to make sure the child was comfortable and calm. By contrast, in the second condition (the "grim interviewer"), the same interviewer became every schoolchild's worst vision of a snarky substitute teacher: distancing herself from the child, talking in a curt, aloof manner, and creating an environment of modest but palpable discomfort. By creating these artificial but convincing conditions, we ended up with four groups of kids, defined by low versus high stress reactivity (dandelions versus orchids) and by nice versus grim interviewer.

Just as we had found repeatedly in our observational, nonexperimental studies, the low-reactivity, dandelion children had competent but average capacities for remembering the details of their lab visits two weeks before, and their ability to remember was completely unaffected by the tenor of the interviewer's style. In other words, it was as if they were less easily affected by the vagaries of life, with less extreme reactions, both positive and negative. When questioned by both the supportive and the snarky interviewer, dandelion children all had just about the same memory performance.

On the other hand, the highly reactive, orchid children had exquisitely accurate, encyclopedic memories of the earlier lab visit when questioned by the nice interviewer, but couldn't seem to remember a thing when interacting with the rude, grim interviewer. In fact, the orchid kids in the supportive condition remembered details that even the lab staff couldn't: the exact order of how the hot chocolate ingredients went into the cup, what the research assistant was wearing that day, the fact that someone had come into the lab session to check on the fire alarm, the precise words the research assistant said when the alarm went off. In the other condition, the orchids remembered hardly anything.

This was our first truly experimental evidence for the exacting sensitivities of orchid children and the effects of social conditions on their cognitive performance (that is, their ability to think, remember, or reason). The orchids remembered nearly everything or nothing, depending upon how they were asked, but the dandelions had average memories in both conditions. With this new finding, we began to understand more fully that orchids and dandelions had very different experiences *of the very same experience* and that this dramatic contrast could be demonstrated in both the natural world and the highly controlled laboratory setting. From the noisy, highly varied consequences of lived childhood adversities had arisen a clear, systematic, and reliable truth about the source of that variation.

The 1913 Paris debut performance of the cacophonous ballet score *The Rite of Spring,* by the starkly modernist composer Igor Stravinsky, was greeted by the audience with screaming, violence, and riotous dismay at its anarchic musicality. The packed Théâtre des Champs-Élysées erupted in protest and anger, house lights had to be turned back on to facilitate an ejection of rampaging miscreants, and a reviewer later referred to the performance as "laborious and puerile barbarity." But Stravinsky was counting on the almost limitless capacity of human sensibilities to discern regularities hidden within pandemonium, to discover the *music* within atonality, dissonance, and disarray. His assumption was keenly sound, and the *Rite of Spring* became one of the most admired works in the historical vanguard of modernist composition.

What similarly began as an effort to discern understandable patterns within the noisy chaos of variation in human health and development has resulted in a symphonic science of individual differences in susceptibility to the social world. Now documented in both monkeys and human children, this differential susceptibility, or special sensitivity, encompasses a substantial subgroup of both species with high reactivity to both the positive and negative features of any given environment—a subgroup we have designated orchids by virtue of their exquisite tenderness to these bivalent aspects of the relational world. Orchid individuals have also been contrasted with another, far more populous group—their dandelion analogues—that displays a remarkable resilience to the trials and threats of life experience. The science describing the phenotypes of orchid and dandelion, and revealing the developmental and health implications of each, has now matured into a credible body of observation and research literature. The next scientific frontier, now already being explored, is the question of where these differences in sensitivity come from, how they are built into the biology of our bodily processes, and whether and when they become enduring features of who we are and will be.

5

Where Do Orchids (and Dandelions) Come From?

We now had reason to believe that the sensitivity of orchid children to life's troubles and hazards was not limited to those occurring in their natural lives, but was responsive as well to the experimental conditions that scientists like me could create. Likewise, the dandelion children residing in our families and communities appeared solidly resilient to childhood's typical, month-to-month events and stressors. But where did these differences in context sensitivity come from? As work by other researchers around the world was by now showing, the genetic characteristics of children created predispositions, but did not necessarily determine outcomes. For example, a consortium of scientists studying Romanian children raised in horribly negligent, sometimes cruel orphanages under the dictatorship of Nicolae Ceauşescu discovered that a shorter version of a gene related to the neurotransmitter serotonin in the brain produced orchid-like outcomes. Children with this shorter allele (an alternative form of a gene) who remained in the orphanages continued on into intellectual impairments and extreme maladjustment, while those with the same allele who were adopted into foster families recovered remarkably, in both development and mental health. Similarly, a team of Dutch researchers studying experimental patterns of children's financial donations in response to an emotionally evocative UNICEF video found that participants with an orchid-like dopamine neurotransmitter gene gave either the *most* charitable contributions or the *least,* depending upon whether they were securely or insecurely attached to their parents—that is, depending on factors that were not genetic.

So the questions still very much in need of study were clear. Was it only genes that made a child an orchid or a dandelion? Were orchids born that way, or do they become orchids by way of early experience? Is it all genetic, or is there something else that happens in early life that pushes development toward the orchid or dandelion phenotype? Were these powerful differences, which appear to influence important outcomes—from infections to behavior problems, and from aggression to charity and compassion—attributable solely to genes, to early childhood environments, or somehow to both? Our first hint at an answer came from an unlikely source: the very first moments of postnatal life.

Right from the Beginning

One of the first skills taught to young pediatricians and obstetricians in training is how to assess the physiological condition of a newborn baby in the first few minutes after birth. When I was a novice pediatrician, it was one of my favorite and most treasured duties—to be the very first living soul to survey the condition of a brand-new, never-before-seen human being, delivered red, squealing, and literally wet behind the ears into this bright, riotous world. At the end of a prolonged, critical, and one-way passage into earthly life, the moment of birth has always seemed one of nearly holy import. Beyond the pediatrician's role in witnessing that moment and in counting toes and fingers, the formal pediatric assessment of the newly born baby is done using the Apgar score, named for its inventor, Dr. Virginia Apgar, an obstetrical anesthesiologist at Columbia University in the 1950s. The score is assigned at one and five minutes following birth and ranges from 0 to 10, the sum of a 0, 1, or 2 scored in each of five areas of immediate postnatal physiological functioning. These are conveniently arranged into a slightly forced acronym—APGAR—which stands for:

A = Appearance, i.e., the pink or blue color of the body, hands, and feet;

P = Pulse rate, i.e., the rapidity of the heartbeat;

G = Grimace (or reflex irritability), i.e., the baby's crying or grimacing response to nasal or oral suction, or other stimulation;

A = Activity, i.e., the degree and vigor of muscle flexion; and

R = Respiration, i.e., the level of the baby's respiratory effort, ranging from none to a strong, lusty cry.

The total Apgar score is an indication of whether medical intervention is needed for asphyxia—that is, the baby's current level of difficulty or ease in exchanging oxygen and carbon dioxide through breathing and crying (yes, that's right: newborns don't just cry from a first outpouring of worldly emotion, but because it is a more vigorous way of breathing). Most babies receive Apgar scores ranging from 7 to 10, with points taken off only for slight blueness in the lips, hands, or feet, less than fully vigorous muscle flexion, or a somewhat sluggish response to stimulation. Babies with scores below 7 may need more active and rapid stimulation or resuscitation, including a warm, heated bassinet or a suctioning of the airway. For scores less than 4, we might insert a breathing tube to support respiration or, more rarely, even begin external heart compressions. Premature babies, as well as those with congenital infections or malformations, can have extremely low Apgar scores, and these are used to guide the intensity and immediacy of the required medical response.

What is especially interesting about the Apgar score, however, is the degree to which the things it measures—heart rate, reflexes, circulation to the hands and feet, and so on—are controlled by the responses of the fight-or-flight, autonomic nervous system involved in dealing with situations of stress. Each of the Apgar subscores (the different measures its acronymic letters represent), to one degree or another, is an indicator of the body's adaptation to the considerable physical (and possibly emotional) stressors of being born, and low scores are a reflection of insufficiently adaptive fight-or-flight responses. After all, birth is an extreme and unprecedented experience for an unborn child, and it is often extreme experiences that tell us most, not just about who we are but who we are as extensions of our individual biology.

Postnatal life begins, perhaps fittingly, with a major, sometimes peril-
ous transit: through the extreme compression and distortion that allows
a seven- or eight-pound newborn to be squeezed through a narrow, anatomically constrained birth canal and to burst wild and indignant into a
cold, noisy, and brilliantly lit world. (And at great cost in pain and effort
to the newborn's mother, we might rightfully add.) Though none of us
can remember even a moment of our own birthing process, it must be,
ironically, a powerfully memorable event, as we are thrust, ready or not,
into what William James called the "blooming, buzzing confusion" of
corporeal life.

This whole process of urgent physiological adaptation to an unanticipated, unfamiliar, and uncomfortable stressor—life outside the
womb—sounds remarkably like a procedure with which we are now
familiar: the stress reactivity testing performed in a research laboratory
by which a child's biological responses to physical and emotional challenges are evoked and measured. Birth, in fact, is a first, telling stress
reactivity trial at the very threshold of postnatal life.

Given that we all begin life by being plunged screaming into an epic
stress reactivity experiment, might we not wonder whether the Apgar
score could tell us more than just whether we need to have our mouths
suctioned or our bodies dried and warmed? If lower scores were actually
reflective of less adaptive, less compensatory fight-or-flight responses,
might they not be telling us about more than birth asphyxia, but perhaps
also about a baby's longer-term proclivity toward maladaptive responses
to the ubiquitous stresses of life? And if this were true, then might not
Apgar scores, over their entire 0–10 point range, predict more than just
neonatal distress? They might even predict far more global, developmentally distant outcomes. Could our first extrauterine moments augur
something important about our whole life yet to come?

That is exactly what we have now found. Careful epidemiologic work
by one of my doctoral students and a former postdoctoral fellow has
found that in nearly thirty-four thousand children from Manitoba,
Canada, five-minute Apgar scores, across their entire 0–10 point range,
were predictive of teacher-reported developmental vulnerability at age
five years for a variety of developmental dimensions. For example, the
teachers of children with Apgar scores of 7 (reflecting perhaps some

bluish color in their hands and lips at birth and a slightly less vigorous cry) identified more areas of developmental vulnerability than they did for children with Apgar scores of 9 or 10. Similarly, kindergartners with Apgar scores of 6—resulting from mild birth asphyxia that caused blue lips and hands, a weak cry, and a slower heart rate—had fewer reported developmental vulnerabilities than did their peers with Apgars of 3 or 4. And importantly, the teachers reporting on their students' development had no prior knowledge of the Apgar scores assigned five years earlier, at birth. The vulnerabilities that teachers reported might have been, for example, a child's slightly lower competence in following rules or instructions; an inability to sit still and focus; a relative lack of interest in books and reading; or an inability to properly grasp and use a pencil. At each lower step on the Apgar scale, the physical, social, emotional, language, and communication domains of development were all significantly more compromised five years later, in the first year of school. Premature and low birth weight babies, as expected, also had lower Apgar scores, but even after statistically adjusting for these variables, the same association with developmental outcomes held. Babies entering the world with greater fight-or-flight instability and less capacity for physiological recovery were more developmentally vulnerable.

So what does this mean? We used to think that any trait or feature present at birth was "congenital" and therefore determined in the genes or somehow fated in the stars. The plays of William Shakespeare and his Spanish equivalent Pedro Calderón de la Barca reflected this kind of seventeenth-century belief, in lines invoking an indelible and relentless tide of destiny within individual human lives:

> What fates impose, that men must needs abide;
> It boots not to resist both wind and tide.
> —William Shakespeare, *Henry VI*

> But Fate shall not by human force be broke,
> Nor foil'd by human feint.
> —Pedro Calderón de la Barca, *Life Is a Dream*

Written in the Stars, or in the Genes?

A more contemporary, scientific version of the same prescriptive vision is *genetic determinism,* according to which all of our differences, in physical traits, capacities, vulnerabilities, and potentials are firmly situated at the time of our conception in the merged DNA we inherit from our mothers and fathers. It is in many ways an ancient vision, in which individual destinies and temperaments are assigned by some inner, Hippocratic mixture of blood, yellow bile, black bile, and phlegm or by the proportional blending of the classical elements of earth, water, air, and fire. You can think of this view of human behavior as the "nature" side of the classic debate over nature versus nurture—that is, whether we come into the world already formed as people, or if the world we live in is what determines who we are and become.

The most recent version of this same deterministic debate was spawned by the advent and completion of the Human Genome Project—the ultimate "nature" approach—from which would eventually emerge, we were roundly promised, the "genes for" autism, schizophrenia, heart disease, and cancer. No such unitary genes have been elucidated, and it is now clear that the role of genes in who we become as individual creatures is not such a straightforward, one-to-one route from genes to behavior, from DNA to phenotype. It is far more complex, more elegant, and more probabilistic than modern minds previously imagined. In fact, scientists are constantly reminded, if they are honest with themselves, that even our most vaunted, prized, and carefully articulated hypotheses pale in the face of the true and exquisite complexities of the natural world.

The old pediatric adage, however, is that all parents-to-be are environmental determinists (everything comes from "nurture"), until they actually have the baby in hand—at which point they all become fully committed genetic determinists (everything from "nature"). Here is what I mean. Before we have children, we're all prone to seeing the misbehavior of children around us as the products of flawed parenting. What about that kid throwing a tantrum at the table next to us in a restaurant, putting a damper on our meal? Obviously it's the parents' fault for not controlling him—their nurture hasn't done what it needed to do. The perspective of those of us who become parents, however, tends to change once we have a child and ours is the felon-in-training throwing the tantrum at the next table or in the adjacent airplane seat. We forget our previous critical thoughts of others and hope that people around us understand that we've done our best, tried our hardest to raise a kid who doesn't throw tantrums and make trouble. This kid just came into the world with this temperament from his genes, and thus our prowess as parents has nothing to do with it. It's far easier and more comforting to ascribe noisy or troubling toddler behavior to genes, for which parents have only passive responsibility, than to their skills and capacities as parents, for which they are far more actively and directly accountable.

But just as genetic determinism has most recently held sway within public minds, there have also been periods when *environmental determinism* was just as powerfully and unreservedly endorsed. When I was a young pediatric resident, steeped in the scientific soup of the 1970s, environmental factors were deemed far more prevalent and causally powerful than genes, especially with respect to disorders of mental health and development. I remember an aging, sanctimonious psychiatrist who ponderously intoned the theory that "cold, distant mothers" were the principal origins of autism and schizophrenia and that, far more broadly, the family environment was the likely unilateral root of all disordered thought and behavior among children. Fixing the family would fix the disorder, and any attribution of psychiatric infirmity to genes, or even to "biology," would have constituted "blaming the victim," a hopelessly unacceptable practice among the medical cognoscenti of that time.

Now, it would have been one measure of certifiable indignity if the so-called refrigerator mother hypothesis (cold mothers cause autism) had simply been wrong. But it was another level of shame altogether that in the hands of that theory, a whole generation of moms (and to some degree, parents of both sexes) with autistic or otherwise troubled kids raised them believing that somehow the parents themselves were the principal reason for what was often a tragic, enduring affliction.

Although the world of pediatrics is everywhere encumbered with stories of parents who harmed or neglected their children, the happy reality is that a truly overwhelming majority of parents treasure their children, protect and encourage them, without any thought for the material or emotional costs to themselves. I remember a request, now long past, to evaluate the behavior of a four-year-old boy who was the first child of two physician parents. As I entered the consultation room, I saw two young parents in their early thirties, the dad holding a sleeping ten-month-old infant girl and the mom struggling, near tears, to contain a writhing, flapping preschooler who hardly noticed my entry. There was an unmistakable pall that blanketed the room.

The boy (let's call him Devon) had been a healthy, robust newborn, brought home with the hopeful anticipation that parents typically have as they head for the first time into one of the greatest and most challenging personal adventures of life. Devon's mom had breastfed him for the first six months but was forced to wean him to a bottle as her maternity leave expired and she returned to an arduous surgical training program. He was an "easy" baby, smiling interactively at six weeks of age, rolling over by himself at four months, undemanding of anyone's attention, and beginning the vocalization of single words at around a year.

Just after his first birthday, however, Devon's parents began to have what were at first modest, but then growing concerns about his development. His use of words noticeably diminished, rather than accelerating as we would have expected in the second year of life; he seldom pointed at toys or objects of interest, as his parents had seen other children of about the same age do with their parents. They found themselves struggling to connect with Devon, who seemed indifferent to their efforts to make eye contact or talk with him or to play interactively at games like peekaboo. Devon was seeming to recede into an oblivion of private thoughts and inner turmoil, unrevealed by the light of language.

By his second birthday, Devon's parents were fully convinced that something was wrong. They wondered at times if he were deaf, as he began to mostly ignore the calling of his name, but audiological testing revealed no deficits in hearing acuity. He had also begun to make repetitive movements, flapping his arms or moving wildly up and down on the balls of his feet. By now, all of his talking had disappeared, replaced by shrill, stereotypical screeches when uncomfortable or frustrated.

His physician, thoroughly well-meaning and schooled in the autism ideology of the day, began to probe the character of Devon's attachment to his mom, her level of presence during his infancy year, her sense of regret as she returned to work. The message was unmistakable: the doctor was seeking evidence of a frosty, distant mother-child attachment. But couldn't Devon's disorder itself result in difficult parent-child interactions? The visit dissolved into a sea of tears, upon which Devon's dad launched a fusillade of anger and indignation on the startled, unnerved physician.

It later became my job to confirm a diagnosis of autism, to absorb and acknowledge the sadness and dismay the news unleashed, to undo the unwarranted and unfair implication that we actually know the disorder's cause, and to help the family move toward acceptance and intervention for their son. However innocent in intent environmental determinism may have been, it was both wrong and harmful, a telling reminder of how theories of disease origins are seldom value- or consequence-free. It wasn't a question of trying to understand Devon as an orchid or dandelion. It was a question of how all children and later adults become who they are, whether they turn out orchid-like or dandelion-like. The answer, as it happened, would be found in the space *between* nurture and nature.

Either/Or or Both/And?

The "Great Dane," philosopher Søren Kierkegaard, wrote his first published book, *Either/Or,* as a discourse on the tension between esthetic and ethical views of life, as individuals grow and mature. He argued that development occurs initially within a hedonistic, subjective kind of consciousness—that is, the mind of a child, with all its quite natural selfishness, is highly attuned to immediate needs and the fulfillment of desires. But Kierkegaard believed that eventually this way of being takes a more ethical turn, one of moral responsibility and duty—toward the mind of a conscious adult, capable of suppressing baser desires and selfish priorities in order to reach a more global, conscientious view. And it is only religious faith, Kierkegaard ultimately claimed, that can rescue us from these two conflictive and incongruous ways of being. The point here is that to fully understand the human condition, we need to dispense with the tendency humans have to perceive—and simplify—the forces that form us as clear-cut dichotomies. Such oversimplistic, binary views in fact run counter to the often profound complexities of our true character.

In a way, what modern developmental and health sciences have similarly faced in recent decades is a kind of Kierkegaardian divide—an "either/or"—urging irreconcilable commitments to either a genetically or environmentally deterministic vision of the origins of disease and disorder. While the environmental view has demanded an allegiance to *external* causes, located within the social and physical contexts in which humans live (like the parenting environment in autism), the genetic view has opposingly asserted that *internal* causes are preeminent, with genomes driving individual phenotypes and lives. To some extent, each position has pursued an insistent muting of the other, and genetic and environmental determinism have emerged as two contradictory, discordant answers to the same fundamental questions: "Where is the origin of human malady and difficulty?" and "Why do some get sick and others not?" And conversely: "Where are the origins of human wellness and achievement?" and "Why are some so healthy and fulfilled, while others are not?"

An initial attempt at reconciling these two rigidly deterministic, either/or views came from the field of *behavior genetics* and from a clever analysis of studies involving human twins. Behavior genetics cogently observed that if genetic determinism were true, then when one monozygotic twin (from a pair of identical twins, formed when a single fertilized egg—the zygote—divides into two separate but identical embryos) developed schizophrenia, then the other should, too. If genetic variation were the sole key to disease causation, then two individuals with identical genomes should always have the same disorder. But most of us know a pair of identical twins who have substantially different personalities and behavioral styles and may even have distinctive mental or physical health issues, despite sharing identical DNA in every cell of their bodies. In contrast to monozygotic twins, when a dizygotic twin (from a pair of fraternal twins, conceived from two, separately fertilized eggs) develops schizophrenia or any other disorder, the concordance rate between the twins (that is, how often the other twin is also affected, if one of them has the disorder) should be only as great as that between siblings who are not twins. On the other hand, if the environment were the whole story, then all kids from a "schizophrenic family" context might be expected to develop schizophrenia.

Instead, the concordance in schizophrenia between monozygotic twins is only about 50 percent, not 100 percent. This means that there is a causal role for *both* genes and environments, in approximately equal proportions. Similarly, the twin concordance for autism is also around 50 percent, again suggesting that both genetic and environmental factors are at work. So behavior genetics strove to better understand variations in behavior and mental disorders by using studies of twins to apportion cause into genetic and environmental sources. With that information in hand, we then could talk about the degree of "heritability" in schizophrenia, diabetes, or obesity, implying a clean split between the genetic and environmental components of their causes.

Even behavior genetics, however, was employing a fundamentally flawed assumption: that the causes of disease are *either* genetic *or* environmental (à la Kierkegaard) *or* some separable combination of both (two parts genes and one part environment, like two cups of water and one cup of oil). It was all just another, slightly more sophisticated answer to the question, "Which is more important, nature or nurture, genes or environments?" To add nuance to this overly simple dichotomy, the Canadian neuropsychologist Donald Hebb, when once asked whether nature or nurture contributes more to human personality, responded, "Which contributes more to the area of a rectangle, its length or its width?" Which, indeed. We now know that it is almost never a matter of either/or, but rather both/and, and one of the most compelling scientific questions of our time is the question of how genes and environments cooperate in the preservation of health and the origins of disease.

Thus, in an enormous, transformative shift in the way scientists think about such origins—of human health and human afflictions—we have now begun to understand that neither genes nor environments, in isolation or even in simple additive combination, can account for the great complexity involved in the causes of disease. Instead, we now believe it is almost always an *interaction between genes and environments.* This interplay is what makes us *us,* for better or worse, and can launch an illness onto its first beachhead within a living body.

For almost every human disposition and every disorder of mental or physical health, it is some intricate interaction between internal and external causes that allows it to take root, flourish, and advance. And ultimately, the key to understanding human differences and to abating and preventing human morbidities will involve a keener and deeper knowledge of how genetic differences and environmental variation work *together* to change biological processes. Whether inflammatory, metabolic, infectious, or cancerous in nature, most human diseases appear rooted in some potently interactive combination of genetic and environmental causes. And whether introverted or extroverted, sanguine or phlegmatic, orchid or dandelion, most human traits and proclivities are likewise grounded in the interplay of genes and contexts. It is this more complex scientific approach to "unpuzzling" human nature and wellness that brings us closer to understanding what makes orchids and dandelions either bloom or wither—or move between these two states over the course of a challenging and changing life.

The Origins of an Orchid, the Seeds of a Dandelion

Orchid children, with their hair-trigger sensitivities to both negative and positive socioemotional environments, may be born with *genetically driven* predispositions toward differential susceptibility, but given what is currently known, there are probably early *environmental forces* that also shape the full flowering of a newly formed orchid. In fact, both orchid and dandelion children are in all likelihood the products of early adaptive interactions between genetic and environmental influences. Both genes and social environments (like family) are almost certainly influential for both of these two phenotypes of children, but it is likely the *interaction* between genes and environments that determine where the kids in my studies ended up on the graphs that we created to chart their behaviors and health.

But what is really meant by this pivotal concept of gene-environment "interaction"? An interaction is a synergy, where two or more components (in this case, genes and environments, your biology and your experiences) converge to have some combined effect. It is where one plus one does not equal two, but rather three or four; where the product is more than the totality of its parts; and where the properties of a novel combination are said to be "emergent," materializing as they do out of a fusion of blended effects.

Water, flour, and yeast, when mixed together and baked in an oven, become bread, a completely novel kind of substance, suitable for eating in ways that none of its components are in isolation (if you doubt this, try a mouthful of hot flour). In genetics, we use the term *epistasis* to describe circumstances in which the effect of one gene is interactively dependent upon a concurrent effect of another. In medicine, drug interactions are the negative or positive effects of taking two medications together—effects that do not derive from taking either one alone. Most often, in each of these meanings of interaction, the actual physical processes or mechanisms by which the interaction actually occurs are tellingly obscure or only partly known. D. H. Lawrence tried to capture this often mysterious nature of interaction in his short poem "The Third Thing":

Water is H_2O, hydrogen two parts, oxygen one,
but there is also a third thing, that makes it water
and nobody knows what it is.
The atom locks up two energies
but it is a third thing present which makes it an atom.

So it is with gene-environment interactions. We have evidence for important effects of genetic variation—that is, differences in DNA sequences—on an individual's vulnerability to a specific disease, on his or her chances for a long and healthy life, and on differences in susceptibility and sensitivity to experiences within social contexts. Nearly always, these genetic effects are due to differences in multiple genes (sometimes in scores or hundreds of genes that together define "polygenic risk"—risk that inheres in many genes), rather than the impact of a single mutation or variant within a single gene. We also have evidence for social environmental risk factors in various mental and biomedical disorders—poverty, child maltreatment, exposures to violence and other adverse experiences, or constellations of such experiences. But it seems highly likely that the most powerful effects of all on health and development are those that involve *interactions between biology and context,* between biological causes, like groups of genes, and collections of environmental exposures. To better understand this, let's consider children's oral health.

The Depravity of a Cavity

Dental caries, the breakdown of the hard enamel layer of a tooth by decay, is the single most common chronic disease of childhood, affecting 60 to 90 percent of children worldwide and influencing long-term adult health status, at least in part through the production of inflammation. There are also large racial and socioeconomic disparities in dental health and caries, with poor, minority-group children having far greater incidences of dental disease. The conventional wisdom in the dental and pediatrics communities is that poor kids get more caries because their parents fail to teach, expect, or enforce good dental hygiene practices, like brushing and flossing. You won't be surprised by now to learn that in fact it's not this simple.

To get a richer and possibly more veridical understanding of how caries come about and why they're more common in kids from disadvantaged communities, we made the slightly strange-sounding request that the six-year-old participants in our Berkeley public schools study send us their baby teeth as they dropped out during the children's first-grade year. We also asked about family stressors and sampled the children's saliva for measurement of the stress hormone cortisol, because cortisol can erode the structural integrity of calcified tissues, like bones and teeth. Not surprisingly, we called this our "Tooth Fairy Project," and we proposed to pay each child $10 per tooth that was brought to us within twenty-four hours of its expulsion from the child's mouth. This was a rate of compensation well above the going tooth fairy market value at the time, and it resulted in a hefty motivation for the removal and conveyance of deciduous teeth. When the teeth arrived at our lab, they were placed in a preserving solution, transported over to the School of Dentistry at UCSF, and the first grader was given a crisp new $10 bill. Presumably under the influence of these market pressures, we received a veritable harvest of teeth, and one tooth submitted by a child came back to us from UCSF with a Post-it that read, "This is a dog's tooth . . ." I'm not sure how he got it, and not sure I fully want to know, but somewhere in Berkeley, there's a dog with a gap in his smile.

Back to the science. In addition to collecting loose baby teeth, we also did a comprehensive dental exam on each child and swabbed the gum margin to look for the presence and number of cariogenic bacteria harbored in the child's mouth. These are the oral bacteria, often acquired from the mother during an infant's first year of life, that lead to tooth decay. On the baby teeth, we measured, with the help of our colleagues from UCSF Dentistry, the hardness and thickness of the various layers of the tooth, using the same computed tomography (CT) scanning that is used to image the inside of a patient's head, belly, or knee joint. What we discovered, much in keeping with the biology-environment interactions highlighted above, was that neither the number of cariogenic bacteria nor the socioeconomic stressors in the child's family predicted the acquisition of dental caries in isolation. Instead, the level of family economic stress predicted the level of cortisol in the child's saliva, which in turn predicted the density and protective thickness of the enamel layer in the child's baby tooth.

This is not unlike the osteoporosis (bone weakening) that occurs in patients with Cushing's disease, who have chronically elevated blood levels of cortisol. The excessive secretion of cortisol in both conditions—in chronic stress and in Cushing's disease—results in a dissolution of calcified tissues, like teeth or bones. Thus the attenuated dental enamel found among children with stress-related elevations in salivary cortisol levels interacted with the counts of cariogenic bacteria to predict who got caries and who did not. It was neither stress-related erosion of the children's enamel alone nor the proliferation of oral bacteria alone that was the culprit. Rather, it was the interactive combination: both stress and bacteria were necessary but not sufficient causes in the process of developing compromised oral health.

Does this not make a kind of perfect logical sense—that our health and survival would be shaken not simply and unilaterally by the presence of an internal vulnerability (like thin tooth enamel) nor by an encounter with some external threat (like oral bacteria)? Isn't it eminently plausible that the genesis of a disease would involve an unhappy and far less frequent coincidence—a synergy, interaction, or confluence—between internal and external causes together? Whether one believes in the wisdom of a divine creator, in the infallibility of evolutionary natural selection, or both, there is something reassuringly complex—like a system of checks and balances—about how disease and susceptibility must be rooted in both internal and external risks.

We know that human infants, even prior to birth, are remarkably and finely attuned to the dynamic features of their environments, first in the womb and later within the nests with which their parents surround them. The brain of the human fetus and newborn is a wondrous developmental "black hole" of sensory capacity, into which is drawn an enormous repository of information about the world that infant will experience and the challenges he or she will face. Between the fifth and twenty-fifth weeks of gestation, new brain neurons are generated from neural stem cells at a rate as high as 250,000 neurons per minute, and slightly later there begins a period of extravagant overproduction of synapses—the connecting points between neurons—at rates of 40,000 new connections per second. The growth of this vast circuitry eventually produces a fully developed human brain of over 100 trillion synapses, 86 billion neurons, and 85 billion non-neuronal cells that together constitute the single most complex physical object in the known universe.

As a result of this remarkable brain growth and neural development, a baby shows an immediate capacity for recognizing and preferring human faces and facelike visual patterns. The newborn can also identify its mother's face by the second day of life, can recognize its mother by the smell of her breast milk, can imitate its parents' facial expressions and behaviors, and can immediately distinguish, by both hearing and watching, its own native language, which it has continuously monitored during intrauterine life. What is even more remarkable is the unconscious capacity of infants to assess their mothers' levels of exposure to adversity (through detecting placental levels of stress hormones), to estimate the environmental availability of nutritious food (through placental transfer of calories and the baby's diet in early infancy), and to detect parental smoking (through changes in oxygen delivery in utero). Human fetuses know and respond to so much about the anticipated environment outside the uterus, even before consciousness can register it!

Because of this vast download of early environmental information, the fetus and newly born infant unconsciously make conditional adaptations in the service of "early life programming." The idea here is that rather than waiting to adjust to the life conditions with which a young child will eventually have to contend, biological adjustments to those conditions begin very early and without awareness, as soon as the fetal or newborn brain begins to detect important adaptive challenges. It's a form of hedging bets, playing it safe, taking no chances. This early programming enhances the likelihood of short-term survival, at least until the capacity for reproducing comes online in puberty, but it may also have the downside of greater risks for chronic adult diseases, such as coronary heart disease, obesity, diabetes, and mental disorders. It is an evolutionary strategy of trading survival in the short run for diminished and less vigorous longevity in the longer term. It works to ensure the propagation of genes but not to preserve chances for a long and healthy life.

We think that differential susceptibilities to the environment—and thus orchid and dandelion children—emerge in this way. As touched upon in chapter 3, there are certain kinds of early social and physical contexts in which important benefits to ensure surviving and thriving might accrue for children with special, enhanced sensitivities to those environments. Children being reared in environments of continuous threat and predation, for example, might logically be protected by the vigilance and hawk-eyed attentiveness of those orchid sensibilities. And back in ancient environments, millennia ago, having a few such orchidish individuals within a hominid band might have even been protective of the *group,* as attacks from animals and other troops arose. On the other hand, being an orchid might also pay great benefit to those living at the other extreme—that is, environments of exceptional safety, protection, and abundance. Here, the propensity of orchid children to be open and porous to environmental events and exposures would garner even greater advantages among that subgroup with orchid phenotypes. Most children would thrive in such settings, but orchids would thrive spectacularly.

Outside of these most extreme rearing conditions, being a dandelion must surely instead yield the greatest rewards and exact the smallest, least taxing price. Dandelions are those who seem impervious to all but the most virulent of threats and insults. Within the typical ups and downs of human societies, these are the individuals who are deemed resilient, hardy, and buoyant in the face of adversity.

Evolution should thus tend to favor a proliferation of orchid phenotypes at the extremes of environmental conditions, while dandelion phenotypes should predominate within the broad middle range of human challenges. Sure enough, there is at least preliminary evidence that dandelions are disproportionately represented in settings where neither menaces nor great fortune predominate.

"Marks" on Our Genes

My life in science and my own personal research agenda were forever changed by a long, formative sojourn in the frigid green wilds of Canada, rich not only in its vast tracts of untouched land and bottomless seas but in a kind of unshackled intellect where ideas grow like rain forests. I was brought to the University of British Columbia (UBC) by my unforgettable colleagues Clyde Hertzman, now sadly gone from this natural world he loved so well, and Ron Barr, a developmental pediatrician whose knowledge and creativity have been an exemplar of pediatric life in the academy. I will remember forever a wintry, blustery late afternoon, looking out on a foreboding black squall gathering on Vancouver's English Bay, when Clyde speculated out loud about whether there might be conceivable circumstances under which I could be lured away from Berkeley, up into that dark green and white Columbian wilderness. Two years and a seeming lifetime of discernment and planning later, Jill and I arrived, against all odds, in the province of British Columbia, where a seven-year season of adventure, both scientific and personal, began. I had there in Canada the truly providential good fortune to meet Mike Kobor and Marla Sokolowski.

Mike is a Berkeley-trained geneticist of European origin, who rowed for Germany in the 1992 World Rowing Championships, studied genetics at the University of Toronto, completed a postdoctoral fellowship at the University of California, and accepted his first faculty job at UBC just prior to my arrival in Vancouver in 2006. As holder of a coveted Canada Research Chair, he teaches and studies the molecular biology of the yeast genome. Marla is a renowned fly geneticist, a distinguished University Professor at the University of Toronto, and daughter of an Eastern European Holocaust survivor. She discovered the foraging gene (known as *for*) in fruit flies and is responsible for the work establishing two major behavioral phenotypes in flies (and other species)—the "rovers" and the "sitters"—that are determined by DNA sequence differences in the foraging gene. Yes, even the tiny yeasties that make our bread rise and the little flies that get in our ears and noses have genes constructed of the same DNA ingredients that make us human.

Beyond the brilliance of both, Mike and Marla had in common an extraordinary capacity for broadly envisioning the implications of discoveries in basic animal models for the larger concern of how functional and egalitarian (that is, democratic and evenhanded) human societies might be built and sustained. They discern our civilizations in our genes. Both have an uncanny ability to teach and convey the intricate complexities of their fields, in language and imagery that is accessible to those unschooled in molecular biology, even to pediatricians like myself. And both had a winsome bent toward the challenging and complex riches of multidisciplinary collaboration.

All of us, as it happened—Hertzman, Barr, Kobor, Sokolowski, and Boyce—soon converged under the sponsorship of the Canadian Institute for Advanced Research (CIFAR), forming the Child and Brain Development Program, which Marla and I co-lead and is now in its fifteenth year of collaborative work. CIFAR is the Canadian brainchild of one J. Fraser Mustard, a blood platelet physician-researcher, founder of the McMaster University medical school, and the late dean of Canadian biomedical science, who recognized in 1982 the need for a kind of scientific and intellectual risk-taking essential for creating transformative knowledge. CIFAR has supported the work of 23 interdisciplinary programs, involving 17 countries and nearly 350 scientists, 18 of whom have become Nobel laureates since the institute's inception. CIFAR has become a dazzlingly unique Canadian idea and organization, with no true counterpart anywhere else in the world.

Under the protective, emboldening freedom of CIFAR's multidisciplinary mandate, the Child and Brain Development Program quickly closed in upon the captivating research question toward which this chapter has been steadily moving:

How do genes and environments, especially environments of adversity and inequality, work together to produce known individual differences in susceptibility, behavior, health, and disease?

The answer to that question has proven key to a provisional understanding of where orchids and dandelions come from and how such differences in sensitivity arise.

We have established that genetic variation—differences in the DNA code that makes up individual genes—surely plays a role in the genesis of orchid and dandelion children. Genes are ordered sequences of four nucleotides, the basic chemical building blocks of DNA—adenine, guanine, cytosine, and thymine. Our individual genetic sequences of those four nucleotides comprise two distinctive, complementary copies—one from each of our parents—that never change from cradle to grave. The entire human genome contains approximately three billion such pairs of nucleotides, and their sequence for each gene, like a word made up of letters, spells out or encodes the instructions for making specific proteins. These proteins, in turn, when produced, or "expressed," change the functioning of cells—functions that influence the physical and psychological features of individual human beings, like eye color, temperament, height, and intelligence. Although many genes likely contribute to the orchid and dandelion phenotypes, those involved in brain development and function are almost certainly implicated. The expression of genes involved in emotion regulation and behavioral control, for example— features highly salient to orchids and dandelions—govern neurotransmitter communications among individual neurons. Differences in these and other genes almost certainly influence a child's orchid or dandelion identity.

But as we have also noted, early environmental exposures and experiences undoubtedly play an additional role, especially exposures to adversity and threat and experiences of family or community support and nurture. Emerging science suggests that genes and environments together contribute to the emergence of orchids and dandelions, both additively and interactively, but up until recently we had no real idea of how this gene-environment interaction actually took place. The research that has now flooded this enigmatic landscape with new light is the field of *epigenetics,* the science of how environmental exposures can modify gene expression, without altering the DNA sequence of the gene itself. The Greek prefix *epi*—meaning "upon" or "above"—connotes how the epigenome, a lattice of chemical "marks" or tags, literally lies upon the genome and controls the expression or silencing of DNA during life.

The fact that individual gene expression can be monitored and changed is essential even to the existence in our bodies of different types of cells and tissues. Remember that every type of cell we possess—blood, liver, lung, skin, and brain cells—contains precisely the same genome, the same collection of genes with the same DNA sequences, half from our mothers and half from our fathers. The only way that the two hundred or so different human cell types, each with a different structure and different functions, could be made from a single genome is if the functioning of our twenty-five thousand genes could be independently controlled. That's where the epigenome comes into play in embryonic development. Stem cells—the primitive, undifferentiated cells from which many cell types and lineages arise—can only become kidney cells or white blood cells through the programmed, epigenetic regulation of those thousands of genes.

Once a stem cell is differentiated—let's say into a white blood cell—the functioning of that cell can also be adjusted (again, epigenetically) to accommodate or adapt to the conditions with which the cell or the whole organism is contending. For example, a child facing a seriously stressful environment might need to change white blood cells' rate of division (thereby increasing the number of available immune cells), change the cells' responsiveness to stress hormones (e.g., sensitizing them to the effects of cortisol), or change their production of the molecules initiating and governing inflammation (e.g., the chemical messengers called cytokines). So the epigenome has two major functions: first, it regulates the *differentiation of cells* into their various types and tissues; and second, it facilitates an *adjustment of cell function* to respond appropriately to the conditions at hand. It is a great and agile improviser. It does both of these functions by regulating the epigenetic chemical tags that attach to the genome, turning up or turning down the expression of the thousands of genes in each cell.

Think of the genome and epigenome like this (and take a minute to study the drawing on page 104). Your genes are like the keys on a piano; each one plays a distinctive note. Remember, too, that although a piano keyboard has just eighty-eight white and black keys, your genome houses around twenty-five thousand individual genes, making it a genetic "keyboard" thousands of times longer and more complex than that of a piano. So in the first kind of epigenetic regulation—cell differentiation—these keys on the keyboard can be played in different combinations, sequences, and timings to create a whole variety of different "tunes"; in fact, there are two hundred different tunes that they play, one for each of the different types of cells in a human body. So one tune corresponds to the production of neurons, another to white blood cells, and yet another to skin cells, and so on. Each cell type and function is a tune played on a keyboard of twenty-five thousand keys.

Once cells are differentiated on this magnificent piano, the epigenome

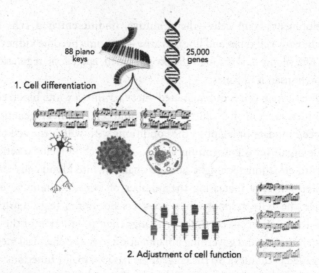

1. Cell differentiation

2. Adjustment of cell function

The epigenome, which regulates the expression or decoding of our twenty-five thousand genes, has two main jobs. First, it controls which of the two hundred different kinds of cells in our bodies an embryonic stem cell will become—a liver cell, a neuron, a white blood cell, and so on. This is like playing the keys of a piano in different combinations and sequences to create a repertoire of two hundred distinctive tunes and melodies. Second, the epigenome calibrates gene expression to adjust various cellular functions in response to environmental conditions. This is like changing the way a single melody sounds by using an audio equalizer to shift sound frequencies and volumes.

is then used for a second kind of regulatory process: the adjustment of cell function to the conditions the organism is currently encountering. Here, the epigenome serves as a kind of "sound equalizer" that adjusts each cell's functions, changing the way the cell's tune sounds, like the levers on an audio equalizer that adjusts the balance between sound frequency ranges. For example, an equalizer can emphasize the treble or bass notes of a song or change their balance to make a jazz piece sound edgy or an orchestral symphony sound elegant and rich. So although each type of cell always plays the same tune—that is, a white blood cell will generally stay a white blood cell and do what white blood cells do— the way that cell functions, and the way the tune sounds, can be adaptively adjusted to suit specific circumstances.

For example, the body of a child encountering a major early life stressor, like maltreatment, might automatically adjust the functioning of many different cell types in order to adapt as well as possible to the experience of being abused or neglected. Adrenal gland cells might be called upon to produce more cortisol (part of the tune that adrenal cells play); nerve cells could activate the fight-or-flight system (the tune certain neurons play); white blood cells could respond to any physical injuries; and brain cells might dampen the child's emotional responses. And these would be only four of the adjustments in cell functions, among probably hundreds that would be occurring, all at the same time.

Beyond the piano metaphor, the way these epigenetic adjustments in cell functioning *actually* take place, at the molecular level within the cell, is shown in the drawing below. Inside the nucleus of the cell, the

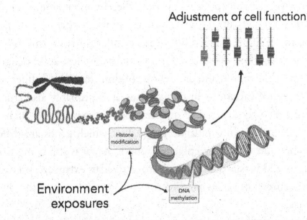

Strands of DNA are tightly packed into chromosomes and cells like a long string of beads called *chromatin*. The string is the DNA, and the cylindrical beads around which the DNA is wound are protein disks called *histones*. When small chemical tags (CH3 or methyl group) are attached to or removed from the DNA string or the protein beads, the packing—or density—of the DNA in the chromosome changes, from loose to tight or from tight to loose. Tight packing makes it physically difficult for the DNA decoder apparatus to reach the gene, thereby silencing or diminishing its expression. Loose chromatin packing, on the other hand, makes gene expression easier. An individual's experience governs the attaching and detaching of the chemical, epigenetic tags and thereby regulates the level of gene expression by changing the density of the chromatin packing. The combined regulation of multiple genes in this manner is like an audio equalizer that adjusts how the cell's "melody" sounds, that is, changing the cell's biological functioning.

long strand of DNA is wound around a cylindrical hockey puck of proteins called histones. Together, the DNA and histone proteins look like beads on a string, which can be either densely or loosely packed within the larger chromosome. Environmental exposures demanding adaptive responses—like a child's experiences of maltreatment or abuse—change the chemical tags that are attached to specific spots on either the DNA or the protein "beads." Depending upon the kinds of experience and the specific genes involved, these chemical tags may be either added or removed, and both can change the level of gene expression to maximize the child's capacity for adaptation. Tight packing physically impedes the molecular mechanism that decodes the DNA, effectively lowering or silencing gene expression. Loose packing, on the other hand, gives that decoding mechanism room to operate, thereby increasing or enabling gene expression. Again, these epigenetic shifts in chemical marks act like a sound equalizer, adjusting overall cellular function through multiple changes in the expression of individual genes. Just as biobehavioral phenotypes, like orchid and dandelion children, are likely influenced by DNA sequence variations in many genes, it is probably also true that the effects of early experience on these phenotypes involve many epigenetic changes within multiple genes. Just which genes are different in sequence and where the epigenetic marks occur is still being worked out, for orchid versus dandelion, introvert versus extrovert, predispositions to depression versus predilections to joy, and many other human differences.

What we now know with some certainty, however, is that most variation in human character, nature, and health will eventually be attributable to an interactive combination of differences in the DNA sequences of multiple genes, along with experience-driven differences in the epigenetic marks that shape the expression, or decoding, of multiple genes. What is wickedly complex in the number of variations involved—how many variants in genes and how many marks in the epigenome—is elegantly simple in design: genes and experience interactively affect human destiny, and the epigenome is the physical link between a gene and its environment. Thus, you can think of human life as the song that issues from the epigenetic piano and its equalizer, the result of a complex compositional process shaped by both genes and environments. Each person is predisposed to play certain types of orchestral scores, like those of the orchid or the dandelion, but there is also abundant space for unique variation and improvisation.

Where It All Comes Together

At the 1889 meeting of the German Anatomical Society in Berlin, an eager and ambitious young Spanish neuroanatomist named Santiago Ramón y Cajal made his first, uneasy presentation of his work to an international scientific audience. Growing up, he had been a rebellious, recalcitrant, and generally annoying adolescent, forever in trouble by virtue of his impulsivity and an intellect that well outstripped his school's and family's capacities for containing and challenging it. He had even spent a night in jail at age eleven, for building a makeshift cannon that he used to demolish the entry gate to his hometown in Spain. So desperate were his parents for some channeling of Santiago's mischief and energy that his father twice involuntarily apprenticed him, without any lasting success, first to a barber and then to a cobbler. But Santiago eventually settled upon pursuing his father's own professional identity as an anatomist and decided to attend medical school. Never fully encumbered, however, by the day-to-day constraints of seeing sick patients or by becoming a clinically active part of a hospital or clinic, he was most enticed by the still impenetrably mysterious anatomy of the brain.

Ramón y Cajal began to seriously challenge prevailing wisdom about the central nervous system's structure. Up until the late nineteenth century, the brain was regarded as a single homogeneous, gelatinous mass—a kind of thinking "pudding," indivisible into smaller units. But using a light microscope and the Golgi stain (a new method for looking at nervous system tissue), Santiago revealed an organ of astonishing complexity, composed of billions of individual cellular units. Thus the work he presented at that 1889 meeting in Berlin confirmed the neuron doctrine, which had predicted that, like other organs and tissues of the body, the brain would have a cellular, atomistic structure, made up of a galaxy of functional subunits, the *neurons*. Perhaps even more surprising and profound in that historical moment, his drawings of the brain's substructure also showed that the connecting points between neurons were discontinuous in nature, made up of tiny, gapped *synapses* across which communication between neurons must occur. With this discovery of the synaptic linkages between neuronal cells, Ramón y Cajal had identified the physical nexus—the material point of connection—between neurons. That discovery ushered in the study of brain circuitry—electrically connected networks of neurons with common, collective functions—and the revelation of synaptic neurotransmitters, the chemical "messengers" by which neurons "converse," and upon which the entire science and industry of psychopharmacology has been built. He had fired a cannon again—smashing the gate of contemporary brain science.

Just as Ramón y Cajal's drawings of brain tissue revealed nearly 130 years ago the system's synaptic channels of communication (like electrical circuitry in the brain), the now flourishing science of epigenetics has identified and made visible the *physical points of connection between genes and environments*—its own network of staggeringly complex connections between genetics and experience. Though earlier studies in human populations had clearly shown that interactions were at play between genes and contexts, emerging epigenetic science has provided our first clear understanding of how such interactions happen. They occur by way of chemical modifications of the genome through lived experiences (family, trauma, and more banal influences) that control when, where, and to what degree specific genes are decoded and expressed. They ensure that who we are—orchids, dandelions, and everyone in between—is responsive to both the settings in which we grow and the genetic differences that delineate who we can become. The result is a symphony of astounding beauty and complexity, a composition finely responsive to all we have heard before, and played on a singular instrument, unique to each of us, with twenty-five thousand distinctive keys.

6

No Two Children Are Raised in the Same Family

With each new breakthrough in the study of orchids and dandelions, my professional journey as physician and researcher became increasingly personal, forcing me to ponder anew the contrast between my sister Mary's life and my own. As we both made our ways, ruefully but steadily, into what we termed "the Middle Ages," the divergences in our life paths had become increasingly perceptible and vivid, one to the other. I was embarked on a frenzied but fulfilling pilgrimage into the crazed cathedral of academic medicine and research. My wife and I had children to raise, teach, and nurture; we had friends to meet, soccer games to coach, and events to attend. And I had become increasingly engulfed in the businesses of managing assistants and students, writing papers and chapters, and becoming an accomplished hunter and gatherer of biomedical research funding. Mary, on the other hand, was by now more contemplative but ominously preoccupied, more reflective but troublingly obsessive. She was becoming progressively more drawn into the dark heart of her essential illness. Though remnants of our former closeness did abide and were at times visible, she had become as lost in the labyrinthine channels of her own psychosis as I had become invested in the urgent and fragile perplexities of university life. Hers was a life of feckless and paralyzing engagement with the demons of disorder; mine was a feverish and consuming allegiance toward a lettered idol.

Though the differences in our lives had nothing to do with virtuosity or talent, it is difficult for me to believe that anyone, given a mythic, all-seeing choice between the two paths, would have chosen Mary's tortured course. But the departure of my life from hers was a choice neither of us consciously or intentionally made. How might the two divergent lives have been different? Was there a single point of bifurcation where a different allele was acquired in that first, preconceptual chromosomal divide, a different, more nurturing parental behavior, or a different embryonic exposure to a virus or stressor that might have changed the entire landscape of our two lives? Or was Mary's plight simply a long, inexorable, and cumulative journey in the direction of malady and disarray? Might such a journey have brought into play differences in the environmental, epigenetic control of our genes' expression, and could that have accounted for the sad parting of sister and brother, of orchid and dandelion?

Mary and I were decidedly *not* genetically or psychologically identical. One sibling was a boy, the other a girl. Both were temperamentally introverted, but one was substantially more shy than even her bashful brother. Both were blessed with an inherent ability to do well in the enterprise of learning, but Mary's was greater than mine. On the other hand, we were also remarkably similar, in age, temperament, behavior, and physical phenotype. Both of us were redheads who were genetically better suited to the Highlands of Scotland than to the beaches of Southern California. As kids, we were freckled and sunburned from June through September and pocked at midlife with the barnacled remains of skin first damaged decades earlier on the sunny easternmost edge of the Pacific Rim. Both of us were bookish and nerdy; both strong-willed but playful; each one the other's closest, go-to playmate in those salad years of our youth. We could amuse each other for hours with a few inverted chairs, covered with blankets, that could become a tunnel, a train, or some secret hideout in which to read an afternoon away. But there was a fragile and shadowed innocence in our play that foretold a complicated and sorrowed future. When we emerged from that childhood "hideout" as adults, we were two very different people.

Mary's orchid nature had taken by midlife a treacherous and destructive turn, toward mental illness and disarray, dependency and self-defeat. She found it impossible to apply for, let alone ably do, a paying job. She was perennially haunted by fears for the future, convinced of her family's malevolence, at war with imagined conspiracies of hostile neighbors and betraying friends. By now, the harrowing, hallucinatory voices that had undone her promising young adulthood had become permanent residents within a broken, disordered mind. How—as I have asked in these pages, and as so many of us ask in our lives—can the paths, the developmental trajectories of two such close and congenial siblings have moved so far asunder? How can a person who was so nearly *me,* or at least a rich part of me, have parted so tragically and irreparably from the wide-open and mostly joyful road on which we had both walked as children?

Beyond the reality that she had the disproportionate sensibilities of an orchid child, and I the relatively hardy indifference of a dandelion, lay another, equally essential thread of our twin stories. Some further part of the mystery these troubling stories tell almost certainly resides in the poignant truth that *no two children are raised in the same family.* Though they live in the same home and may be born of the same parental blood, two siblings can grow up and develop—by virtue of vast differences in treatment, biology, and circumstance—in very different realities. Beyond our differences in sensitivity to the subtle variations in social contexts, I was a firstborn son and Mary a middle-born daughter. Despite my rank as the first of my parents' three children, I was far from a son who would become my dad's chosen favorite. That distinction was to reside in our younger brother, who became the acorn that fell not far from the tree, the son whose temperament and demeanor recapitulated uncannily our dad's hardy beneficence and generosity of character. But as for me, my mom had an evident admiration for the young man I seemed to be becoming. It was at times an ambivalent admiration, based as it was on her assessment that I bore strong physical and temperamental resemblances to her father, whom she both loved and feared. But it was admiration, respect, and dependable love nonetheless.

So although inadvertently and as a consequence of unintended psychological complexities, the family within which I grew and matured was almost entirely distinctive from the one that Mary knew. At birth and in early life, Mary and I shared certain clear commonalities in temperament and disposition, but our foundational biology (for example, in genetic makeup) was likely different, as were our potentials for epigenetic adaptation. And in life, our later selves were shaped by significantly different experiences during childhood. Very different epigenetic "switches" were flipped. She was an orchid planted in family terrain from which it was hard to bloom. I was from the beginning a mostly resilient dandelion, within an enduring climate of sunlight favorably cast by parents who tried hard to nurture and sustain.

Most contemporary parents hew to an egalitarian ideal of "treating all of our children the same." We strive, at least at the outset of the childbearing years, not to play favorites, to give all of our kids what we give to each one. Few modern parents would take any open pride in finding a visible unevenness in our gifts to our children, in our attentiveness to their safety, or in our care for their education and welfare. And yet despite this powerful adherence to a seemingly pervasive principle of parenting equity, the children from any given family often become as remarkably different as Mary and me.

One day in around 1991, as I sat in a carrel in the UCSF Library, looking out over the foggy green expanse of Golden Gate Park, I was mulling over this irony. By some pleasing serendipity, I happened upon what is now a dog-eared and famous paper by behavior geneticist Robert Plomin, who asked in 1987, "Why are children from the same family so different from each other?" The answer the paper delivered was a new science that explained, in part, how Mary and I had drifted onto different developmental paths. It argued that a major source of variation between siblings—in personality, psychopathology, and cognitive ability—comes from actual differences in their *experiences* of the same family environment (what behavior geneticists have called the "nonshared family environment"). The nuance was key; it wasn't just different events, but different ways of internalizing events, both shared and nonshared, in the brains and bodies of siblings.

Beyond the differences in genetic background, which even children from the same family often have in abundance, there are important and substantial differences in the way siblings experience, are treated, and feel within their family settings. It turns out that by virtue of differences in gender, birth order, behavior, adaptive "fit," and likely a slew of other, sometimes subtle peculiarities, kids growing up in the "same" family, with the "same" parents, at the "same" time have very different impressions and experiences of that very same family. These differences shape them epigenetically into the people they will be as adults. So we are products not only of the differences in our genes, but of differences as well in how our families imagined, saw, helped, and treated us—and how we encode and hold on to those experiences in our epigenome. And then of course there are also the "external" and incidental facts of life that are beyond choice or decisions yet affect us internally: a family tragedy, neighborhood violence, economic hardship, and many other traumatic events.

Geneticists' best illustration of this is the natural experiment in which two unrelated kids from different biological parents get adopted into the same family. In these circumstances, they don't share the same genes, coming as they do from entirely different biological lineages, but the adoptees do share the same family environment. Because their genes are not shared, any commonalities between them in psychological outcomes—like personality, mental health, or IQ—must be due to the shared effects of their common rearing environment. But in reality the similarity in such outcomes between adopted siblings is near zero! We know there are family environmental effects on psychological development, since even identical twins don't have the same personalities, mental health, or IQs—so it can't all be due to genes. So what does this mean? It means that the family environmental effects on a child's development are not shared between siblings—there are clearly family effects, but they are different for each kid. Children growing up in the same family actually experience that family in dramatically and consequentially different ways. These nonshared environmental effects must be attributable to differences in children's gender, birth (or adoption) order, or treatment by parents and siblings.

Might these differences in children's experiences of a given family affect the epigenetic processes that regulate gene expression, in the brain and in tissues throughout the body? Could the epigenome be a common pathway for the nonshared environmental effects that shape the development of personality, psychological well-being, and the risk for disease and disorder? Might differences in our early experiences of family, neighborhood, or community define our eventual divergences into the orchid and dandelion patterns of sensitivity to the world? And if that were true, could it change forever our liabilities to "suffer the slings and arrows of outrageous fortune"?

I Just Don't Have Time to Lick These Pups!

The most celebrated and widely known research revealing the effects of early family environments on the epigenetic shaping of behavior is the rat model of maternal licking and grooming pioneered by psychologist Michael Meaney and molecular biologist Moshe Szyf at McGill University. The model illustrates the behavioral and biological consequences not only of the differences *between* families in parenting behavior, but also of the differences *within* families in the parents' treatment of individual children. The model shows us how maternal behavior toward rat pups epigenetically regulates the kinds of adults they become, but also how mothers' individual treatment—and thus the pups' profiles of epigenetic marks—varies from one to another within the same litter.

Rat mothers, like human mothers, differ pretty dramatically in their approaches to taking care of their litters. Some care intensively for their young—engaging almost continuously in the activities of licking the pups' anogenital areas, grooming their scant fur, and assuming an arched-back position that allows maximal access to her teats for nursing. Other rat moms, by contrast, show precious little licking, grooming, or nursing—only that amount required to keep the pups alive, growing, and healthy. It is a continuum of mothering behavior, with most rat moms somewhere in the middle and smaller numbers at each end of the licking and grooming spectrum. I, for one, have always been grateful that licking my two kids was not among the behaviors required of good human parents.

While we're comparing the standards of good parental behavior between rats and humans, let's take a moment to contemplate the similarities and differences between the various species we've been considering thus far and ask what can be legitimately learned about the human condition from a pink-eyed mother rat and her fleshy little pups, each no bigger than our fingertips. Humans, monkeys, and rats are all *mammals,* along with their evolutionary cousins—porcupines, whales, and reindeer, plus another fifty-four hundred species or so. All female mammals nurse their babies with milk from mammary glands (breasts), and the majority of mammalian species have placentas that feed their fetuses inside the womb as another, earlier means of nurturing and supplying their young. Mammals also all have middle ears through which sound is transmitted to the brain, and all give birth to living newborns, not eggs.

Differences in the genetic sequences of DNA between humans and our closest primate ancestors are far fewer and smaller than most of us realize, with genomic *dissimilarities* between humans and chimpanzees currently estimated at just over 1 percent. In other words, we're 99 percent genetically the same, but that small difference makes, well, a big difference. For scientists who have studied both human and nonhuman mammalian species, what is always most striking (and humbling, I suppose) is the astonishing level of concordance between species—in social structures and behavior, physiology, anatomy, and molecular biology. As one who has scrutinized at length the behavior of both human children and young monkeys, it is simply enthralling to watch how groups of young macaques will play, argue, form friendships, and compete in a manner exactly replicating their human counterparts.

Meaney and Szyf's landmark insights were derived from comparing the behavior, physiology, and epigenetic marks of pups cared for by rat mothers at the two extremes of the mothering continuum. First, take note of the fact that there is nothing especially lethal or beneficial about any location on this continuum of maternal behavior. Both high and low licking, grooming, and nursing rat moms (from here on, let's just call them *low* or *high licking* for short) are displaying behavior that is typical of their species, and the pups from both kinds of litters generally survive, thrive, reproduce, and "succeed" irrespective of their moms' early attentiveness. Nonetheless, Meaney and Szyf discovered that when compared to grown-up pups from high licking mothers, those from low licking moms had higher resting cortisol levels, greater cortisol system reactivity to stress, more anxious behavior, earlier sexual maturation, and more aggressive, dominant behavior that could bolster reproductive success. All of these characteristics in pups from low licking moms seem to point toward the pups subconsciously preparing for a life of scarcity, threat, and reproductive urgency. It is as if their young, developing brains have detected an early environment of scant nurturing, unreliable food, and frequent stressors and are calibrating the pups' behavior and biology to maximize their chances of survival and reproduction.

The intriguing findings, however, don't end there. Female pups from the same litters of low licking moms, when observed several weeks later at reproductive maturity, showed the same low-intensity mothering behaviors when caring for *their own* offspring. The grown-up pups replicate the maternal behaviors they received from their own moms. So here was evidence—albeit in rodents—that maternal treatment in early life was directly correlated with young rats' levels of stress response, sexual precocity, anxiety and aggression, and parenting behavior as they moved into adult life. As a rat pup, who you are mothered by has direct implications for who you become as you grow, mature, and become a parent. If you happened to have a mom who is less interested in caring for her pups, you become an adult with heightened reactivity to stress and challenge, more anxious behavior, and a diminished predisposition to intensively parenting your own young. It looks for all the world like an intergenerational transmission of risk.

Maybe, you might speculate, the low licking moms had low licking pups simply because they were genetically related, and their shared genes gave rise to the same behaviors in both generations. But in a series of ingenious "cross-fostering" experiments, Meaney and colleagues were able to prove that the conveyance of parenting behavior across generations was *not* due to the genetic commonality between moms and pups. When pups from low licking moms were transplanted early in postnatal life into the litters of high licking moms, they grew up to show high licking behavior—the same as their foster moms. Similarly, female pups from high licking biological moms, when foster-reared by low licking moms, matured into rat mothers with low licking behavior. Here, nurture proved stronger than nature.

Finally, Meaney and Szyf established that these effects of maternal licking on aspects of their pups' behavior, maturation, and stress biology are due to *epigenetic changes* that are switched on by the physical sensation of the mother tending her pups. Recall the chemical tags of the epigenome, from the last chapter, which attach to the DNA or histone proteins and govern the expression or decoding of genes by controlling how tightly the chromatin DNA is packaged. Low levels of maternal licking lead to DNA methylation in the pups' gene that produces the cortisol receptor—a kind of molecular receiver, where cortisol "plugs into" the neurons of the pups' brains. The DNA methylation results in lower expression of the cortisol receptor protein, which in turn leads to greater cortisol reactivity and higher levels of anxiety. Further, when the female pups of low licking moms grow up, they themselves become low licking moms. So the mother's natural level of physically licking and grooming her pups over the first few days of life creates two different phenotypes of adult rat by changing the pup's epigenetic regulation of the cortisol receptor gene. The effect is a wholesale alteration in the pup's lifelong vulnerability to stress and anxiety.

The other biological agent that plays an important role in the regulation of maternal behavior is the so-called peace and bonding hormone, oxytocin. Discovered at the turn of the nineteenth century, oxytocin (which means "quick birth" in Greek) is a protein molecule that is manufactured in the brain's hypothalamus and is implicated in multiple reproductive processes, including contraction of the uterus during birth and milk letdown during breastfeeding. It is the hormone responsible for the feelings of contentment, euphoria, or even sensuality experienced by new moms during breastfeeding. Oxytocin is also responsible for the lifetime pair-bonding between males and females that occurs in some species (it is released in humans after sex, presumably to promote feelings of closeness) and, in part, for differences in maternal behavior among female rats. As with the effects of licking and grooming on the cortisol receptor expression in pups' brains, oxytocin's role in the origin of maternal behavior appears related to epigenetic changes controlling the expression of both the hormone itself and its brain receptors.

Might the human epigenome similarly bear the marks of early differences in parental care? Could variations in the attentive or neglectful behavior of human parents regulate stress biology and behavior in their human newborns? And do the differences in early parenting sustained by human "pups" have something to do with the emergence of orchid and dandelion phenotypes? If my sister, Mary, had been somehow transplanted into a different family at birth, might her life as an infant orchid have been fundamentally transformed? Although it is impossible to say, this question has gnawed at my memories as I reflect back on our early formative years and as Jill and I parented our own children through those same crucial years. The remarkable sensitivities of an orchid child can amplify even subtle differences between family settings, and those differences can, for some children, result in life-changing developmental effects. Could they be the difference between a stable career and family and a life of chaos and disconnection? And if the answer were yes, could knowing this help us improve the outcomes for children from the very same "litter" but who grow up in "different families"?

Changing Lives and Growing Brains

Although human parents are not required to lick their pups, there is strong evidence that the adequacy and abundance of caring parental behavior can profoundly influence the development of children's brains, intelligence, and behavior. The Bucharest Early Intervention Project, mentioned earlier, has sadly shown how early neglect and impoverished parental care can fundamentally change neurodevelopment among children growing up in institutional conditions. In a famously misguided social manipulation, the Romanian government under Nicolae Ceauşescu attempted to augment the national workforce, and thus boost the national economy, by mandating higher numbers of pregnancies and births. The result was a generation of children for which families were economically unable to care and provide. As many as 170,000 Romanian children were abandoned to orphanages, where the ratio of children to caretakers was on the order of 15 to 1. Imagine the attentiveness to a child's needs and well-being available in a family of fifteen children, all of about the same age, and with one mom! The physical conditions in these orphanages were bleak and dismal, with children sometimes tied to their beds and days organized into efficient but lifeless routines of silent meals and assembly-line baths.

UNICEF estimates that over 150 million children worldwide have lost at least one parent, and 13 million have lost both, as a consequence of war, economic abandonment, or disease pandemics. Children who are institutionalized as a result of these parental losses can develop profound developmental deficits, ranging from intellectual impairments to severe, autism-like mental disorders and behaviors. One need only think of the famous studies conducted by psychologist Harry Harlow in the 1950s and '60s, in which infant monkeys developed physical and emotional bonds with inanimate wire surrogate mothers and over time showed increasingly autistic behaviors. Just like Harlow's young monkeys, children raised in conditions of institutionalized deprivation develop abnormal behaviors, such as rocking, head banging, finger sucking, animal-like vocalizations, and extreme attention seeking. They have been noted to be unusually impulsive and are dangerously willing to follow any stranger who shows attentive behavior toward them. Ultimately, such children show excessively high rates of stunted growth, chronic physical disorders, and serious psychopathology.

On the other hand, human infants who grow up in families in which parents are attentive, responsive, and caring can thrive, develop, and grow in so many remarkable, seemingly miraculous ways. I am now the proud "Papa" to four young grandsons between the ages of nine months and four years, and I have been struck once again by the exquisite and powerful dance between parents and babies. I am dazzled by how the rapidly unfolding behavioral and interactive capacities of young infants can pull forth powerful parental love and care that the parents never knew they had. It is like watching a fully grown person discover that she can speak fluently and eloquently in a language she never knew existed or never learned. Watching a young father discover the sheer wonder that is his young son is like seeing a student discover a secret field of study, perfectly aligned with his own natural talents and proclivities. The six- to twelve-week-old human newborn begins to smile and unleashes a torrent of love and endearment from his stunned, adoring parents. A five-month-old infant learns to babble in his first, primordial imitation of his parents' speech, and the mom and dad become unabashed wellsprings of baby talk, spoken in long, delighted paragraphs. The one-year-old takes her first halting, foolish steps across a living room carpet, and an entire three-generation family erupts in loud, celebratory approval. The toddler, in reply, discovers a bright new yearning to run headlong into the charmed future of her life.

Whether it is the sad, stunted decline of an abandoned orphan child in an institution or the developmental explosion of a thoroughly loved and carefully attended infant, much of what we see unfolding in the early lives of children, for good or ill, is the result of epigenetic processes regulated by the paucity or plenitude of parental care. We now know that these environmental events and the conditions of early life release whole orchestral scores of coordinated epigenetic events, turning genes on and off and ensuring a child's evolved, unconscious adaptation to the world into which he or she has been born. For every child, the object is to do as well as he or she can within the setting that he or she has been given, and the epigenome is the means to that end. These tiny molecular events and adjustments are the critical mechanisms that allow both a Romanian orphan and a treasured North American newborn to survive and thrive as best they each can do.

What's Wrong with Sammy?

Even *within* each kind of setting, whether barren of or lavish with love and sufficiency, there are striking differences in the adaptive prosperity and well-being of individual children. Some dandelion-like children thrive even in orphanages despite the dismal sterility and coldness of their "home." Others, in relatively protective and nurturing families, devolve into fragile, troubled lives despite their material and emotional wealth. As a dandelion child reared in a typical but often stressful home, I was able to surmount the adversities and conflicts, but my sister, Mary, with the delicate responsiveness of an orchid, was not. Such differences, as we have now seen, arise from a combination of special biological sensitivity to those social settings and cues (the orchid phenotype) and the reality that a single, seemingly unerring environment is in fact *not* the same for each individual child.

I remember the early years of an endearing little girl who had been abandoned by her native family to the care of a rural Nicaraguan mission hospital in which I was working for a summer as a senior medical student. Even as a preschool-age child, Marta, as I will call her, had a happy, bright spirit to which people were drawn in spite of themselves, especially given her tenuous and unpromising circumstances. She wasn't the first or last child to be jettisoned into the care of this medical staff on the Rio Coco, but she had a kind of sparkle as she made her coy, playful rounds each day in the various quarters of that miniature hospital. I would see her in the early morning, diligently sweeping the hospital dining room with a little preschool-sized broom someone had fashioned for her. Later, there she would be again, in the corner of the clinic waiting room, chatting up the sick and the halt in her native Miskito tongue. And in the evening, as I made my last rounds on the sickest of kids in the children's ward, there Marta would often be, curled up tiny and asleep in one of the clean unoccupied beds. She drew from that primitive, medical environment as much attentiveness and care as a "home" without parents could muster.

In a small miracle of hope for this young institutionalized life, Marta was adopted that summer by a wonderful, loving North American family with five other kids. That Moravian family had trundled their ample entourage, in an old Checker cab with three hundred thousand miles already in its rearview mirror, all the way from North Carolina to the boonies of the Nicaraguan outback. Over that summer, they fell, collectively and progressively, in love with the tiny waif Marta and decided that they could not abide the thought of returning home without her. In a colossal and wearing effort of engagement with the Nicaraguan government and the U.S. embassy, they secured permission to adopt her legally into their family and added yet one more small passenger to the cargo of an already overstuffed vehicle, headed north. She grew into a lovely young woman who remains to this day a cherished, life-giving member of her North Carolina family, in a home nearly thirty-five hundred miles away from her infelicitous beginnings. The stark, impoverished, and seemingly hopeless character of growing up alone in a bleak Central American outpost hospital was simply not the same gig for Marta as it had been for a dozen other orphaned children left for dead or useless over the years in the very same remote place. That same hospital "family" was uniquely different for Marta from what it had been for others similarly marooned in early life. Just because a child has an inauspicious beginning does not foreclose on the future she has yet to experience.

I remember seeing, as well, during my years as a pediatrician providing primary health care to children in multiple North American settings, a family who brought their four kids, ranging in age from kindergarten to early middle school, into our clinic for a single concurrent well child visit and examination. As I entered the room, there sat four somewhat snaggle-toothed, grinning brothers bearing a clear family resemblance, like four charmingly scruffy crows on a wire, arrayed along a continuum of S to XL. The smallest one, on one end, beamed with alacrity at the prospect of seeing and talking to "the doctor," while the big one, serving at that moment as the other bookend, had the kind of sullen, permanently eye-rolled countenance of a junior high house ape. One of the two in the middle, a boy of about eight, had missing teeth that he had forfeited to a fall while trying to pee off the roof of their home, much to his brothers' delight. He made furtive glances up at me from under an overhang of greasy brown hair disarrayed in what would today be regarded as a fashionably messy hairstyle. As I began a conversation about the boys' health, their experiences in school, and their growth and development, the mom said, in a definitive tone, "They're all pretty healthy, except *that one!*"—pointing as she said it to the dodgy, midsized culprit in the middle. We'll call him Sammy. "I just don't know what's wrong with Sammy," she said with a kind of half-plaintive, half-accusatory voice. "All the boys get sick occasionally, but *he gets everything,* always has something broken, always breaking out in *rashes,* and gets in trouble at school to boot! Please tell me, *what's wrong with Sammy?*"

Well, there was nothing wrong with Sammy. He was a healthy, robust seven-year-old boy who was growing fine and doing reasonably well in school, despite recurrent trips to the principal's office for various minor infractions. But it was clear, as I got to know him better, that his experience of his family was quite different from that of his brothers. He was an artist, not an athlete; a cat in a family of dogs; an introvert poet in a posse of people-person cowboys. His older brother picked on him relentlessly, and when Sammy tried to do the same to his younger brother, he was invariably caught, tried, and incarcerated. In school, he was always a distant second fiddle to the older brother's reputation as a talented jock and stand-up comedian. Even the youngest, the kindergartner, found ways to torment Sammy, colluding with the others to put worms in his yogurt or feed him grass clippings while the others held him down. It was as if Sammy were living and growing in a different family altogether.

In fact, to my recollection, there has not been a single instance in all those years of caring for kids and young families in which a parent said of a second child, "Oh, this one's just like the last one." And this is more than parents simply endorsing the individuality of their kids. Apart from similarities in a family's physical appearances, two consecutive children born to the same parents seem hardly ever to be alike, as if there were an inviolable law of the universe that children from the same family must be forever different. If the first is irritable and colicky, the second is easy and placid. If the first sleeps through the night by six months, the second waits until her second birthday. If the first is a gregarious entertainer, the second is a silent, humorless introvert, never speaking until spoken to. Children in the same family seem never remotely congruent—in temperament, disposition, or approaches to the world.

So how does the story of a mother rat's pup-licking practices help with understanding the Sammys of the world—that is, with how early parenting might create children's differences *within* families, rather than *between* families? It seems that even in rat families, the differences in experiences of maternal licking, grooming, and nursing are just as dramatic among pups within a single litter as they are among pups from different litters and different moms. There are sometimes threefold differences in the amount of licking and grooming that individual pups receive within a given litter, even from rat moms that over a reproductive lifetime show extreme differences in their average levels of commitment to the care of their young. Both high and low licking and grooming mothers show substantial variation in how vigilantly and intensively they care for individual pups within a given litter.

This new line of research on within-litter differences in maternal care also shows that male pups are often licked more frequently than females, that differences in the care of individual pups are stable over the their entire ten-day newborn period, and that the differences in within-litter maternal care have the same expected and long-term effects on behavior and biology in adult life. Pups within a given "sibship" that were less attentively licked and groomed grow up to be less socially adept, show more anxiety-like behavior in novel or challenging situations, and have greater emotional and cortisol system reactivity under conditions of stress. These studies also confirm that the observed differences in biology and behavior among pups shortchanged on maternal attention are due to epigenetic differences that control the expression of brain proteins like the cortisol and oxytocin receptors. Finally, although differences in maternal behavior toward individual pups can calibrate their biological and behavioral responses to the conditions of adult life, it has also become clear that innate differences in the pups themselves—like the natural intensity and pitch of their crying—can influence the level of maternal care they receive.

As it is with a litter of eight or ten baby rats, so it is with human children: no two of them grow up in the same family. Not only do orchid and dandelion children experience their natal homes in vastly different ways, but the developmental emergence of their very identities, as orchids or as dandelions, is shaped in part by their unique niches within multidimensional family "nests." Is the child a boy or a girl? Was she born first, second, or third? Into a one- or two-parent family? Awash in wealth or pinioned by poverty? My orchid sister, Mary, for all of her tenderness and brilliance, was reared in a different family—albeit nominally the *same* family—from that of her dandelion brothers. And the effect of that difference was to set her upon a path toward disappointment and disease, disallowing thereby the brilliant and healthy future she might have otherwise rightfully claimed in another more support-

ive and forgiving home. All of these finely tuned environmental parameters conspire, along with the inherent constraints of a child's unique
genomic identity, to produce distinctive human organisms—as different
in provenance and in destiny as the kaleidoscopic varieties of snowflakes
and stars.

These differences are what make our species adaptable and our individual lives unique and meaningful. But they also make us vulnerable in
ways that science hasn't previously understood—and certainly in ways
neither Mary, I, nor our parents understood. But who are the orchids
and dandelions beyond the family nest, and how are they formed by the
external worlds of school and friendship? How can we ensure that they
prosper and bloom?

7

The Kindness and Cruelty
of Children

In the winter months of 1987, an eight-year-old Vietnamese girl—I'll call her Lan—visited my pediatric office with a complaint of chronic, recurrent abdominal pain. She had striking brown eyes, wore an adorable dress, and nervously kicked her legs as she sat waiting on the examining table. Her mother was very worried. Lan's pain, while easily localizable (in the midline, just below the center of her breastbone and rib cage), had confounded all efforts to identify its origin. Using the best of a modern medical laboratory and diagnostic imaging, her primary care pediatrician had diligently and skillfully searched for ulcers, kidney stones, inflammatory conditions, and infections—to no avail. Lan had had no fever and described her pain as a dull central abdominal "aching," accompanied by an occasional sharper cramp. Her pain bore no relation to eating, urinating, or bowel movements and had been attended by no weight loss, joint pain, or other symptoms. She had not yet started her menstrual periods, and her physical examination was that of an entirely normal prepubertal girl. All of Lan's laboratory blood and urine tests were also normal; there was no evidence of anemia, inflammation, or infection; and an ultrasound imaging of her abdomen had revealed no abnormalities. What was going on in this child's belly?

After speaking with Lan and looking over her chart—I wondered if it soon would end up being one of the "doorstop" files I'd come to associate with some orchid children—two additional pieces of history came to light. First, the pain had sometimes been sufficiently severe to keep Lan home from school, and while at home with her mom, she had from time to time voiced concerns about the other kids at school. She alluded to "the big kids" who treated younger, smaller children with disdain, excluding them from games and bullying them with derision, taunts, and the kind of nonphysical childhood aggression teachers know well. As Lan's mother was describing the primary school social world with which her daughter had had to contend, Lan was at work in a corner of the exam room with the paper and crayons I always keep at hand. Although I wasn't able to offer an unequivocal diagnosis, I had a hunch about what might be causing the stomach ailment. But I didn't want to voice it quite yet, so we made a follow-up appointment to check in again soon. As Lan and her mom left the clinic, she shyly handed me a folded drawing, as if slipping me a note with a secret message. I waved goodbye.

Back in my office, I examined the drawing. It seemed to confirm my hunch. It depicted three older girls, two in red dresses and one in blue. Next to them was a portrait of a small, crying girl. Right away, I realized that it was a self-portrait—of Lan and her experience at school. Each "character" had voice bubbles. From the big girls' mouths came the words, "You cant play your too small to play!" "You cant play you dont have click clack shoos." and "You cant play your not tall." (By the way, "click clack" shoes are actually a known category in the taxonomy of young girls' shoes—they are the dressy, grown-up shoes that make "clickity-clackity" sounds as their owner walks on hard surfaces. It was news to me.) Below the picture were Lan's words: "I got left out when the big kid teas me and my hart is like bracking."

Lan's stomach pain was as physical as a skin wound or a broken bone, but its cause wasn't straightforward, like stepping on a nail or falling out of a treehouse. It was her emotional experiences transformed into a physical malady. She was an orchid struggling to blossom in a harsh, unfriendly place. How did this happen exactly, and what was the solution?

A drawing by my eight-year-old patient "Lan" of
her distress at being excluded by the bigger girls.

Survival of the Fittest . . . in Preschool?

Lan was what psychologist Elaine Aron influentially termed a "highly
sensitive child," and within our lexicon of special sensitivity or differential susceptibility, Lan would be regarded as a quintessentially orchid
child—psychologically unprotected, biologically attuned and reactive
to environmental adversity, and exceptionally susceptible to social pain.
The disabling pain in Lan's belly was being caused not by a disease, but
rather by her unconscious physical embodiment of the social stress she
was routinely encountering at school.

Emotional and physical pain are in a certain sense the same thing—
not just for orchids, but for everyone. Neuroscientists have in fact shown
how the pain of social exclusion can activate the same brain regions as
those affected by acute and chronic physical pain. In a similar vein,
researchers have shown that taking a pain relief pill like acetaminophen

can reduce an emotional hurt, like heartbreak. Thus children like Lan experience both bodily and psychological pain within the same brain circuitry—regions called the anterior cingulate and prefrontal cortex that lie toward the front of the brain. We can think of this as a kind of "ouch zone" in the brain. It is a very important tool that we have evolved, since knowing when we are hurt, physically and emotionally, was key to our survival in the distant past, and of course still is today. This commonality in the brain regions underlying emotional and physical pain makes it readily apparent how exposures to school bullying can be somatically experienced as chronic abdominal pain. It sometimes physically hurts to be marginalized, left out, or ostracized, especially if you're a sensitive eight-year-old girl.

So what do we do with this knowledge? I teach the science of child development to medical and public health students, as well as to pediatric and psychiatric residents in training. Although it is sometimes relegated to one of the arcane subspecialties of medicine, child development is actually the foundational science of all pediatrics and child psychiatry. It teaches about the remarkable breadth of normal variation in the behavior and development of children, about the profound influence that relational experiences in the early years can have on health and achievement, and about how a child's genetically appointed propensities interact with the nature of his or her external world to determine health and illness, accomplishment and disappointment, success and failure over the entire course of life. The orchid and dandelion subtypes of children are just one example of how wide-ranging "normal" can be among those with differing sensibilities and temperaments.

The science of child development helps doctors, teachers, and parents to discern where a child lies on the developmental spectrum from normative to disordered, delayed to advanced, orchid to dandelion. Sometimes an odd behavior is simply that—unmistakably odd, but within the normal range for children of a given age. Other times, such aberrations, if persistent or severe, can presage the advent of a psychiatric disorder, a neurodevelopmental impediment, or a significant, remediable obstacle to successful development and growth.

So much can be learned about this normal variation by simply watching children as they play, learn, and interact, in a doctor's office, a family's living room, or the play yard of a school. I have often used observation in a community preschool as a means of teaching the range of expectable, typical behavior in young children. Students watch a classroom of twenty or thirty three- and four-year-old children as they go about the business of being preschoolers: playing house; engaged in games, construction, or demolition; making art; sharing news in "circle time"; eating snacks; or napping. The behavior we watch is both the average of the age-specific, developmental group and that of the unique individual child—how some children always run in packs, while others play alone; how some are immediately responsive to teacher instruction and requests, while others seem completely oblivious; how boys are prone to physicality and competition, while girls are often keen, intuitive observers of subtle social complexities (or how, sometimes, it's just the opposite).

Among the broad expanse of behaviors a medical student can witness in two or three hours of careful, anonymous observation within a preschool setting are children's unmistakable predispositions to form hierarchies of social power and influence. It is the characteristic of child behavior that medical trainees most hate to discover, because they believe almost inevitably in a prevailing conventional vision of the young child's natural innocence, benevolence, and predilection to democratic behavior. I point out an almost continuous stream of examples of how children array themselves in despotic pecking orders of dominance and social position, and my students often vigorously protest, unwilling to acknowledge the Hobbesian societies that three- and four-year-old children almost universally form. "But kids are so sweet," my soon-to-be doctors protest. "They still have the innocence we lose as adults." And it falls upon me to dismally disabuse them of this notion.

Even preverbal human infants have ways of recognizing and thinking about social dominance, using relative size to predict the outcome of conflicts between agents with opposing goals. One group of scientists used computer animations of cartoon figures, each with a mouth and eyes, to portray dominance contests between pairs of agents. When shown a competition for an object between two figures, infants as young as ten to thirteen months could predict (measured using eye tracking and the infant's looking time at the two figures) that the bigger of the two would prevail and claim the desired object. This shows that even in the first year of life, human infants understand dominance and anticipate the outcome of competitions for scarce resources. Even before social contact with peers has been extensively experienced, very young children have a seemingly built-in cognitive capacity for thinking about and judging who's on top and who's at the bottom. Yes, children are innocent; that is exactly what makes them unconcerned with cloaking their behavior in the deceptive niceties of adult life. But they offer a nakedly honest glimpse into how humans interact competitively in the social field in which orchids and dandelions grow and encounter each other, expressing some of the raw truths of human nature.

Just as with the animated cartoon figures, any pairs of real children will reveal winners and losers, the powerful and powerless, leaders and the led. Visit any preschool, observe any kindergarten classroom, and it becomes apparent that Susie always leads and Emma always follows; in the competition for a scarce resource—a coveted toy or the teacher's attention—it is consistently John, Catherine, or Paul who gets the most access; when a game begins among five kids, it is always Kirsten who sets the rules. Though my students sometimes despair that I am tarnishing the ideal of egalitarian childhoods, preschool and kindergarten teachers will always confirm the reality that within two to three weeks of coming together into novel social groups, such as a new classroom at the beginning of a new school year, children intuitively establish dominance and subordination relationships within linearly ordered hierarchies of social position.

Although there are functional, socially stabilizing aspects of these early childhood hierarchies, of which we will soon take note, they can also act as the backdrop for a more malevolent social dynamic—the bullying or coercive domination of one child by another, or by a group. It is sometimes this darker side of childhood pecking orders that becomes salient and operative in the lives of dandelion and orchid children, like Lan. And, as we'll see, also in the lives of orchid and dandelion adults.

Who Gets the Bananas?

Even where bullying and marginalization are rare, however, there is
still an underlying predisposition that *Homo sapiens*—even diminutive
Homo sapiens children—seem to have: to create ordered social relationships along a gradient from dominant to subordinate, bigwig to earwig,
top dog to underdog, big cheese to cheeseball. This will likely remind
you of the allegedly more primitive world of the animal kingdom, in
which there are no hospitals, therapists, or parent-teacher conferences.
In fact, the behavior of animals, much like that of children, reveals a
vivid picture of who we are and where we've come from, even as we resist
our call of the wild.

During my year working with and observing monkeys at the NIH, I
received an object lesson that I was able to apply across species. Through
that most coveted of things—food—we ascertained where individual
monkeys lay on this continuum in a very simple but effective and quite
visible way. We loaded a couple of full branches of ripe bananas into a
wheelbarrow, transported them down to the natural habitat where the
troop of thirty to forty animals lived, and chucked the bananas over the
enclosure fence. What happened next was a vivid illustration of how social
hierarchies work in monkey societies. The number one, alpha male, to
whom everyone else deferred, would casually saunter over to where the
banana branch had landed, the very picture of nonchalance. He would
then sit down and proceed to gorge himself on as many bananas as his
ample belly could hold. Sometimes this number was twenty or thirty
bananas, creating a scene not unlike Paul Newman's bet in *Cool Hand
Luke* that he could eat fifty hard-boiled eggs in an hour. Once sated,
the alpha male would produce a noisy belch, defecate impressively, and
sleepily sashay away from the site, whereupon the number two monkey
would get his or her turn. This continued, one monkey at a time, in an
absolutely orderly fashion, until the last, omega monkey got what was
left, which was often not much. Being among the low-status animals
also didn't just assign you to a life of leftover bananas. In the day-to-day

activities of being a monkey, these were the ones who were last into the shelter during a rainstorm, the least desirable playmates, the last male to leave the natal troop during adolescence, and the most unlikely to have access to "reproductive opportunities."

The animals at the top of the pack were not necessarily the biggest or the meanest. When it came to acquiring status in a rhesus monkey society, it was not so much how fierce you could be, but rather whom you knew and how effectively you led. Having the right mother, making the right alliances with your peers, and using the right swagger as you cruised the compound on Friday nights were all more important than size or ferocity. And though an individual monkey's status was largely stable over time, the hierarchy *could* change in certain opportunistic circumstances. Primatologist and molecular biologist Robert Sapolsky tells the story of a strictly and ferociously hierarchical troop of Kenyan baboons, whose high-status animals took to aggressively excluding others from access to a tourist lodge garbage dump, where the CEO monkeys were feasting in comfort and exclusivity. It turned out, however, that the meat in the dump was contaminated with bovine tuberculosis—like Wall Street bonuses delivered with a touch of the plague. The dominant animals eventually became sick and died, resulting in far more egalitarian, supportive relationships among the troop's remaining members—a more pacific "culture" that has lasted for more than two decades.

Similarly, Steve Suomi relates the discovery that one morning in 2009, a "palace revolt" had occurred on the grounds of the NIH primate field station. As the event was reconstructed from webcams by center staff, a provocation had occurred during the night between two monkeys, one of which was a member of the dominant clan. That clan's hold on the top positions in the troop had been recently eroded by the removal of one of its members for the treatment of a kidney disorder and by the progressive aging of its alpha male into an arthritic, less aggressive shadow of his former self. When a fight erupted with a member of the dominant group, a clan two ranks down in the hierarchy saw its chance. A violent brawl broke out, involving every one of the adult monkeys. The melee resulted in the deaths of two dominant animals and forced the rest of their cabal over the electrified field station fence and into temporary exile in the parking lot. When the primate center staff arrived on site the following morning, there were injured, penitent, and formerly top-dog monkeys lurking everywhere on the grounds outside the habitat. In the years since, the formerly number three clan has maintained a firm, visible grip on the leadership of the troop.

Sapolsky's and Suomi's monkey revolution stories also illustrate another dimension of social position in monkey societies. *Where* an individual monkey resides within the hierarchy of its social group and the *circumstances* under which he holds that position have a lot to do not just with how many bananas he gets to eat or how many females with whom he gets to copulate, but also with his health and longevity. Across the animal kingdom, from roundworms and fruit flies to fish and nonhuman primates, social groups form hierarchical organizations that, to one degree or another, ensure unequal access to scarce resources and create visible inequities between their dominant and subordinate members. Why there is such an overpowering, instinctive urge to form these hierarchies, across so many simple and complex animal species, is not completely understood. But from an evolutionary perspective, dominance hierarchies have likely been conserved over millennia because of the adaptive advantages they serve—dividing labor and social roles, providing leadership to the social group, and controlling aggression through predictable and enduring social positions. In other words, we didn't spend eons just evolving as individuals, but as groups. We survived as tribes, and for these tribes to work, apparently not everyone could be the leader. The question this raises for modern life is how we can preserve the positive qualities of social ladders, while softening their collateral damage on the eight-year-old Lans of the world, who need bananas (literally and metaphorically) just as much as the rest of us.

Occupying subordinate (low-rank) positions within those hierarchies has been shown to have a panoply of physiological consequences. These range from a chronic, persistent stirring within the cortisol and fight-or-flight reactivity systems, to a lighting up of critical stress response centers in the brain, to a kind of DEFCON 1 level of threat alert that is shuttled from cell to cell throughout the immune system. Such "biological embedding" of low social status can have big effects on the life course of individual animals. It has been shown in monkeys, for example, that being put in a marginal social position can increase the risk of physical and psychological/behavioral disorders and can exacerbate chronic preexisting conditions such as high blood pressure, coronary heart disease, diabetes, immune deficiencies, and disorders of reproduction. As Sapolsky has pointed out, being the underdog doesn't *always* produce these health downturns; the virulence of social subordination also depends on the species, the specific social group, its despotic or egalitarian culture, and an individual's other, socially supportive relationships. The deaths of the garbage-eating baboon CEOs and of the two previously dominant monkeys during the palace revolt at the NIH are real-life demonstrations of how being on top can also be dangerous when there is "political" upheaval and a dramatic change in the group power structure.

For human counterparts of such stories of lost grace and fallen power, we need look no further than to the tragedies of two very human Richards: Shakespeare's Richard III and the American president Richard Milhous Nixon. Richard III—the play's tragic, scoliotic protagonist who aspires at all costs to the throne of England—effects a reign of terror, brutally murdering all those who would thwart his ambitions to ascent. In the end, he is feared and loathed by his countrymen, and following a night in which he is terrorized by the ghosts of all those whose lives he has taken, he is himself killed by the invading forces of the Earl of Richmond. In the final scene, Richard laments:

> My conscience hath a thousand several tongues,
> And every tongue brings in a several tale,
> And every tale condemns me for a villain.

Richard Nixon, himself a tragic sovereign of Shakespearean proportions, resigned the U.S. presidency in 1974 in a tide of shame following revelations of a politically motivated criminal break-in at the Watergate offices of the Democratic National Committee. In a final lugubrious but pitiable speech to his White House staff, Nixon exhorted, "Always remember: others may hate you, but those who hate you don't win unless you hate them, and then you destroy yourself." Within days of his resignation, Nixon had developed a deep vein thrombosis in his leg, leading to a life-threatening pulmonary embolism from which he only narrowly recovered.

Clearly, there are liabilities and snares at both ends of the sociopolitical spectrum, and occasionally—though not occasionally enough, it seems—those at the top are justly "rewarded" when malevolence and duplicity guide their rules. But more often than not, the chronic, measurable costs—in health, illness, and longevity—of being on the lowest end predominate.

Lower Status, Bigger Problems

There are remarkable parallels between the health effects of social status in animal species and those found in relation to socioeconomic status (SES) in human societies. Where you fall socially and economically affects how healthy you are when you're alive, as well as when and how you will die. Just as troops of monkeys, schools of fish, and human preschoolers are hierarchically organized, contemporary adult human societies also show some degree of layering or partitioning of power, deference, and access to resources by an individual's SES—generally measured as a combination of one's educational level, job prestige, and income. In fact, SES is the single most powerful predictor of human health and development we have, at every stage of life. It is so powerful a predictor—of acute and chronic disease, physical and mental health, accidental and violent injury, academic achievement, reading and literacy levels, and longevity—that we question any other observed linkages between a risk factor (like cholesterol levels or high blood pressure) and health outcomes unless researchers have first controlled or adjusted for SES. You can't understand the course of an individual human life—or death—without looking at that person's position in society.

And yet we only began studying this powerful factor in its own right over the past twenty or twenty-five years, even though it has likely shaped human life and health from the distant recesses of hunter-gatherer societies. I remember attending a meeting convened by my UCSF colleague and friend Nancy Adler, where we were asked to think together about the determinants of health, broadly defined, at the level of human populations. Professor Leonard Syme from UC Berkeley said to the gathered group, "Well, if you want to know what predicts human health and illness, I can tell you the answer right now, and we can all go home: it's socioeconomic status."

Len had begun his career as a UCLA- and Yale-trained medical sociologist, the son of a blue-collar electrician in the then-backwater Canadian town of Winnipeg, Manitoba. Early in his professional life he was recruited to the NIH to form the first epidemiology study section and become the first sociologist to enter the U.S. civil service. Enthralled by his reading of Émile Durkheim and other early theorists, Syme became convinced that the social conditions of life—the availability of social and financial resources, exposures to stressors and adversity, and the character of close relationships—were the principal environmental factors that determined who got sick and who remained well. Over the years, Len became, along with John Cassel of the University of North Carolina, one of the founders of the new discipline of social epidemiology—the field that studies the social determinants of health and the origins of the well-recognized socioeconomic disparities in health and development. The list of Len's former students reads like a who's who of the field. So when Len Syme said, "It's socioeconomic status[, stupid]," everyone listened.

Seizing Syme's admonition, Nancy Adler went on to lead a thirteen-year MacArthur Foundation Research Network on Socioeconomic Status and Health, which explored the biological basis of SES-driven health disparities and established the important additional role of *subjective* social status (that is, the self-appraised social position you confer upon yourself) as a predictor of health outcomes, over and above its objective measurement. Sir Michael Marmot, a former Syme doctoral student at Berkeley and now a knighted and renowned professor of epidemiology and public health at University College London, has repeatedly demonstrated a strong, graded association between employment level in the British civil service and virtually all forms of human malady—physical and mental, acute and chronic. His research has systematically revealed the developmental and health sacrifices that stem from having low social status in human societies. Marmot's work shows, for example, that the effects of social position are not simply those of poverty affecting health and longevity—the self-evident example to which people usually jump—but rather that the level of illness varies along a continuous gradient of SES. Even the children of doctors and lawyers have more injuries and more chronic, limiting health conditions than do the children of the most highly paid CEOs and bankers. It's clearly not that the rates of chronic disease are flat until we reach the most impoverished, low-SES children, in whom the incidence sharply increases. Rather, kids at every level of SES have higher rates of chronic morbidities than those just above them in family wealth and education, and lower rates than those just below them. It is not simply poverty that drives health inequities; it's the entire spectrum of societal inequality.

In fact, Richard Wilkinson and Kate Pickett of the University of Nottingham have convincingly shown in international studies of countries rather than of individuals that different countries' levels of income inequality are powerfully linked to measures of health. Summarizing a veritable mountain of epidemiologic data from around the world, they demonstrate that what matters for health and mortality within a given country is less the overall wealth of the country, as conventional wisdom would usually assume, but rather how evenly or unevenly wealth is distributed within its citizen population. People living in socioeconomically less equitable societies have poorer overall health, lower educational attainments, more chronic, disabling diseases and injuries, and shorter lives than populations from more egalitarian nations. This is true for measures of health and well-being that range from obesity to mental health, from academic performance to teen pregnancies, from criminality and violence to drug abuse and life expectancy. Remarkably, even the most affluent subpopulations of citizens are healthier and more fulfilled when societies are less unbalanced in their allocations of resources and wealth.

Noting the current U.S. trend toward increasing income inequality—in fact, the most inequality since the years of the Great Depression—Wilkinson and Pickett trace the health consequences of such inequality to the erosion of trust, the breakdown of social connections, the increase in social anxiety, and the marginalization of disempowered outsiders that reliably accompany the partitioning of societies into small minorities of the ultra-wealthy, surrounded by all the rest with distinctly modest lives. The generational expression of dismay over this national, and to some extent international, shift toward inequities in wealth and power has been the Occupy Wall Street and Black Lives Matter movements and their demands for greater social justice, more egalitarian economies, and an end to institutional racism. This would also explain the unexpectedly successful campaign of Senator Bernie Sanders to become the 2016 Democratic presidential candidate. Although he lost to Hillary Clinton, no one expected that a balding, gruff-voiced social activist in his mid-seventies would inspire such fervent admiration and following. As his supporters filled concert venues, stadiums, and city squares, they reflected a sea change in what many Americans wanted for leaders. Given what we know about the effects of socioeconomic status, they weren't just rallying for a United States with greater income equality. They were gathered to express their desire for a society with more equitably distributed health, more justly allocated life chances.

Much debate has gone to deciding whether the differences in health that attend societal inequalities, minority subjugation, and the cavernous gap between levels of social position are due to the material surfeits and deficiencies of life or to the psychosocial differences in experiences of happiness, contentment, and sense of place in the world. The answer is likely that both forms of deprivation are involved in social inequalities. Children lower on the SES scale, like the twins I helped deliver as a young doctor in the skies over Colorado, are compromised by any number of material differences in their lives: poorer nutrition; larger and more sustained exposures to toxins like lead; crowded, noisy, and suboptimal housing; and fewer dollars to spend on less accessible health care. But the same kids also face a full complement of socioemotional assaults: witnessing neighborhood and family violence; sometimes poor or unenlightened parenting; less effective schools; and disproportionate exposures to stress and adversity. As Nancy Adler and her colleagues in the MacArthur Research Network have shown, even your subjective intuition about where you stand on the scale of SES—in your country or in your community—is often a more powerful predictor of health and morbidity than your objective social position as measured by education, job prestige, or income. One systematic review paper found, for example, that perceiving oneself to be low in social status compared to one's country or community was associated with significantly increased risks of coronary heart disease, hypertension, diabetes, and blood cholesterol imbalance, even after taking into account the individual's actual, objective SES. Although the health of an aging African American janitor from Oakland can be impaired by the paucity and instability of his income, his health may be protected, or even bolstered, by the social connections that proceed from his work as a deacon in his local Baptist church. The truth is that all of these factors—material, psychosocial, and subjective—are at work in the undermining and the sustaining of children's health in their positions on the rungs of the social ladder.

The "Micro-societies" of Childhood

Children's health, however, is not affected only by the social status of their parents and families. The hierarchical "micro-societies" (in the classroom, for example) that small groups of children and youth form when brought together into novel social settings—just as do monkeys, fish, and fruit flies—appear to have effects on health and development that parallel those we have come to expect from socioeconomic status in families and adults. And what a Vietnamese girl named Lan with a bellyache had taught me was that the hierarchical severities of even such peer relationships—even at a very early age—can have visible, palpable repercussions in children's health and well-being. Fast-forward to 2003, when Nancy Adler, postdocs Nicki Bush and Jelena Obradović, researcher Juliet Stamperdahl, and I designed a study that would carefully observe and measure the effects of dominance and subordination on the health of over three hundred children in almost thirty of the kindergarten classrooms of the Berkeley, California, public schools.

We decided to measure the kids' position in their classroom dominance hierarchies in two quite different ways. First, we sent graduate student research assistants into each of the classrooms with a chair to sit on and a digital tablet on which to record the child-to-child interactions they saw. Their instructions were to talk to no one and to avoid eye contact with any of the children. It doesn't take long before an otherwise interesting twenty-something grad student can turn into a "potted plant" when she or he is completely (and sometimes frustratingly) unresponsive to children's questions and attentions. Our research assistants were taught to scan the classroom and playground over the course of three or four hours for any forms of physical or verbal interactions taking place among two or three children. These observations targeted both the obvious exchanges from which the comparative rank of the children could be inferred, like one child physically attacking another or taking away a toy, as well as more subtle interactions, like one child being imitated by another. These exchanges thus included self-evident assertions of dominance, where one child triumphed and the other was vanquished, but also encompassed less obvious interactions such as one child leading, following, physically displacing, or instructing another. We watched and recorded as one boy taught another how to play a new ball game, as a single girl led a gaggle of four others in a boisterous circumferential run around the play yard, as one child emerged glum and defeated from a brief physical altercation with a playmate. We included, as well, bouts of "relational aggression" that sometimes occurred, like the exclusion of a third girl from a play activity so that two girls could maintain a smug illusion of exclusivity, or a physically big boy pointedly ignoring a smaller classmate as a means of asserting control.

We had really smart and really hardworking research assistants—UC Berkeley grad students and young postbaccalaureate geniuses on their way to brilliant careers. And in the course of hours of in-class observations, they collected data on nearly thirty-three thousand paired dominance interactions between five-year-olds, which were then fed into a computer algorithm that told us the social position of each child vis-à-vis the rest of his or her classroom. Now, mind you, no single one of these recorded interactions could tell us much about the longer-term relationship between two kids or about their locations on the classroom social hierarchy. But when the data were averaged over all thirty-three thousand interactions, a rather clear picture emerged of the dominance landscape in each of our classrooms of twenty or thirty children. Neither a child's gender nor his or her family SES determined classroom dominance status; boys and girls were equally likely to be high or low in the computed hierarchy, as were kids from more wealthy and more disadvantaged families. So with each child's classroom dominance position now in hand, we could use that measured rank to analyze whether dominance and subordination were related to health outcomes over the course of those children's first year in school. More about those analyses in a moment.

In a second approach to identifying classroom status positions, we brought groups of four or five kids of the same sex and close in social rank together in a room where they were introduced to a big, mysterious white box. Inside the box, the currently most enthralling video for five-year-olds (in 2003, it was *Finding Nemo*) was being played. There were two peepholes at eye height in the box's front through which the movie could be watched. The "problem" was that the video played only when two buttons on the sides of the box were pushed, and the buttons were too far away from the peepholes for a single child to be able to push the buttons and view the video on his or her own. So the kids had to figure out how to make it all work. They were universally eager to see the video, but they had to talk at least two of the other kids into helping them watch it by pushing the buttons on the sides.

We told them how it all worked and that they had fifteen minutes to do what they'd like. Every group was immediately gripped by a single-minded obsession to *see that video*, and all went to work finding a solution, though there were clear differences by gender in how this was accomplished. Not always, but in general, the boys approached the dilemma like a gang of housebound, suddenly liberated prepubescent monkeys. There were loud cries and instructions, everyone running excitedly around the box, pushing, shoving, jumping—you can visualize the scene. The girls, on the other hand, generally arranged four small chairs in a circle, sat down with their hands in their laps, and had a civilized, deliberative discussion about how they were going to do the task, in as orderly and polite a fashion as possible. (If you don't believe my accounting of five-year-old male and female approaches to the movie viewer, try it yourself with a convenient group of untrained kindergartners.) For both boys and girls, and over the fifteen-minute procedure, the research assistant stood by and recorded with a stopwatch how many seconds and minutes each child got to actually view the film, and the children were assigned rank positions 1–4 (or 5) based on their viewing time.

As we analyzed our data from this kindergarten hierarchy project, clear themes began to emerge in our results, reflecting the biological and psychological costs of finding oneself at or near the bottom of the kindergarten social ladder—as well as the biological and psychological virtues of being at the top. We first noted that children's previously measured levels of cortisol system response to our stress reactivity protocol clearly varied by children's positions in the movie viewer lineup. Kids who got the least viewing time had the highest cortisol reactivity scores, those with midlevel viewing times had medium scores, and the ones who got the most viewing time actually had *negative* reactivity scores (meaning that their cortisol levels went *down* over the course of the reactivity session). So the subordinate children in the movie viewer foursomes, who always got the dregs of leftover viewing time (a bit like leftover bananas), had shown us substantially greater cortisol reactivity to stress. By contrast, the highly dominant kids, who had gotten the most video viewing, had shown not just low stress reactivity but rather its opposite—lower cortisol levels at the end of the reactivity protocol than they had had at the beginning. Being low on the movie viewer hierarchy was linked to more dramatic reactivity to psychological stress.

Even more compelling with regard to children's health and well-being, we found in our classroom observation work that children whose daily behavior showed frequent acts of subordination (not just in the movie viewer situation) showed significantly more teacher-reported symptoms of depression and inattention, poorer peer relationships, and less positive academic competence during their kindergarten year than did their counterparts with higher dominance status. The subordinate children—those who sifted down through group processes to the bottom of their class status hierarchy—were substantially more troubled in their classroom behavior, in their new friendships at school, and in their progress toward the goals of reading, beginning to write, and understanding numbers. Here was previously undiscovered evidence that the stratification of even the tiny micro-societies of kindergarten children operated in the same manner as the social stratification of nations—that is, relegating a subset of their members to lesser social positions resulted in more frequent and more severe disorders of health and development. At the levels of both low SES in adult societies and subordinate positions in kindergarten classrooms, being low in rank and prestige had measurable aftereffects in the health and well-being of individuals.

As these results emerged, I could not help but remember my sister, Mary, who had struggled mightily in her early, primary school relationships with other, often more dominant and assertive kids. She managed to make good and sometimes lasting friendships, but her enormous sensitivity was frequently a complicating and obstructing element in her efforts to negotiate the intricate complexities of those early social connections. In my own detailed tracking of the developmental progress and health of 340 kindergarten children—forty years or more beyond my sister's first, tentative year of school—the story of one little boy we'll call Diego stood out as illustrative of what we discovered. Diego was a shy boy whose preschool experience had consisted of peaceable independent play, with occasional forays into the confusion of group dynamics, but usually within a group of only four to six other kids. Under the preschool staff's watchful supervision, Diego accommodated with reasonable effectiveness to the demanding novelty and constant press of social interchange with other kids. But kindergarten, in a larger public school, with whole battalions of larger, fearsome fifth and sixth graders and giant "upperclassmen," was a new and stiffer challenge. Suddenly immersed in a seemingly hostile sea of new peers, Diego withdrew into spaces where he could hide.

His new classroom, however, was not an easy place to disappear. More children, smaller spaces, and diminished oversight by a busy teacher created minimally regulated bedlam. The more domineering children regularly seized Diego's toys, paints, or seat, and he was persistently reminded of his lower standing by routine physical assaults, verbal coercion, and social exclusion. He emerged from the year even more reticent to engage (or certainly confront or compete with) other children, less confident in his own abilities and value, and worried about his prospects for a safe and happy future in school. There are real and consequential effects of where a child lands in the hierarchical self-organization that characterizes every school classroom, and to his parents' dismay, Diego had landed close to the bottom, in a social space that threatened to undo his comfort and success in school. Thankfully, however, there are important differences, in both the constitution of the child and the character of the classroom, that can blunt or even reverse the unhappy results of social subordination.

Haseya and Jacob

One way of thinking about the nature of a dandelion child is as one who is constitutionally *untethered* from the implications of his or her life station. Dandelion children reared in harsh, impoverished settings can be anomalously healthy and strong, as if impervious to the damaging effects of those environments. Not every poor child founders on the shoals of poverty or subordination. But dandelion children in wealthy, advantaged contexts can be anomalously ill or imperiled, because they are similarly unyoked from the socioeconomic benefits of their circumstances. Not every child born into eminence and ascendency has a life unfettered by illness and misfortune. Two children from my past perhaps helpfully illustrate how dandelions can sometimes elude either the jeopardy of disadvantage or the shelter of abundance. Let's call them Haseya and Jacob.

Haseya (whose name means "she rises" in the Navajo language) was a ten-year-old girl I had cared for in 1978 and whose quite traditional family was an unmitigated disaster. The dad drank instead of working, and the mom physically clobbered the dad whenever she found him drunk, often resulting in his loss of consciousness, lacerations to his scalp and face, and even greater dimming of an already fading cognition. One of

Haseya's older brothers had jumped from his girlfriend's moving car as she broke up with him, sustaining serious head and neck trauma and landing him permanently in a wheelchair. Try pushing a wheelchair through desert terrain for the rest of your brother's life. Even worse, the family's well water exceeded standards for arsenic levels, they used abundant pesticides to protect their meager single-family garden, sheep wandered in and out of the family hogan at will, and their hygienic practices were pretty much nonexistent.

But despite a life of rank poverty on a windswept, godforsaken piece of land, compounded with a family life of chaos and mayhem, Haseya, a lovely bright-eyed and pigtailed Navajo girl, was the picture of health. She had come into the world as a healthy baby, with a hearty cry and a resilient temperament. She had a few routine pediatric illnesses during her early years in school but had never once been seriously ill or hospitalized. And she was doing quite well in school, to boot. The impression was one of an affable, sturdy Native American girl who could have thrived almost anywhere—a bright yellow dandelion growing steadily upward from the desert floor. She was the very embodiment of what has conventionally been called "resilience."

Another memorable young patient from a well-to-do San Francisco family—Jacob—was afflicted with acute and chronic health conditions throughout his childhood and adolescence. Despite uncompromising health care, a home in an enviable neighborhood, a supportive family, and a top-notch, expensive urban preschool, Jacob developed a long series of ear infections that were resistant to most antibiotics and even to surgical implantation of ear tubes. These chronic infections eventually led to an extended period of hearing impairment and a delay in language acquisition, which in turn necessitated speech and language evaluations and a course of speech therapy. By the time he started school—a private primary school with a teacher-to-child ratio of 1 to 12—he had been twice hospitalized with pneumonia and was falling behind in his academic progress. In middle childhood, he occasionally showed defiant behavior, ignoring parental and authority figure demands, and in high school he moved for a time from experimentation with cannabis to the regular consumption of cocaine. Despite his having almost every advantage that early life can bestow on a child, his health had been of concern to both his parents and his pediatrician—concerns that thankfully dissipated as he became a young adult. By midway through his college years, Jacob had found his way into a steadier, more promising life: he began to do well in his classes, gave up the drugs, with the exception of an occasional social toke, and found a girlfriend with whom he fell fervidly in love.

Jacob revealed, in a sense, the other side of the dandelion "coin." His early health was unbound to the social world in which he resided as a child, in this case one of wealth and privilege. Despite these early advantages, he was afflicted with recurrent illnesses that exposed his dandelion insensibility to the socioeconomic assets that fully surrounded him. Like Haseya, Jacob had a constitutional indifference to his social, material position, but unlike Haseya, that position was one of privilege, not poverty. Their convergent stories reveal how the essential core of the dandelion's nature is not so much "resilience" as an impermeability to and disengagement from the circumstances of life. It is this resistance to environmental influence—this detachment of early conditions from later consequences—that so characterizes the dandelion child, the Swedish *maskrosbarn*.

Orchid children, whose smaller numbers and keen susceptibility distinguish them from their more plentiful dandelion peers, might have had severe, chronic, and disabling health problems in the setting of Haseya's impoverished Navajo family. Such an orchid might also have exhibited quite exceptional health and unfettered developmental outcomes in Jacob's prosperous Bay Area home. For orchid children, with their exquisite engagement with the social settings that envelop them, so much depends upon the inherent qualities of those settings—whether pernicious and threatening or nurturant and sustaining. Their outcomes are tightly bound to what lies outside them. Dandelions like Haseya and Jacob, on the other hand, have a hardiness that defies to some degree the capacity of social environments to malign or magnify their prospects and potentials. They are comfortably and safely insulated from the extremes of their childhood social conditions and generally see their way through to lives of substantial health and solid accomplishment. And just as such dandelion children remain relatively impervious to the larger hardships or blessings of their families' socioeconomic conditions, such children also go through childhood reasonably unscathed by the sometimes coercive experiences of subordination and dominance at the hands of their young peers.

Within the sometimes severely stratified and hierarchical structures of adult societies and kindergarten classrooms, we expect orchid children to fare far worse or far better than their more abundant dandelion peers—for two possible reasons. As suggested in chapter 3, orchid children, with their high sensitivities and often inhibited, less assertive behavioral styles, might be expected to sort disproportionately down into the marginality of lower social ranks. Like their rodent and monkey counterparts, human orchids may be overrepresented within the subordinate lowlands of their early childhood social groups. It may also be true, however, that orchid children are sometimes disproportionately represented in the *highest* ranks of peer hierarchies, given their careful attentiveness to social dynamics and to the possibilities for leadership that such attentiveness conveys.

Orchids subjected to the exigencies of steep competition for dominance positions may also be substantially more jeopardized and undone by the difficulties that accompany such competition. Thus orchids relegated to low-ranking roles, where marginalization and social isolation prevail, may more often experience subjugation, stress, and symptoms of despair, leading to psychological and physical duress. On the other hand, orchids achieving high social ranks may be more visibly rewarded with the strong mental health and developmental achievements that such ranks engender. And yet dandelions, like Haseya and Jacob, could be expected to reveal largely blunted or muted consequences of either low or high life stations.

The Unsung Valor of the Kindergarten Teacher

Teachers—perhaps especially kindergarten teachers, poised as they are on the very threshold of children's first experiences with "real school"—

are hugely influential people in the lives of the twenty or thirty five-year-olds with whom they are charged each year to care for and instruct. In many ways, early primary school teachers bear the seriously instrumental task of setting the educational and developmental trajectories of every child that they touch and teach. Although the average U.S. salary for a kindergarten teacher is around $52,000 per year, their potential for influence on individual human lives and on the character of the larger society is enormous. In fact, the Stanford economist Raj Chetty has calculated that our society's return on investment in a really top-notch kindergarten teacher is about $320,000 per classroom per year. In other words, every classroom staffed with a truly skilled, highly educated teacher generates $320,000 per year in national benefits and savings—$320,000 worth of higher test scores, greater educational achievements, more college graduations, and better economic productivity. Having a highly qualified kindergarten teacher results in students who, over the long term, lead more successful and productive lives, become single parents less frequently, are more likely to be saving for retirement, and, perhaps most strikingly, by age thirty are earning higher salaries. All this from one early year with an excellent teacher of young children! Preschool and kindergarten teachers earn the very smallest paychecks of those who staff our national system of education, and yet they are the educators most likely to profoundly shape young minds and lives, during the most neurobiologically formative period of early learning.

Kindergarten teachers are also acutely aware of and contribute most to the interpersonal politics and organizational structures played out in their classroom settings. Early in the course of our Berkeley kindergarten project, research assistants began returning from their classroom observations of five-year-old children with clear impressions of their social hierarchies—who was on top, who on the bottom. But they also were noticing something else. They came back to their university home base noting that the culture or spirit of the classroom—the way each class seemed to feel—was strikingly distinctive. Some of our assistants told stories of cold, steely classrooms where authoritarian teachers maintained unbending daily schedules, largely avoiding frivolity and laughter and reinforcing the special status of certain high-ranking children by showcasing their gifts and strengths, while ignoring the less visible qualities of others. In other classrooms, however, assistants reported a lighter, more informal tone, where teachers delighted in their students' differences and seemed to pointedly acknowledge the admirable abilities of even the most peripheral, marginal, and low-ranking kids. Where a child stood in the social hierarchy seemed to matter little in some of the observed school settings. In these classes, the social groups were more pliable and less predictable—mostly girls playing with girls and boys with boys, but without the same clubby, invariant social groups forming day after day.

As we discussed together what lay behind these kindergarten cultural differences, we began to understand, as education scholars have carefully shown, that while some teachers were exploiting the children's social hierarchies as a means of controlling child and group behavior, others were explicitly attempting to minimize the visibility and potency of the hierarchy by employing more child-centered, egalitarian teaching approaches. Some teachers, for example, might quell a disagreement by taking a dominant child's side or might avoid a conflict or disappointment by allowing certain kids to be marginalized or excluded. Others, by comparison, seemed to consciously employ techniques and strategies for undermining or challenging their students' hierarchical order. This could occur if the teacher publicly noted a subordinate child's special artistic or intellectual or athletic gift, or banned exclusionary social behavior, establishing a classroom policy in which "you can't say, 'you can't play.'" There were striking classroom differences in how attentive and fair the teachers' practices and policies were, and the more sensitive, orchid children appeared to thrive far more readily in those child-centered, equitable classrooms. There were still student hierarchies in all the classrooms, to be sure, but in some they were far less visible and virulent.

The result of these classroom differences was quite readily seen in the research results that our project began to uncover. We found, for example, that a child's classroom social rank and level of depression-like symptoms and behaviors (e.g., feeling sad, lonely, or unwanted, or being afraid to try new things for fear of making mistakes) were significantly linked. Not altogether surprisingly, kids occupying the bottom rungs of these little classroom communities were substantially more likely to show symptoms of depression than were kids at the top. By contrast, children who enjoyed the loftiest, most dominant ranks in their classroom hierarchies were the most mentally healthy. Even after statistical adjustment for sex and family socioeconomic status, higher-ranking children showed fewer depressive behaviors, better abilities to attend to lessons, more positive peer relationships, and greater overall academic competence.

But it wasn't in every classroom that life at the bottom came with more loneliness, more fearfulness, and more social isolation. In fact, the experiences of subordinate children were highly dependent upon their teachers' use of child-centered, egalitarian teaching practices. In classes where teachers ignored, or even fostered, dominance relationships, the linkage between subordinate rank and depressive behavior was very strong and quite predictive. On the other hand, in classrooms where teachers were committed to more child-oriented, hierarchy-undermining teaching methods, depressive behaviors and symptoms appeared almost unrelated to a child's social rank. The more hierarchical the teacher's approaches were, the steeper was the slope of the statistical line relating rank to depression, but the more actively egalitarian those approaches, the flatter that line became. In other words, in classes where teachers practiced evenhanded, child-centered teaching approaches, where you landed in your new kindergarten classroom's social hierarchy mattered very little with respect to mental health symptoms. We were beginning to see quite vividly how powerfully influential teachers' practices, philosophies, and approaches were. In that first, impressionable year of primary school education, teachers' styles and methods were crucially instrumental in shaping a child's early development, mental health, and academic success.

Gone to Seed: Orchids, Dandelions, and the Exigencies of Life in Stratified Societies

Clearly, the perils and provocations of dominance hierarchies are not limited to childhood or to the often intense relational ferment of kindergarten classrooms. Children grow up, and in adult places of work and in the architectures of broader societies, the insidious but unavoidable processes of dominance and subordination are also pervasively at work. Both the evolution of our species and the demands of organizational structure and stability have mandated, at least in modern cultures and nations, an almost inevitable emergence of a stratification in which a society's rewards are unevenly distributed. And there are vaunted benefits of such "free market" competition that are roundly hailed within the economies of Western societies.

But while there appears an almost lawful proclivity to the layering of human groups along gradients of power, wealth, and esteem, we have no reason to believe that the linkage of health and human development to one's social position is a necessary or universal reality. Indeed, the striking differences between nations in the slope or strength of the graded connection between social status and health suggest that they are largely able to be separated under the proper conditions of egalitarian tradition and just social policy. Though dominance and subordination may be the inevitable by-products of a long evolutionary history, the coupling of social position with health and development should not be regarded as inevitable or inviolable. Though renouncing illusory visions of a "flat" society, where individual efforts go unrewarded and "tall poppies" are cut down to ensure uniformity, we should not ignore the disproportionate ill health and early mortality that is unfairly borne by the poor and disadvantaged.

Nor should the respective special sensitivities and hardinesses of orchid and dandelion children be overlooked in our efforts to create more equitable nations and fairer childhoods. Just as orchid children suffer greater ill health and poorer developmental achievements in conditions of adversity, experiences of poverty and subordination also disproportionately affect such children, with their greater sensitivities to dominance relations. Eight-year-old Lan is just one example of a child whose special susceptibility to the painful realities of social position and bullying resulted in bodily symptoms requiring medical attention. As we now know, it is also likely that orchid children like Lan could disproportionately benefit from egalitarian and evenhanded social circumstances. And just as dandelion children maintain a relative impermeability to the effects of adversity, such children are also proportionately less affected by uneven societies and more despotic social relationships. In fact, one of the possible reasons that unjust societies have so often survived—be they in classrooms or nations—is the preponderance of dandelion-like citizens who find ways of thriving and succeeding even in the direst and most rapacious of social conditions.

We all travel, one way or another, along the same human path, continually transacting with others the struggles for power, the contests of will, the tournaments of control that so characterize and permeate hominid life. One need only scratch the surfaces of courtship and marriage, offices and corporations, legislatures and governments to reveal the abiding, smoldering cauldron of dominance and subordination. To be sure, the fruits of such relations are not universally destructive. In fact, we look to dominance and subordination for leadership to emerge, for creativity to triumph, for stability to reign. But the costs of bullying and coercive social control—that is, dominance and subordination run amok—are abundantly evident, both in contemporary societies and in the cultures of primary school classrooms. Such costs are evident as well in the words posted on the internet by a young German student the evening before he went on a shooting rampage in 2009, killing fifteen people. He wrote, "I am sick of this messy life. Always the same. Everyone makes fun of me. No one recognizes my potential. I am serious." It is sadly tempting to speculate on what might have allowed this boy's potential to blossom forth instead in creative, positive acts, how his life might have changed had his school been more able to recognize and reverse the perceived injustices that undid him. What might be done—in kindergartens, families, and societies—that could heal these wounds of social subordination, plant the seeds of more equitable human relationships, and attend to the special susceptibilities of their most sentient and vulnerable members?

8

Sowing and Tilling the Gardens of Childhood

I've been bowed down to but so misread,
Treated like a rose, as an orchid.

—Alanis Morissette, "Orchid"

Having now considered the features, origins, developmental assets, and liabilities of orchid and dandelion children, we now come to the parenting puzzle akin to what rock climbers call the "crux" of a climb—that is, the route's most difficult and demanding move, requiring courage, agility, and strength. In ascending a several-thousand-foot wall of Yosemite granite, that crux may be a blind reach onto the face of a three-foot overhang; in the parenting of children, it is having the knowledge, intuition, and capacity for adaptively supporting the growth and development of a houseful of very different and needful young creatures. My Texas friend and wedding best man, Bruce, once shared with me the insight, which has served me well from a scientific point of view, that the four principal developmental stages of childhood are: rug rat, ankle biter, house ape, and honyock (a colloquial label meaning "rustic oaf"). Some authorities would add curtain climber in the third position between ankle biter and house ape. The technical, relational, and crux-like challenge to parents is that not only are their children's parenting needs dramatically different in each unique developmental phase, but their needs are also remarkably dissimilar from one child to the next. It is like conducting an orchestra one musician at a time, but with all of them playing.

Though arduously trained as pediatrician and a specialist in children's development, I am compelled in addressing the challenges of parenting orchid and dandelion children to acknowledge at the outset that it has been my amazing and lovely wife, Jill, from whom I have learned most about the ins and outs, the secrets and lessons, the traps and tangles of sowing and tilling a garden of small human creatures. As I write this book, it has been nearly thirty-nine years since she and I embarked on that most taxing and rewarding journey of two lives together, a journey that began with the screaming predawn entrance of our son, Andrew, into what Shakespeare called "this breathing world." That hot, bright August morning in the Sonoran Desert launched all of us—Andrew, me, and Jill—into an adventure for which no one of us was fully prepared. Two years later, on a cold, arid night just before a mesquite-smoke-scented Tucson Christmas, our daughter, Amy, took a first tremulous breath and followed her waiting brother into the feast that is life on this dear earth. Nothing has ever been the same since.

Jill's and my lives were utterly transfigured by those two sudden, chaotic, and exhilarating arrivals. Raising and parenting two irreplaceable children into adulthood—one dandelion and one orchid—has been at once our lives' most formidable and most joyous task. There have been moments of hilarity, pride, and unmitigated delight, as Andrew and Amy discovered what it is to be alive and conscious in the world, full of intention, sorrow, will, and desire. There is no experience in life that transcends a parent's jubilation at seeing his infant's smile in response to his own, his toddler's first, risky steps toward walking, his son's or daughter's first, thrilling glimpse of place and vocation in the world.

The Agile Parent

I have already noted how parenting practices within a family can have profound but differing effects on the development of individual children. While orchid children are differentially affected by even subtle differences in their parents' approaches to childrearing, dandelion children can march through childhood relatively unperturbed by their parents' skills and foibles. Parents, grandparents, and other significant caregivers can, like teachers, optimize the health and development of children, especially when those caregivers are armed with a clear and present understanding of how orchids and dandelions differ in their needs, responses, and susceptibilities to parenting strategies. The optimal parenting approaches to children of different sensitivities and temperaments are a focus of ongoing research by many developmental scientists in multiple areas of the world.

First, parents of all nations, of both sexes, biological and adoptive, of every race and ethnicity, whether wealthy or in poverty, are together compelled to stay "light on their feet" in the face of the long, colossal task that lies before them on the first day of a fresh new life. I remember diapering Andrew for the very first time, when he was two or three days of age, newly home from the hospital at which I practiced. I was a fully certified pediatrician with twelve years of higher education and professional training and three years of practice behind me, much of it focused specifically on the care and husbandry of infants and children. This was also the twentieth-century, pre-Pampers and pre-Huggies era, when cloth diapers were the diapers du jour. They were made of real cotton cloth, which you sealed with two large blue-headed safety pins and, once used, threw in a big, disgusting bucket at the side of the changing table.

With all the care of a first-time father and all the confidence of a highly trained baby doctor, I placed little Andrew on the neatly folded diaper, brought the back part up and over the front part edge, and thrust the sizable pin through the diaper . . . and through my little newly born son's skin and out the other side, creating, in effect, entry and exit wounds. He turned a deep crimson color from head to toe and howled, as he had every right to do, like a screaming stuck piglet on its way to slaughter. I quickly withdrew the instrument of torture and inspected, horrified, the first, cruel injury Andrew had ever sustained . . . at the hands of his embarrassed, devastated, and deeply contrite pediatrician-father. I think both of us have had a touch of post-traumatic stress disorder ever since, though he denies all flashback memories of the event. Parenting is no day at the beach, even for those of us specifically trained in the care of babies.

So I should acknowledge at the outset that no instinct or experience, no knowledge or class, no book or podcast ever fully prepares us for the enormous challenges of bringing a newborn human being into earthly life and rearing that child into a healthy, long-distant maturity. Every child born into this living world is a wonder of absolute singularity, an exquisitely unique organism with a complexity that we can only glimpse and estimate. We must therefore greet every new birth with the humility and awe that is borne of our overpowering limits and terrible constraints. I have never examined a newborn infant without muted reverence for its glistening newness and unfettered promise.

As I have argued from the outset of this book, orchid children—who comprise, as best we can tell, about one child in five—bear uncanny and double-edged sensitivities to both the social and physical worlds that they encounter in their young lives. They possess a kind of porous receptivity to external encounters, a receptivity that renders them acutely, sometimes painfully aware of physical sensations, such as touch, sound, and taste, and relational experiences, of nurturing, warmth, malevolence, and indifference. It is a thorough openness to the world that fosters a fragile duality of outcomes: in strong, supportive social settings, they thrive like no other child, but in critical, undermining settings, they can devolve into lives of disorder and despair.

My sister, Mary, was of course one such child. Though she held within her the possibility of brilliance and greatness, she found herself embedded within a family where critique and disapproval, though unintended and perhaps largely unconscious, were the order of the day and where a female orchid was bound, perhaps inexorably, to a life of disappointment, failure, and ill health. A backward look at her life sees her forever poised on a sharpened borderland between genius and disarray. There were periods of great lucidity and creativity, during which she traveled, worked, and taught, but these were interspersed, with declining frequency, between years of craziness and mayhem, when she was repeatedly hospitalized and powerfully overruled by the demons that had made a home in her head.

Most orchid children by no means teeter between the extremities of health and dysfunction that my sister visited over her fifty-three years of life. But what many such children have in common with her is this exceptional variation in possibility, created by their sensate receptivity to the character of the surrounding social world. What might have saved my sister? What might have allowed her life path to follow its longing for success and artistry, which it might well have achieved? What are the elements of parenting or teaching (or brothering) that might have turned an unhappy life tide toward one of promise and brilliance?

As is true for all children, there are no easy, formulaic approaches to helpfully parenting or teaching an orchid child. What there is, however, is the garnered wisdom of parents and pediatricians, like me, who have found ways, through intuition and insight, to care for and protect young orchids. There are also the accumulated wisdoms of families and siblings, also like me, who have struggled to understand and interpret the experiences of a fragile sister, brother, niece, or nephew. And there is the experience of teachers who have found, over years of pedagogical experience, ways of recognizing orchid children, supporting their learning, and fostering adaptation. What follows, then, is my own personal collection of parental and teaching approaches, which are offered to readers as strategies to try, possibilities to explore, methods to assess. The list is neither exhaustive nor foolproof, and what may work well with one orchid child may fail with another. But it is a compendium of practices borne of many years of watching, listening, and aiding the "orchids I have known": my sister, my own child, and those many orchid children who have honored me with their trust as a doctor.

1. The Menace of Novelty and Comfort of the Ordinary

First, among the sensibilities that roil the lives of orchid kids is their sensitivity to whatever is new and unexpected. Jerome Kagan referred to this phenomenon as "neophobia"—a deep-seated dread of the unanticipated or previously unencountered. My own daughter, Amy, showed us how aversive novelty could be for a little girl with orchid leanings and how comforting stability and reliable routine could be. New, previously unknown babysitters were particularly loathsome in Amy's early world. They were full of strange smells, unreadable faces, uninterpretable speech, and peculiar, unknowable bedtime rituals and, as such, were to be avoided whenever possible. Every school year also began with Amy's adjustment to a new teacher, who inevitably changed the learning approaches and classroom conventions that the prior year's teacher had progressively instilled. New foods, especially those somehow exotic in taste, color, or texture, were especially suspect to Amy and were avoided at all costs. Unfamiliar kids and novel social settings were causes for retreat or hiding. By age three and the onset of her preschool experience, my daughter had become a committed neophobe.

Oddly, the source of such thorough dedication to neophobia was never timidity or lack of courage. Amy was and is as courageous and full of adventure as her more dandelion brother, Andrew. In fact, both displayed a level of bravery at times that parents come to dread—pole vaulting over fifteen-foot bars, jumping out of airplanes, precariously scaling climbing walls and rock cliffs, skiing double-black-diamond runs, and diving into thunderous surf. It wasn't courage that Amy lacked; it was a basic, trusting comfort with previously unconfronted social settings and experiences.

The answer to this fear of the new was, for Amy—as it is for kids with more frankly orchid constitutions—a counterbalancing reliance on *sameness and routine.* We made conscious commitments to family routines, like eating dinner together every night, attending church together weekly, giving our kids regular daily and weekly chores they were expected to complete on schedule, having a regular nap or quiet time, going to the same father-daughter group event together each month, having standard bedtimes and regular sequences of bedtime rituals (e.g., putting on pajamas, brushing teeth, and getting into bed, followed by reading, a tuck-in, and lights out). Nothing very fancy, complicated, or out of the ordinary. In fact, it was all rather mundane and pleasingly unexceptional. But it is remarkable how often in contemporary family life these routine, predictable elements are overlooked and omitted from a family's collective life. Routines provide a child with a sense of control and a backdrop of certainty and sameness in a world sometimes maddeningly disordered, unpredictable, and inchoate.

I know one family that offers back to their child a modicum of control over daily life by arraying on a felt board images of all the tasks needing to be done at a given moment or on a given day—for example, the teeth brushing, breakfast eating, dressing, and lunch making that comprise the drill of departure for school. But their son is allowed to physically sequence the several tasks for that morning, by ordering their representative images on the board in the kitchen. It all must be done, every schoolday morning, but it is accomplished in the child's own manner and arrangement. It is a small relinquishment of control to the child, in exchange for a timely completion of a complex daily routine.

Fathering a child in need of ritual was not my first encounter with the psychological benefits of family routines. Back in the 1970s, when I was working with John Cassel in North Carolina, we thought of stress and adversity as aspects of what were then called "life changes"—that is, the life events or shifts, both negative and positive, that challenge an individual's adaptive capability. There was, in fact, a whole body of research by adult psychiatrists Thomas Holmes and Richard Rahe and psychiatric epidemiologist Bruce Dohrenwend enumerating "life change units" as an index of stressful experience, and we had used a pediatric modification of their scale in weighing adversity exposures among the children we studied. As noted earlier in chapter 2, a collaboration with a fellow researcher led to a proposal that if stress could be operationalized as life change, then perhaps the opposite of change—life stability and family routines—could serve as protective, supportive factors for children in the midst of great adversity. Sure enough, routines were shown, in that study of rural Chapel Hill children and their families, to blunt or soften the effects of stressful life changes on predispositions to respiratory illnesses. Barbara Fiese, a developmental psychologist at the University of Illinois at Urbana-Champaign, has gone on to document, in an elegant, career-long series of studies, the beneficial and protective functions of family routines.

2. The Love of a Child

A second parenting practice that offers reassurance and support to children with orchid-like qualities is simply the pervasive presence of a parent's *attentiveness and love.* Although all children crave and need their parents' attention and care, orchid kids are especially in need of parental affection and time and particularly benefit from their effects. Such attentiveness may come principally from one parent or from both, or may be the special gift that a grandparent, godparent, or nanny bestows. There is abundant evidence in the writings of child psychiatrists like Harvard professor Robert Coles that even a single supportive adult can have a transformative influence in the life a child. It is this *steadfast love* from a caring adult that can transfigure the life and development of children, especially orchid children.

One of the abiding cultural legends of our time is that a parent's lack of time with children, due to job pressures, social obligations, and the general busyness of life, can be counterbalanced by spending what has come to be known as "quality time," that is, special, arranged time when a parent and child can engage in meaningful conversation and activity together. But as I wrote in a 1990 opinion in the *American Journal of Diseases of Children:*

> I would like to debunk what has become enshrined as an almost holy artifact in the mythology of contemporary life. Quality time is simply a cultural myth. There is no such thing and never has been. So we should not count on it happening and should not try to create it.

The reality is that the very best of moments with our children come at unplanned, unexpected times—during the car ride to a Saturday morning soccer game, in the middle of an otherwise uneventful bathing of a toddler, or while scrambling to get breakfast and the kids off to school. Try as we might to orchestrate such times, the closest, most cherished moments with our children come during intervals when they are least expected. Such moments cannot be arranged or planned. They simply surface out of the normal, monotonous flow of daily life, when sufficient *ordinary time* has been passed between parent and child. It is during such ordinary time that these moments of extraordinary communication and intimacy can occur.

I remember one such time with my son, Andrew. On a brief, overnight backpacking trip one weekend, to a primitive campsite along the rugged, windswept coast of Northern California—an activity in which we fairly regularly engaged as a family—Andrew, who was then about eight years old, and I were hiking along the trail. The western sky over the Pacific Ocean had begun to color as sunset approached. The earlier, reliably frigid fog of the coastal summer morning had cleared as the expected afternoon winds picked up, and our campsite could be seen appearing just over a rise, at the distant end of the path we were walking. The gathering beauty of the sun's descent prompted Andrew to pause and take me deeper into his inner world.

"You know, Dad," he said, "I really like to draw and paint. I really like doing art."

It was a sensible but unforeseen disclosure—a literally momentary interlude within a four- or five-hour expanse of time—possibly anticipating, or trying on, the direction of a future life and career. It would likely not have happened without the long prior car ride, followed by tedious slogging through several miles on a foggy footpath. I said I knew he had some real talent for art and that lifelong vocations in art were entirely possible.

Then, noting that the entire dome of the Pacific sky was turning a bright, translucent orange, Andrew again surprised me. "Yeah," he said, "orange is the most misunderstood color."

What a revelation! Here was a kid—my son!—who thought about colors like most of us think about people. It had honestly never occurred to me that orange could be misunderstood, or even understood, for that matter. He was and is a brilliant and imaginative artist, and he went on to become a graduate of the Yale School of Drama, an award-winning theater set designer, and now a professor of theater at a major university.

A bumper sticker from years back proclaimed, THE BEST THING YOU CAN SPEND ON YOUR KID IS TIME! However sloganish such an assertion is, there is truth in its message. Happily, a general consensus among those who study the various relational dimensions of family life is that contemporary parents are probably spending somewhat more time accessible to their children than parents did three or four decades ago. It may also be the case, however, that parents' hours of engaged, participatory interaction with children has diminished. Interestingly and possibly counterintuitively, there is also evidence that the salutary effects of parental time—on child outcomes such as behavioral and emotional problems—increase during adolescence, where parental time and monitoring appear to diminish risk-taking behavior that can lead to delinquency, substance abuse, and other adolescent morbidities. These are examples of T. Berry Brazelton's developmental "touchpoints" that occur between parent and child, between physician and parent— the moments of special susceptibility and memorable time, which are marked by heightened receptivity to the communication and influence between children and the adults who care for them. Early in his work, Brazelton noted predictable periods during development when a child will do something new, like starting to walk, shortly after that child stops doing something else he or she has been doing for months, such as sleeping through the night. Another example might be the eight-month-old baby who begins night-waking again, just as she becomes more emotionally aware of the difference between Mom and a stranger. These are the touchpoints that characterize moments of qualitative leaps forward in a child's development—moments when parents, working with skilled clinicians and counselors, can learn much about their child's needs, strengths and weaknesses, capacities for mastery, and expressions of feeling. But such learning, and the stabilization of the family system that it fosters, cannot occur without parents' substantial investment of time and attentiveness.

In response to the sociocultural "mommy wars," through which young moms have been subjected to the twin, irresolvable imperatives of active careers and intensive mothering, some social scientists have presented evidence that, especially in early life, a mother's presence has little bearing on healthy developmental outcomes. Single studies do not a truth make, however. We certainly have evidence, through work such as that by Charles Nelson and colleagues in Romanian orphanages (chapter 6), for the devastating effects of the institutional, nonparental rearing of small children, on everything from physical growth and brain function to socioemotional well-being. There is simply no question that the presence of at least one loving, responsive parent in a child's early life is essential to normative, positive youth development. Beyond that, we enter the realm of more subtle differences, more difficult to detect in observational or experimental studies. Nonetheless, many studies find that more optimal outcomes are found among children living in a family with two married parents, a conclusion with which I concur. We also know that child development and health are heavily and negatively affected by children being raised in "risky families," that is, those characterized by aggressive conflict and cold, unsupportive relationships. There is also substantial evidence that the presence of fathers in the home has measurable benefits for developmental and health outcomes in children.

A brief word, however, about single or LGBT parents. Some of the most heroic, wonderful, and effective parents I have known are raising their children alone, without the benefit of another adult in the home. That missing second parent can, in the best circumstances, fulfill a panoply of needs for both kids and partners: backup parenting when energy fails or coping flags; a second opinion on gnarly parenting dilemmas; the ability to "divide and conquer"; an alternate adult model of being and becoming in the world; and a source of support and resolve when parenting gets tough. Though these advantages of coparenting are powerful and real, there are situations where two parents remaining together undermines rather than enhances child well-being. And there are millions of remarkable single parents who, through grit, grace, and perseverance, raise strong, capable children of which any nation or community should be proud. Similarly, though I am no expert in parenting by couples from the LGBT community, my observation as a pediatrician has been that committed, caring coparenting by two individuals of the same sex produces healthy, developmentally typical children, whether biologically related to their parents or not. Kids raised in such homes are generally healthy, happy, and equal in physical and mental well-being to their peers from majority family configurations. Again, however, the same advantages and strengths of dual parenting apply: LGBT couples will parent together more adaptively, easily, and better than will most single LGBT parents alone.

Most important to our concerns here, however, is the reality that all of these effects of parenting—both subtle and dramatic, positive and negative—are amplified several times over for orchid children living in the same family configurations and types. Orchid kids, by virtue of their great openness and susceptibility to the social world, derive even more of the benefits of having two parents who attend to their needs, encourage their interests, and unconditionally love who they become. The very same orchid kids, when sufficiently unlucky to be born into a cold, conflictive family environment, bear even more of the risks inherent for all children in those settings. Some of my orchid patients have been fortunate enough to have had a mom like Jill. For it was most often she—though sometimes vigorously at odds with our kids during their teenage years—who had the tenacity of kindness, the *caritas,* or charity, to offer up a kind of unfettered, steadfast love: the kind of love that orchid children so need to grow and thrive. In recent years, I have also watched with awe as some of my earliest orchid patients have been fortunate enough, later in their young adulthoods, to find and marry partners equally filled with the great gifts of caritas—those of empathy and love. Orchid children are our tender "canaries in the mineshaft" whose sensitivities—to both caring and destructive environments—show a context's earliest and most visible effects. They are the harbingers of both grace and ill will.

3. A Responsiveness to Differences

A parent's third means of supporting and caring for an orchid child is to *recognize and honor the goodness of human differences.* Remembering that no two children are raised in the same family, parents are called upon to discern, name, and celebrate their children's distinguishing features, one from the other. There is a lovely little book by Canadian children's author Jean Little called *Jess Was the Brave One*. It is the story of two sisters: the older, more fearful but imaginative Claire, and the younger, more fearless Jess. Jess can watch scary movies without averting her eyes, gets shots at the doctor's office with courageous aplomb, and can climb to the highest branches of the trees around their home. Claire, by contrast, reacts to hypodermic needles as if they were daggers and finds tree-tops intimidating, but also has a vivid imagination and loves to listen to and reenact her grandfather's stories. Most of the admiration between the two sisters flows from Claire to Jess, the "brave one." But one day, when the neighborhood bullies snatch Jess's "Pink Ted," her beloved rose-colored teddy bear, it is Claire, in a burst of imaginative brilliance, who crafts an intimidating story about the girls' brawny, heroic cousins who will surely soon arrive to forcibly reclaim the stuffed bear. The multilayered moral of the story is of course the adaptive utility of variation in sibling characteristics; the context-dependent nature of heroism and valor; and the recognition that every child is exceptional. Though the fearful orchid Claire is bereft of bravery in most day-to-day scenes of play and family, she is the one in a moment of crisis who summons a great reservoir of stalwart, inspired bravery and saves the day.

As with Claire, it is easy for an orchid child to feel diminished, a lesser being, against the backdrop of a family's field of dandelions. But like the best of the teachers in the Berkeley kindergarten project, parents are called upon to recognize, acknowledge, and praise the special skills and strengths of their orchid kids. Though orchids may sometimes appear weak or inconsequential within the buzzing, feverish activity of family life, they always have an array of gifts and potencies of great significance and advantage. Parents can uncover and reveal those gifts in their interactions with their children, in the ways they refer to and describe their children, and in the trust they place in each of their children's individual competencies. It is this parental "sensitivity to sensitivities" that allows the effective, responsive mom or dad to notice and answer the broad differences in needs that their children present. Only by seeing such differences and affirming their legitimacy can both orchids and dandelions flower and flourish.

4. A Grounding in Forbearance and Freedom

Fourth, the orchid child will flourish whose parents offer *acceptance and affirmation* of the child's true, tenderhearted, and creative self. Orchid children are sharply discerning of their parents' judgments and opinions and respond to these in ways that are both receptive and vivid. They are also often creative, imaginative children and have needs for findings ways to express and use their creativity. If such a child discerns that parental expectations demand unerring alignment with the parent's own desires and ambitions, that child's hopes, dreams, and creativity may become stunted and bound. Alice Miller's work in *The Drama of the Gifted Child* describes the psychotherapeutic process for a type of highly reflective and sensitive adult patient whose parents' expectations created, in the patient's childhood, the "tragic and painful state of being separated from his true self." Orchid children—"gifted" in their attunement to others— can easily become trapped in their family's expectancies, imprisoned by their parents' intolerance or heedlessness, and fail to experience and express their own, often powerful feelings and hopes. It is the freedom to become thoroughly and openly oneself for which the orchid tacitly longs.

An orchid child's parents must therefore respond with a special forbearance of their child's own sensitivity, and often in ways that can exceed the needs of their other children. This might happen by ensuring that at the family dinner table every child gets a chance to talk and express what is on his or her mind. It might take the form of seeking opportunities for the child's creative expression, in music or painting, dance or theater. It could involve consciously creating a family culture in which freedom of expression for emotion is carefully sheltered and dissonant opinions or feelings are valued. I know one family in which this culture of expression takes the form of a "talking stick"—a kind of tangible license to speak—that is passed around the table at dinnertime, thereby guaranteeing each of its members a chance to voice his or her own thoughts, news, or opinions, freely and uninterrupted. The family protects and reserves a kind of temporal space in which its orchid members are empowered to speak and express themselves. So the nurturing of an orchid child should involve not only the parents' actions and sensitivities but extend as well to siblings and the family at large. Orchids grow on rocks and trees, not in soil, and orchid children similarly require different, more solid structures and "groundings" in which to prosper and bloom.

5. The Finely Drawn Line Between Protecting and Provoking

The families of orchid children must also seek and achieve a well-tempered *balance between measured protection and emboldened exposure.* On the one hand, because orchid kids are prone to an easily triggered physiological reactivity, a certain level of parental insulation from the world's abundant challenges is often a needed and helpful protection. Knowing that my child has strong biological responses to overwhelming social settings might prompt me, for example, to identify paths of escape, held in abeyance until the need arises. Such paths might take the form of visually monitoring his arousal and withdrawal, periodically checking in to assess his level of discomfort, offering a means of early departure if fear begins to predominate over fun, or sometimes providing an option to decline an invitation to an especially challenging event.

On the other hand, the parenting of an orchid child must never be solely about protection and sheltering; parents must also know when to push, when to nudge, when to encourage a child's venturing into unknown and even uncomfortable psychological or physical territory. For it is the successes in such terra incognita that will foster the child's growth, revealing her capacity for mastering situations that seem at first impossible to abide.

All parents of orchid children walk this fine, constantly shifting line between sheltering and provoking. It is a border that is relevant to the rearing of all children, but especially so in the case of orchid children, who show so much greater variation in response to parenting practices. Too much sheltering has the liability of becoming coddling, but excessive pressure toward exposure can overwhelm. As Robert Frost wrote in his poem "The Fear," "Every child should have the memory / Of at least one long-after-bedtime walk," by which he meant that part of childhood is the mastery of fear and the confrontation of a darkened unknown. All children need to know that they can bear risk and face unknown and fearful perils.

This is at least part of the reason for the current backlash against the overprotection of children, against "helicopter parents" who hover constantly and protectively above their children's activities, guarding against the menace of "stranger danger" that so constrains the space, time, and variety of contemporary children's play. Parents of orchid children are thus called to find an often delicate middle ground between pushing their naturally reticent child into activities or events that might be overpowering and being so protective that the growth-producing aspects of novel, risky, or even difficult experiences are seldom encountered. It is a hard line to discern and walk, but with experimentation and careful observation, most parents can achieve a finely tuned approach that is most helpful for their particular orchid.

6. The Potency of Play

Finally, the parents of orchid children, as well as parents of all children, must be schooled in the *great virtues of play, fantasy, and imaginative fun*. Among the many reasons that we in the adult world can be so charmed and captivated by the presence of children is their more natural, more unencumbered access to the fantastical, playful corners of life. Sometimes it seems that we who write and teach and sell and make have relinquished too early, too easily the frivolity and innocent pleasures that all of us once knew. We love and yearn for children because they show us who we once were and where we've been. They remind us of another way of being, a kind of "home" to which we once belonged.

And as we've seen repeatedly, what is true and needed in the parenting of all children is especially and intensely required for the orchids we raise, teach, care for, coach, or encourage. All kids—dandelions and orchids alike—are surely as fed and nurtured by imaginative play as they are by food and love, because play, like dreaming, is a way of bringing the realities of life down to size, a means of emptying the poison from fraught conflicts and indignities. A band of feral boys enacts the siege of an enemy encampment in part to drain the death from war. A group of children engage in a circle dance, singing, "Ashes, ashes, they all fall down," unaware of the dark historical meanings their lyrics invoke—of the nineteenth-century bubonic plague and epidemic mortality. A child ritualistically and fastidiously cares for her or his favorite doll as a kind of rehearsal—both joyful and earnest—for the childrearing and parenting that will one day come. Play is an enchanting, if momentary, holiday from the serious and real business of life, of which children, especially orchid children, are keenly aware.

It is thus no accident that therapeutic work with troubled children often takes the form of play. Those who have survived a natural disaster or a near-fatal car accident find their way back to an untroubled life through the medium of make-believe—reenacting and reliving moments of peril and fright. Young children whose parents have separated or divorced find in play a means of resolving their grief, comprehending the always-present but never-welcome truth of a parent's departure, and reconciling themselves to a life with a mom *or* a dad, one at a time. Both dandelions and orchids use invention and pretense as means of accommodating the very real difficulties and vivid emotions of life, and parents who welcome and engage in their children's play are thereby fostering a means of grace that is both thoroughly childlike and full of healing and hope.

These then are the potent secrets of raising, teaching, or shepherding a happy and healthy, if delicate, orchid boy or girl: the power of sameness and routine, the gifts of attentiveness and love, the celebration of human differences, the affirmation of a true and genuine self, the balance between protection and emboldening challenge, and the beneficence of play. In the great and honorable charity of caring for a child, we are all, one way or another, invited back into the magic and holiness of our own beginnings.

9

The Arc of Life for Orchids and Dandelions

All parents yearn for their children's achievement of what poet Mary Oliver called a "wild and precious life"—a life of attainable happiness, sturdy health, fulfilling relationships, and some measure of success and meaning. This is the hope that stirs each mother's, each father's heart as they gaze for the first time into the miraculous and enigmatic face of a tiny, newly born child. It is the hope that sustains their attentiveness and love through long nights of scant sleep and a baby's cry, the agony of a fevered illness besetting a fragile toddler, the tedium of Saturday mornings installed on the sidelines of the year's twenty-third baseball game, and through the dark, lonely worry of watching an adolescent find her stormy way. It is the hope that moves the parent of every child—orchid or dandelion, boy or girl, biological or adopted—to dream of love and safety for that child, to long for fulfillment and favor, prosperity and virtue. Rare is the parent who dreams otherwise or fails to dream at all. Almost universally, we crave goodness and light for our children's childhoods.

Among the reasons that developmental scientists like me are also preoccupied with beneficence and care in the experiences of early life is the reality that the trajectories of the entire life course are set largely in those first few, irreplaceable years, which come and go like the tender green leaves of passing seasons. What happens in early life is never confined in its influence to the first few years, like the events of infancy that no one can remember. What happens in childhood never, ever stays simply in childhood.

As the new field of developmental origins of health and disease asserts, the events, exposures, and experiences of youth echo down the corridors of life, into the farthest reaches of our middle and elder years. This area of study was launched by epidemiologist David Barker and his formative observation that undernutrition of the fetus, reflected in poor fetal growth and low birth weight, might be causally connected to the origins of coronary heart disease decades later in the life course. What had always been regarded as a disease mostly of late adulthood— the cardiovascular events from which far too many still die—turned out to have its origins in risk factors incurred during prenatal life and in the first few postnatal years. In other words, what happens in childhood lasts a lifetime.

The broader assertion—that the events and experiences of very early life are powerfully linked to later disorders and afflictions—is one that has crossed the boundaries of discipline, geography, and historical time. Ethologist Konrad Lorenz famously recorded an instinctive "imprinting" of young goslings on the first perceived moving objects in their immediate environment in the hours following hatching—resulting, experimentally, in several broods of young geese that learned to follow Lorenz himself instead of the mother geese their imprinting was meant to target. Biologist René Dubos argued that adverse exposures in childhood can produce neurobiological risks that persist even when those exposures are later abated or removed. And three major research reports, in the United States, the United Kingdom, and Canada, have forged a strong consensus that the experiences of early life, rendered remarkably different by aspects of socioeconomic status and social position, result in societies with widely divergent developmental and health outcomes.

So we know with conviction and ever-growing scientific proof that children's experiences in their first few years of life, perhaps even in their mothers' wombs, continuously reverberate into their subsequent decades of life, affecting health, accomplishment, and well-being over the entire life span. What implications might there then be for those of us—and those of our children and loved ones—who find themselves imbued with the sensibilities and signs of the orchid or the dandelion? How does the tenderness of the orchid child play itself out in the developmental paths of young adulthood? How does the durability of the dandelion child project itself into the second and third decades of a dandelion life? And what are the ramifications of these dandelion or orchid constitutions over the long span of an individual life? These are important questions, with big implications. For how we parent, how we teach, and how we care for the young orchids and dandelions within our reach likely play critical formative roles in the kinds of adults they will become, the kind of health and well-being they will enjoy, and the kinds of successes and failures they are likely to experience.

It was of course these same powerful questions that propelled me into a life in medical research nearly forty years ago, eventually leading to a study of preschool children in the San Francisco Bay Area. Out of that research, as described in chapter 3, we discovered the orchid and dandelion children (and their successors in many later studies) who became the foundation of this book. As the pages of that story slowly emerged, I began to wonder what had happened to all those now grown-up children in the years since we studied them in the late 1980s. How had their lives turned out thus far, and what might we possibly learn from them? These newer questions prompted my colleagues Abbey Alkon, Aaron Shulman, and me to begin a search for a small number of representative millennials who had been preschoolers in that first study in which the orchid/dandelion contrast had come to light. We wanted to know what they remembered of their distinctive and quite diverse childhoods and to hear the stories of their young adult lives. Had there been orchid stories as sadly disheartening as that of my sister, Mary, or were there orchid kids we once studied who had thrived and soared? Now, three decades later, what had been their triumphs and failures, their joys and sorrows, their proud successes, their laments and regrets?

We began by literally dusting off a crinkled, yellowing reprint of our twenty-eight-year-old 1995 scientific paper where differential susceptibility had been first tentatively proposed (see chapter 3, page 48). How many of these "kids"—now thirty-something years of age (the same as

my own children)—could we even find? Would any of them want to talk
to us or remember who we were? What stories might they tell, and what
life lessons might they have learned over the three intervening decades
since they were tested and observed? I knew that we couldn't come even
close to interviewing all 137 of them from that first preschool study, so
we had to come up with a way of narrowing the field. We needed to win-
now the study sample down to a representative and crucial few individuals whom, if we tried long and hard enough, we might be able to find
and contact.

So, first resurrecting the data we had collected and analyzed for that
original, formative paper, I divided them into the kids whose fight-or-
flight and/or cortisol reactivity profiles in the laboratory stress experiment had been especially low (the dandelions) or especially high (the
orchids). Recall that the measured, laboratory reactivity was in response
to tasks such as tasting a drop of lemon juice, watching a sad or scary
movie, or having to memorize a string of numbers. Next, I grouped them
by the level of stress and adversity we had measured in their homes and
preschools. Home stressors were challenges like moving to a new house
or apartment, seeing or hearing their parents frequently argue or fight,
or a parent becoming seriously ill. Preschool stressors were events such as
embarrassing problems with using the toilet, changes in the preschool's
daily routine, or being disciplined by a teacher. These two groupings—by
reactivity and stress exposure—produced four batches of kids: low and
high in stress reactivity and low and high in naturally occurring early
adversity. Think of the four groups as dandelions planted on meadows
or freeways and orchids raised in tropical rain forests or frigid Alaskan
offices. Finally, we sorted the four batches into those children who, during that preschool year long ago, had had low or high levels of respiratory
illnesses, like colds, sore throats, ear infections, and bronchitis or pneumonia. The orchid kids, as we now know, had either very high or very
low rates of illness, depending upon their levels of home and preschool
stress, while the dandelions had moderate rates of illness, irrespective of
their stressful experiences. As shown in the now familiar graph on the
facing page, from the four batches of kids, we chose eight young adults
who nicely represented these patterns of illness among orchid and dandelion children. The graph shows the fictitious names of these young

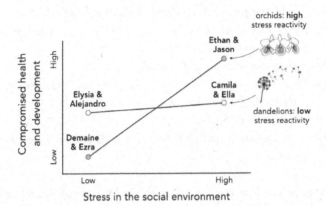

Fictitious names of the eight former preschoolers followed up thirty years later; four groups divided by stress reactivity (low = dandelions; high = orchids) and adversity exposures in the early social environment. The graph shows which individuals correspond to the four previously noted groups defining the relations between stress and health among dandelion and orchid children.

people superimposed on the earlier graph of stress in the social environment predicting compromised health and development.

We then set out, with some trepidation, to see whether any of these eight young people could now be found for interviews. Try sometime chasing groups of adventurous, nomadic millennial preschoolers into the thirty-year diaspora of their young adult lives; it is neither easy nor obvious how to proceed (though social media and the internet certainly helped). Nonetheless, our team was able to locate all eight of the long-lost study kids, and each one participated in a one- to two-hour intensive interview—interviews that proved interesting, emotionally potent, and provocatively instructive. All of the interviews were conducted by the one of us closest in age to the interviewees themselves (that is, Aaron) and who had thus never known them while they were enrolled in the research project three decades past. The interviewer was thus "blind" to—with no knowledge of—the study group to which each of the interviewees belonged.

The conversations began with a series of open-ended questions on a broad range of topics, starting with their earliest memories:

How would your parents have described you as a child?

What were some of your proudest successes and greatest challenges as a child, teenager, and adult?

Where have your interests and passions gone?

What have been the joys and struggles in your personal relationships?

How has your health been over the years?

What has your work life been like?

Who have you found yourself to be and how do you feel about your present life?

These questions were starting points that led to a set of natural, reflective, and remarkably frank conversations.

All the interviews, which comprised three young women and five men, were recorded and transcribed for later analysis. This research design, in which a small number of participants are intensively interviewed to acquire a high-resolution understanding of their life experience, thoughts, and observations, is termed *ethnographic research.* Though such a study differs substantially from the more quantitative, empirical research that I have pursued over much of my career, there are reliable, scientifically valid observations that can only be acquired in the kind of in-depth, penetrating, and responsive conversations with individual people that were conducted in this follow-up study. If you want to learn about a forest, you count species, record seasonal growth, and measure air temperatures, but if you want to learn about a particular tree, you spend a lot of time sitting beneath it. We paid each participant a small honorarium for their time and commended them for their openness and forthrightness in diving deeply into their first three and half decades of life. Here is what they told us.

Preschool Dandelions, Growing in Meadows

As a three-year-old, Elysia* had been a seemingly confident little girl with lots of pluck and an easy friendliness. She had the usual colds, coughs,

---

* All names in this section and those below are pseudonyms.

and dribbling noses of a preschooler exposed to an ocean of previously unencountered viruses, but she was sick no more and no less than most of her tiny schoolmates. In her early thirties, Elysia had become a very articulate, self-aware, and introspective young woman, sharply dressed, with stylish glasses and a mane of wavy chestnut-colored hair—the perfect image of a young professional who knew how to position herself in a modern urban milieu. She turned out to be the only participant of the eight who actually remembered being a part of the original study. She recalled her childhood as having revealed a strong need for personal control. She still had memories of the adorable, if amusing behavior of not liking to go to the bathroom when very young, since she thereby ceded control of substances that were "hers." Partially as a consequence of this trait of control and the strong work ethic conveyed by her father, she never had any difficulties achieving academic success. In her early relationships with her peers, she often assumed nurturing but submissive roles with girlfriends, sometimes leading to what she considered "unhealthy" relationships. She had a vivid imagination and was drawn to fantasy and art, which she later studied in college and still pursues as a hobby.

Just as she was entering middle school, Elysia's family moved to Europe, which entailed for her a number of adaptive challenges, including the pressure to strengthen her language skills (she spoke the language of her new country at home with her parents, but had grown up studying only English in school) and to weather the loss of her familiar surroundings and friends. At the same time, she was entering puberty and experienced all the bodily changes for which no one had fully prepared her. Nonetheless, she ultimately adapted well, enjoying the social liberalism of European life. She maintained an exciting social life—going out with her teenaged friends to clubs blasting European dance music—yet without undue experimentation with demanding relationships or recreational drugs. She had a very good college experience back in the United States and, following graduation, moved to New York City, where she took her first job.

In that corporate position, she fell into a "toxic relationship" with her boss, who took advantage of her youth and inexperience, forcing himself upon her emotionally and inappropriately crossing professional boundaries. Thankfully, she also met the man who is now her fiancé. Feeling the need to break with NYC and all the bad associations that had come to define it, she picked up and moved across the country, in a kind of homecoming, back to the San Francisco Bay Area she had left as a kid. This was a considerable risk: her relationship fell briefly apart, and she couldn't control the outcome of the transition. She controlled only the decision she had made that she had to move. But the change was all she had hoped for: an escape from the abusive boss, a job switch to the nonprofit sector, and opportunities for meeting new people and friends. Eventually her New York boyfriend joined her in San Francisco, and they reestablished a very happy life together. She is pleased with her life and proud of the way she rerouted her path when it strayed from what was good for her. In her resilience and success, she is similar in many ways to her fellow dandelion Alejandro.

Alejandro has a friendly voice that makes you feel as if you've known him for longer than you have, which in his burgeoning career as a psychiatrist surely equates to a comforting bedside manner. His first life memory was of the Loma Prieta earthquake, the catastrophic seismic rumble that shook the Bay Area one October afternoon in 1989 while he was playing with friends in his preschool play yard. He remembers the whole playground of kids beginning to cry as the ground moved, but then being reassured and comforted by teachers and parents after the quake ended. He believes his parents would have described him all those years ago as a "sweet kid" who presented them with few if any difficulties or challenges. He confessed to an early tendency to "zone out," resulting in periodic momentary attentional absences, both at home and at school. He also remembered having an early preoccupation with fairness and a strong need for equitable resolution of conflicts with his friends and parents. It was this penchant for fair play and evenhandedness that, he believes, set him on his present path toward practicing medicine within underserved communities.

He remembers, as well, his parents as being protective—perhaps sometimes overprotective, as when they failed to disclose his beloved grandmother's death for several days. But his family life was stable and caring; his parents had a strong, supportive marriage; and he established a generally healthy and harmonious relationship with his high-achieving older brother. Alejandro also had solid academic and social successes throughout his period of growing up and beyond, spending a year in South America as a Fulbright Scholar and later beginning medical school and residency. Especially during his postgraduate residency training, he had to confront multiple concurrent trials that would perhaps have required another person to take time off or return home. After a cross-country move, which entailed starting over and moving away from all of his friends, he plunged into the demands of an intensive educational program, only to then face the suicide of his new roommate, who jumped off a building. And then, to boot, he and his girlfriend broke up. Nevertheless, he persisted calmly in the face of adversity, getting involved in a therapy group that helped him and his fellow classmates process the roommate's suicide, and people commented on his equanimity in dealing with these sorrows.

Alejandro also began, in high school, to experiment actively with his own sexual orientation and eventually concluded that he is bisexual or "queer." This has occasionally led to a lack of understanding from those close to him, as well as his own internal questions as he lived out the realities of being attracted to both sexes. But he exudes self-acceptance and is now happy and comfortable in his early adult life, with the only challenge being his continuing dilemmas over sexuality and how to find and sustain a lasting relationship.

Elysia's and Alejandro's young adult lives illustrate nicely many of the themes we have come to recognize in the stories of dandelion children with sheltered, stable childhoods. These are kids who grow up secure and self-reliant, able to address with aplomb the challenges and difficulties that their lives inevitably bring. For Elysia, these were the adaptive challenges of moving in early adolescence to an entirely new society and home and confronting an emotionally assaultive authority figure who took advantage of his power. For Alejandro, it was the puzzle of his own sexuality and his adjustment to the exigencies of medical school and his proximity to a very traumatic incident. But the most prominent and important theme is that despite these inescapable and often trying life strains, both Elysia and Alejandro have found within themselves capacities for adaptation and renewal. Both have sustained powerful problems and survived. Both have found their ways through to satisfying and meaningful adult lives.

Preschool Dandelions, Planted on Freeways

Camila has penetrating eyes, loves to cook and go to live concerts, and had just started graduate school. She told us, when asked about what kind of kid she remembered herself having been, that she was a "teacher's pet"—a hardworking achiever who always sought approval from authority figures. As a preschooler, she had sustained perhaps more than her share of stressful or annoying events at school—but her health history was neither better nor worse than that of any of her pals. Her family home was tranquil and stable, and her mother functioned as her most ardent cheerleader. In school, Camila tended to gravitate toward more dominant, ringleader kids, preferring to occupy a more subordinate, following role. She admitted that at times, feeding off the potency and reputation of her higher-status friends, she engaged in the bullying of younger or less powerful peers. Timid by predisposition, Camila learned, through her connections to her friends, to shed her wallflower image and to become far more talkative, approachable, and outgoing. She was very decisive and proactive in this regard. After middle school she wanted a new, extroverted persona, so she refashioned her public self.

Yet Camila, like most of us, wasn't able to fully rewrite her inborn tendencies. Her social proclivities toward subordination to more powerful friends resulted, in late adolescence, in a pivotal and shaming incident. She became close with a male friend who had a thrill-seeking penchant for shoplifting, and she let herself get pulled along for the ride. One day, they walked into an electronics store, lifted some valuable external hard drives, and left. Yet out in the parking lot after their successful mission, they were on a high that made them want an even greater high—so they went right back in and stole more hard drives. This time, however, they were caught. What seemed like a juvenile if risky game was suddenly a serious adult problem. She and the friend were handcuffed and questioned, and she spent a night in a communal jail cell, in a prison uniform.

This was a shattering experience for her and her parents. For a kid from a solidly middle-class, responsible family, it was a powerful and unforgettable event in which she was charged and convicted (the crime was technically a felony, but was negotiated to a lesser charge), which deeply troubled her parents. There followed long, expensive efforts to expunge this from her record, with the humiliation of the conviction periodically reemerging during job applications and licensure exams. Though Camila is now proudly completing a graduate degree and though she performed beautifully in a case worker job for five years before, the shadow of her crime and arrest have not readily or easily faded into the past. Nevertheless, she takes full responsibility and has tried to use this wayward moment of her life as something to learn from, even though she wishes she could take it back.

Camila also confronted, during a period of her early life, body-image and eating issues as she struggled with being overweight. Supported by her mother, however, she has been able to lose much of her excess weight and has overcome to a large degree the insecurities surrounding her body and image. She is now in a rewarding and satisfying relationship with a young man from a different ethnic culture and has become a smart, reflective, and emotionally self-aware young person.

Ella, like Camila, faced an undue share of preschool stressors when we first knew her at age four, but was only modestly reactive in the lab and had an average allotment of respiratory illnesses. Also like Camila, Ella has contended with substantial adversity in the years since, though you wouldn't know it from just spending a few minutes with her. She is smiley and curious, with a punky style (jean jacket with patches, big black boots) that projects a quiet, happy confidence. She described herself as a young child as shy, but strong of character. Her mom said that she was a "firm" and solid little girl, never one to hold back how she felt inside the family. She had no trouble academically but found social situations somewhat challenging and still considers herself a textbook introvert. When she was eleven, her family moved back to South America, from whence they had come to San Francisco for part of her father's training (curiously similar to Elysia's move to Europe around the same age). This was an important and onerous transition for Ella, requiring a deeper immersion in her parents' native tongue, an acquisition of culturally distinct social and academic skills, and an accommodation to the developmental reality that the female classmates who surrounded her were substantially more advanced sexually than she had yet become. She was a bit of a tomboy who loved playing out in the streets with her cousins, but now she was expected to be a conventional young woman with values and behaviors with which she didn't identify.

Ella was sixteen years old when her family suffered a profound tragedy: her father died, suddenly and unexpectedly, at age forty-five. It was a blow for everyone, and each member of the family, including Ella, retreated into her or his own grief and mourning. The family home became a collection of silos, each person suffering in silence the father's abruptly imposed absence. Ella coped with this great loss in her life by moving gradually into her father's prior world: studying in a program he had helped establish, working in a laboratory with his own colleagues, and gravitating toward his professional area of science. She felt terribly and, at times, desperately unprepared, however, to occupy her father's shoes, and she attempted to weather those feelings of inadequacy with alcohol and marijuana during her college years.

After graduating, Ella moved back to San Francisco, like so many of her itinerant peers, and experienced a reverse culture shock, all over again. She had to master anew the intricacies of different social expectations, the nuances of changed English slang, and the conventions of behavior and tradition. She recalled how the word "shady" had come into popular use while she was away. At first somewhat aimless and at sea, still using alcohol and cannabis as a crutch, she was plagued by insecurities regarding her future and her fate. But she secured a job as a laboratory technician, and one day her older sister, also living in San Francisco, gave her a bicycle. As if the wonderfully intuitive gift were a magical spell, Ella's life began to transform. After a few exhausting days on the bicycle in which she thought she might die out on the roads, she got the hang of it. She rode the bike six miles to and from work each day; she began rock climbing and got in shape; and she saw a therapist who helped her reestablish a sense of self and purpose. She had a tumultuous romantic relationship along the way, but is now single, and has finally achieved stability and happiness.

Again, the stories of Camila's and Ella's young lives, still very much being written, reveal the resilience and adaptability of the dandelion child. Both of these young women faced in their early years, during their participation in our preschool study, substantially higher levels of exposure to family and school stressors than were typical of their peers. Such early stressors can take the form of acute adverse childhood events, such as parental separations or divorces, witnessing conflict or violence, or having a parent struggle with alcoholism or substance abuse. Or they can be adversities that are more chronic in nature, such as parental mental health disorders or long-term child maltreatment. Whatever the specific toxic stressors experienced by these two children over the course of their preschool years, neither sustained the inordinate levels of respiratory illness that sometimes accompany exposures to acute and chronic stressors. Both maintained, as dandelions often do, relatively robust health despite the significant perturbations in their socioemotional lives.

Remarkably, the same pattern of rugged resistance to life challenges and difficulties appears to have persisted into both girls' fourth decades. Camila sustained a humiliating prosecution for shoplifting as a nineteen-year-old first offender, unleashing a trail of legal and emotional complexities with which she still contends. She has also struggled with the difficult and tenacious problem of becoming overweight. Ella, for her part, lost her dad when she was sixteen and twice migrated between North and South American cultures. Losing a parent is difficult and painful at any age, but for a teenage girl to have her father die midway through her adolescence, without warning or preparation, was a powerful and disquieting tragedy. But there is no evidence in either Camila's or Ella's past years of a developmental arrest or a compromising of developmental achievements over time. Both appear to have absorbed big losses—for one, the tarnishing of her innocence and virtue with respect to law and society; for the other, the death of a deeply beloved parent. But both also found ways of transmuting those losses into life lessons that usefully chastened or deepened their identities.

Preschool Orchids, Growing in Tropical Rain Forests

When he was four years old, Demaine was among the healthiest preschoolers we encountered in our early study. Despite his clearly extravagant fight-or-flight responses in the reactivity lab, which identified him as an orchid child, he had virtually no illnesses during the entire year in which we observed and regularly examined him. Indeed, he had fewer colds and viruses than the entire field of dandelions in which he was immersed at his San Francisco preschool. This was truly an uber-healthy little boy. His near-flawless, record-holding picture of health as a four-year-old preschooler was likely attributable, in part, to a supportive, virtually adversity-free life at school and home, along with his orchid constitution that rendered him intensely susceptible to the protective effects of these nurturing, stress-free early environments. This despite the fact that he was then, as he surely is now, an exceedingly gregarious and charismatic young fellow, who was quite generously exposed to red-eyed, mucus-nosed classmates who suffused the very air Demaine breathed with cough- and sneeze-launched pathogens. Even three decades later, and even while recalling his parents as somewhat disapproving and critical of him, this was a vigorously healthy young man with a larger-than-life life. And when we met him again, he welcomed the chance to recount the story of his dazzling, fast-paced, and high-stakes existence.

Right from the beginning, Demaine, who is prone to dramatic gestures with his hands and body, felt like a misfit in the world of childhood and children. It was as if he had been born to the world a thirty-five-year-old profligate Gatsby in the dissembling body of a young boy. He found peers frivolous, children's play boring and unchallenging; he much preferred the more sophisticated and intriguing company of his parents' friends and adult relatives. He didn't like the things with which boy children are usually preoccupied: sports and video games, dinosaurs and dragons. He preferred adult garden parties in homes with elegant features and antique furniture. He had an innate, congenital need that his surroundings, things, and friends be perfectly orderly, grand in scale, and spectacular in refinement. He had an obsessive revulsion for unseemly conditions or events and recalled staying home for a week after one of his schoolmates vomited in class. He readily admitted an early, constitutional intolerance for all things and people that were banal, nasty, or common.

An extrovert with certifiable ADHD, Demaine couldn't sit still, either in life or for our interview. But his fidgety restlessness had propelled him into jobs in high-priced restaurants, as a means of meeting wealthy and influential friends—preferably older. He interned in the offices of a San Francisco political figure, yet for a time this didn't seem to lead anywhere, since his hyperactive nature made it hard for him to hunker down and focus. After college he lived at home and amassed massive credit card debt, spending money he didn't have in order to live the high life that beckoned him. But his strengths paid off as if this had been the plan all along. In his late twenties, he finagled his way into reality TV, which gave him sudden stardom and vast new entrée into exotic travel, speaking engagements, business opportunities, and the subtle, distinctive aroma of money. He had an indisputable knack and craving for the theater and pageantry of public life, especially the lofty public life of celebrity and glamour.

As a graduating high school student, Demaine had been voted "Most Likely to Become a Millionaire," a prophecy promptly fulfilled (or exceeded) by his current salary, which lies substantially north of $500,000 per annum. If a bit nervous by nature, he was likable and magnetic in our interview and had the grace and shiny, smooth surfaces of a natural schmoozer and practiced communicator. Everything about him telegraphed sensitivity, taste, and elegance, although he did express considerable anguish at the fact that he does not like San Francisco, but must stay in the city for the time being, since it is where his work is based. He is now well on his way to achieving the "special" and charmed life that he had imagined and begun to search for even at four years of age.

The only downside he found in his penchant for elegance and notability was the discomfort he registered in working for someone else and in adhering to the demands and schedules of a corporate life. He craves, and undoubtedly will one day attain, the control and dominance that attends ownership and leading. Though he worries over the potential losses involved in the conventional life of having a wife and family—which would likely include less jetting and a less chaotically fast pace, which is ironically essential to his emotional stability—he is in a deeply caring relationship with a woman who may well become that wife.

Ezra, Demaine's counterpart in the category of exceptionally healthy orchids, offered both an interesting contrast and a notable parallel as we heard the story of his first decades of life. As with Demaine, we found Ezra engaging, reflective, and self-aware, though he had a calm presence and an understated, clever sense of humor. He also had a self-possessed serenity, and he never rushed himself to speak if he wasn't ready with his thought. Unlike Demaine, Ezra has found the economic climate of American society, post–Great Recession, to be challenging and, to some degree, disappointing. Born in Eastern Europe, he immigrated to the United States with his family at age three, and his earliest memory is the bittersweet scene of bidding his extended family a permanent farewell at the airport as he and his parents, who were Jewish intellectuals, left in the run-up to a communist government collapse. They boarded their plane, flew over landmasses and oceans, and landed on another continent, with another language and an unknown life awaiting them.

The contrast to this story of sudden and disruptive flight from a native country on the brink of dissolution is the more proximal reality for Ezra of parents who loved and encouraged him, who sought his welfare and protection, and who sacrificed homeland and familiarity for a chance at raising him and his sister in an atmosphere of freedom and opportunity. Their transition to American society was overwhelmingly successful, with Ezra attending a bilingual private school on scholarship and discovering a previously unrecognized passion and talent for dance that led him to the San Francisco Ballet. He became a young dancer in the company and seriously considered a longer-term path toward becoming a professional ballet dancer, until a significant injury in late high school ended his dancing career. This didn't stop or slow him down, however, since dancing was only one of his many talents.

From his early years as a young immigrant, Ezra, who is confident and naturally sociable, engaged readily and thoroughly with the city of San Francisco and made it his home. With a picturesqueness that is hard to imagine in a kid's daily life, he rode one of the city's famous trolleys up its hills to school each day, admiring the town houses and buildings around him. The trolley conductors even knew him by name. Perhaps it is no coincidence that he is now pursuing his other artistic interest, architecture, and maintains a large, diverse social network with which he shares the architectural landscape and culture of the city. He has continued to have no real health problems as a young adult and is currently in a serious, committed relationship. He is somewhat discontented with his present economic situation, which he attributes to the remnants of the 2007–08 global financial crisis, and laments to some degree his apparently permanent implantation into San Francisco and the Bay Area.

Demaine's and Ezra's stories—so different in their origins and endpoints—nonetheless reveal commonalities that unearth and illustrate the complexities of life as young orchids. Neither young man, in either his early or his present life, could possibly be seen as average or unexceptional. Both lives stood out from the vanilla backdrop of boyhood. Demaine dreamed of a life beyond the mainstream, stylishly peculiar in its character and direction. Ezra, born into a gray, post-Soviet chaos, escaped to the flamboyance of San Francisco and became a cosmopolitan, trilingual ballet dancer. Both impressed us as having a graceful, easy aptitude for interpersonal connection, and unlike many of the young, shy orchids I have known in their earlier, childhood years, both had become by their fourth decade of life comfortably extroverted. Both had within themselves a strong sense of uniqueness and personal destiny, as if there were a secret, special role for which each one was solely made. And both revealed an impressive commitment and capacity toward enacting and making real these special visions for their lives. Neither were loners, neither inhibited. And both were embedded in apparently committed and enduring romantic relationships. We came away from these interviews impressed not only with the degree to which each young man had thrived and flourished, but also with a strong sense of how "special, in special ways" each of these orchid lives had become.

Preschool Orchids, Growing in Frigid Alaskan Office Buildings

Ethan was as biologically susceptible to stressors as any child we tested for our preschool project. He showed strong fight-or-flight responses to even the modestly challenging tasks we asked him to complete and was visibly affected by trying to describe an emotionally difficult event. He seemed to have a vivid imagination for both the good and the bad things that can happen in a four-year-old life. He also encountered more than his fair share of adversity within the preschool setting: sometimes excluded or bullied on the playground, upset by changes in his drop-off or pickup routine, and with a small teaching staff that was simply unable to attend to every child's distress. Perhaps as a consequence of these conditions and the immune compromises that may have accompanied his stress reactivity, Ethan was perennially unwell. Especially during the winter months, he seemed to sustain one viral illness after another, often with complications such as ear infections or sinusitis. He seemed an unusually fragile little boy.

Three decades later, Ethan chatted reflectively with us in the living room of his Bay Area apartment, which was overflowing with books and DVDs. With a collection of freckles scattered on a kind face, he had grown up to be a healthy, composed young man able to connect with others even as his head seemed full of private thoughts. He was the youngest of a large family of siblings and half siblings, and the first of his memories was of his baptism at eighteen months of age—an exceptionally early memory, given the well-recognized phenomenon of "infantile amnesia." For most people, the earliest recallable episodic memories begin around age three or four, but perhaps Ethan's exceptional sensitivities have allowed him to retain traces of experience that fade away for most of the rest of us. Even so, Ethan didn't remember his participation in our study, though his parents certainly did. The night before the recent interview, they had told him how overwhelming the laboratory tasks had been for him. Ethan had many childhood memories of being "overstimulated" by situations; he recalled being sensitive to and overwhelmed by many experiences of early life, especially those in crowded or tumultuous settings. He also recollected having had an explosive temper, which he attributed to his frustration at not being able to control certain situations. He found the school day, beginning in preschool and continuing thereafter, draining and difficult and would have preferred to be home alone, watching TV or reading. He had a powerful capacity for empathic connection with others and a lively imagination—confirming our earliest impressions of him as a four-year-old—and by the end of primary school he had set his life course. In late elementary school, he ended up in a theater class and at once felt like he had found his way home. He was to become an actor.

In spite of this newfound sense of direction and purpose, middle school for Ethan was very challenging, both academically and socially. He was distracted from his work by incoming sensory stimuli, was bullied on the play yard and during transit to school, and remembered feeling that "I just couldn't find my way in." Lonely and somewhat isolated, Ethan found companionship in the company of "weirdos"—social outcasts who existed, resentful and estranged, on the margins of the middle school and high school societies. His parents, concerned for his well-being and safety, moved him for the remainder of high school to a "hippie school," which offered a more flexible and accommodating educational model, but still engendered for Ethan a lack of belonging. In the new setting, he felt increasingly alone and depressed, and at the bottom of this darkest of periods he entertained thoughts of suicide. He recalled an emblematic moment from this time, at a summer camp for families, in which he accidentally dropped his plate of food on the floor in the cafeteria. In a bout of well-meant teasing, the other diners began applauding. Ethan stormed off to the bathroom, full of self-loathing, and punched a hole in the wall.

Thankfully, soon after, he himself came forward to his parents to say he wanted to see a therapist, and they listened and acted. He was referred to a therapist who helped him find his way back into a plausible and genial life. Midway through high school, he found his first girlfriend, established a new sense of confidence, and slowly surfaced from his depression and hopelessness. His grades began to improve, his academic potential became more evident, and in his senior year he put in a sustained effort and was accepted into a dramatic arts program at a major university. College was heaven for him. He had finally found his people, and he thrived in the theater department. Following college graduation, he worked for a time in Los Angeles, but found the acting scene there fiercely competitive, with jobs dependent upon a talent for empty communication that Ethan clearly lacked. He returned to the San Francisco area for a part in a play and has stayed, able to sustain and comfortably live his life on the proceeds of acting and waiting tables. He still feels a fundamental sense of identity, however, with the weirdos in life—the artsy and whimsically strange people who color and decorate our societies and communities.

Like Ethan, Jason was among those orchid children identified in the preschool project—showing florid reactivity to challenge in the laboratory, experiencing a disproportionate share of stressors, both at home and at school, and one of the kids with a constant dripping cold. Also like Ethan, Jason was the youngest of multiple siblings in a blended family. The others were sufficiently older that he spent much of his youth feeling like an only child. He believes his parents would have called him "needy" and "spoiled," particular as he was about his requirements and the demands of his family. He was heavily involved in video games and baseball (watching, not playing) and made a young best friend, who remains his best buddy even today. In person, Jason was jovial, leaning back happily in his chair and talking rapidly.

He attended a parochial middle school and high school, and in rebellion against those restrictive academic environments began drinking lots of alcohol and smoking lots of weed. His social group while at his university was the hippie bunch (the slacker crowd, rather than Ethan's artistic gang), who regarded school as a tolerable rite of passage but retreated to the California desert to eat mushrooms, smoke, and scramble up and down enormous boulders. Following his graduation from high school, Jason's parents moved full-time to the East Coast, leaving him the San Francisco house to which to return, where he continues to live even now. He spent a year living in the urban east with his parents, but he found the environment overstimulating. All the traffic, people, and noise wore him out.

On the one hand, Jason's life has become stable and productive, settled as he is into an administrative post at a local university. He has a serious, responsible job and a foreseeable and secure future, working his way up on a long-term employment trajectory that is reputable, if modest in slope. He is comfortable and steady in his present life. On the other hand, his story has just a whiff of disappointment and resignation. His parents worry from afar over his consumption of alcohol. On a typical day, he'll return from work, smoke a bowl of weed, down a few shots to induce relaxation, and then settle into a hypnotic evening of TV sports. Jason acknowledges that he won't be forever able to live in his parents' San Francisco home, but he understandably cites the exorbitant rent market and his personal need for saving money as reasons for staying put, at least for now. Regrettably, his longest romantic relationship has lasted only three or four months, which he attributes to his comfort being alone. He is politically well-informed and a thoughtful atheist, with little appetite or need for spiritual practices or experiences. He has developed, in his young adulthood, a "sensitive stomach" of unknown origin, which gives him occasional GI symptoms that are annoying. He likes routine and appears quite risk-averse. At thirty-four, he is an articulate and talkative young man, without being verbose, who has a nervous laugh that sometimes exaggerates the humor of a given moment. As secure as his life now appears, he seemed a young guy who has for the moment lost his bearings within a lifestyle that is sometimes lonely and unreflective of his real potential.

As we have recognized from the beginning, the quality of orchidness—some children's exceptional susceptibility and tenderness to the character of the world that surrounds and infuses them—has a double-sided character, rendering possible the exceptional outcomes and brilliant accomplishments that orchids often achieve, but conveying as well the possibility of misfortune and a liability to defeat. Neither Ethan nor Jason reported life histories that we would deem troubled or failed. Both have good jobs with steady incomes, and both are productive citizens of our society and world. But at the same time, both have struggled to find joy, and, in Jason's case, passion as well. Ethan more than Jason is embarked on a life dedicated to a long-term dream, but neither is wholly embedded in a job or family to which their lives are perceptibly devoted.

Both told stories of modest achievement and pride in their work and purpose.

Deeper Lessons from Young Lives

All eight of our young refugees from a formative study of preschool stress and illness, now three decades in the past, have lives that lie still mostly before them. As human longevity continues to increase, each of these young women and men could plausibly claim a half century or more of living yet to come. Thus any conclusions about life paths that we might reach from our present scrutiny and siftings of their interview transcripts are provisional at best. Our hope for them, along with those of their parents and loved ones, is for long, productive, and satisfying lives. Tentative and incomplete as their stories are, at present, they are stories that together comprise nearly 250 years of individual human history, and are thereby, as the lyricist portrayed them, "laden with happiness and tears." Though now less than half the length of their likely eventual span, these young lives have been already marked by the complexities, joys, and sorrows of their presence on this green earth.

What new insights might we harvest from our eight adult "kids" that could illuminate the larger story of orchid and dandelion children? Knowing how they varied so substantially and consequentially in their early sensitivities or indifferences to the circumstances of their homes and preschools, how might their stories aid our understanding of the arc of life—the trajectories of misfortune and well-being—for young orchids and dandelions? Several such fresh longitudinal reflections might be legitimately and helpfully gleaned.

First, it is immensely clear, as I noted in a previous chapter, that "orchid" and "dandelion" are best seen as locations on a continuum of special sensitivity, rather than as "buckets" of human phenotypes into which each child can be empirically placed. Demaine, Ezra, Ethan, and Jason were cataloged, at age three or four, as orchid children for the purposes of a developmental study of neurobiological reactivity, and each bore certain hallmarks of what we've come to recognize as an orchid profile. Each had exaggerated, heightened responses to mild laboratory stressors in their now distant preschool years. Each of them had special sensibilities that led, in the case of Demaine, to an intolerance for the pedestrian and the "normal," or for Ezra to a talent for ballet, and for others, to a sense of easy overstimulation or being overwhelmed in intense or crowded conditions.

Our hardy dandelions—Alejandro, Elysia, Ella, and Camila—had all, in their early years, revealed impassive, minimal biological reactivity to the very same laboratory challenges that triggered vigorous responses in the orchids. And all now reported life experiences reflecting some aspect of steady, resilient reactions in the face of real adversity. For Alejandro, it was wanting his grandmother's death to be revealed to him, not hidden, so that he could genuinely experience and grieve her loss. For Elysia, it was successfully adapting to a new life in Europe, even as she was contending with the dramatic changes of puberty. And in Ella's life it was the far too early loss of her dad to his unsuspected, unanticipated disease.

But equally telling was *the striking diversity of the orchid and dandelion groups*. The orchid child Ethan was socially withdrawn and responded by achieving a hard-won comfort on the very public theatrical stage. But another orchid, Demaine, had little time for childhood comforts and moved confidently, even ferociously, into adult life. Dandelions Ella and Camila both had experiences of genuine trauma in their childhoods or adolescence. But Ella responded to her father's death by immediately redoubling her personal and professional (and likely therapeutic) identity with her dad, while Camila's arrest and conviction became a gnawing, persistent stain on her otherwise purely remarkable life. Each individual, it seemed, was some mosaic of orchid- and dandelion-like traits. Though all eight sorted visibly and recognizably, even thirty years later, into the categories to which our lab procedures had once assigned them, no one of the eight was a pure, unadulterated specimen of one flower or the other. Each was located somewhere on a spectrum of orchid to dandelion sensibility.

Second, and of little surprise to the developmentalist, all of these young adults had lives and identities that had changed perceptibly over time. Some became progressively and emphatically more like the

children we had known in the late 1980s, but others displayed striking differences, in temperament and behavior from the youngsters we
had observed them to be at age three or four years. Camila was a high
achiever and a teacher's pet right from the start of her primary school
years and went on to the pursuit of a graduate degree in a rigorous field.
Ethan had discovered theater and acting even before he finished his elementary education, but, unlike many others who flirt with a theater or
film career, he deepened and magnified his commitment to acting over
time.

In contrast, Alejandro had an early, noticeable proclivity toward a
wandering, unfocused attention, a tendency, as he put it, to "zone out"—
hardly an asset for an academic vocation. And yet he became a Fulbright
Scholar and is now a resident physician in a major psychiatric training
program. Ella began life shy and anxious and found social situations
threatening and difficult. But she now has a vigorous interpersonal life,
with good friends and valued colleagues, and is successfully engaged in
the socially intensive biotech industry. Sometimes we are surprised by
the remarkable transformations—both welcome and lamentable—that
can emerge as children grow into the mature, adult versions of themselves. We all have heard the stories of plain young wallflowers who grow
into corporate leaders of stunning attractiveness, or class presidents who
become white-collar criminals and miscreants.

But the perhaps most conspicuous and poignant contrast among
pairs of our young interviewees was that which emerged between the
two orchid boys, Ethan and Jason. Both had had relatively high adversity
lives in their preschool years, and both were uncommonly afflicted—
not with serious, chronic diseases, but with just one after another of the
perennial fevers and respiratory illnesses that are endemic in preschools.
Both boys had school and home environments that were notable for
their challenges, adversities, and stressors. And both fell into high school
groups that existed on the reclusive and unsettled margins of their peer
societies.

But these two conversations diverged strikingly in what Ethan and
Jason reported about the current state of their lives and about the family
and peer relationships that had ushered them toward their present life

circumstances. While both had taken up with peers who lived on the isolated outskirts of their high schools and colleges, Ethan's group was artists, with eccentric identities that they had chosen to adopt. Jason's group, on the other hand, was engaged in more genuinely antisocial and risky behaviors, involving the frequent use of recreational drugs and a predisposition toward withdrawal from the larger society. While both young men have maintained ongoing relationships with their parents and families, we were struck by the remarkable lengths to which Ethan's family had gone over the course of his childhood to ensure his ongoing connection and sense of identity with them. They adopted, for example, a mealtime practice of passing around a kind of microphone that gave everyone, even the youngest (Ethan), a chance to speak and be heard. During his period of serious depression, Ethan's family moved quickly and assertively to identify a therapist and support his recovery. His family, throughout his young life, stuck faithfully with him, supporting and encouraging him (and his artistic idiosyncrasies) in a wide variety of ways. By contrast, Jason's family, while clearly caring and involved, was and is more distant, more emotionally and geographically removed from the day-to-day realities of his life, less likely to adhere effectively to a sometimes struggling young son.

The upshot, we believe, has been a perceptible divergence in the life paths of these two preschool orchids, who were affected even thirty years ago by disproportionate exposures to adversity. Ethan adopted, as early as primary school, a committed life path that has propelled him toward meaningful and successful work in theater and film. But Jason's trajectory, at least for the present, is disquieting in its overinvolvement with alcohol, its lingering attachment to his parental home (though minus the physical presence of his parents), and the sense that he is still searching for direction and meaning. Here, surely, is a rich example of how differences in the nurturance and support offered by families can appreciably affect the life course of highly sensitive young orchid children.

That said, it is also important to acknowledge and remind ourselves that in many ways the lives of Ethan and Jason are still just beginning, and that we all grow and develop at decidedly differing paces. Even beyond the fourth decade of life—that in which these two young men currently reside—*we are, each of us, always "becoming," forever changed from the person we once were, but not yet transformed into the individual we are still to be.* Parents and grandparents watch, entranced, as their children and grandchildren unfold over the years of their early development, in sometimes spectacular and often unforeseen ways. Change and development in the first decades of life are especially breathtaking in their pace and scope. But that development has both continuities and discontinuities, and the young people we knew in our own sixties are both replicas and departures from the children we knew in our thirties. Tiny infants with red hair and sunny personalities become the ginger teens we always knew and hoped they would be. Whiny toddlers beget gnarly adolescents. But sometimes we are surprised. Or disappointed. The sensate orchid four-year-old, so visibly overflowing with emotion and delicacy, can become a stalwart and courageous adult leader, seemingly unencumbered by uncertainty or hesitation. And the resilient preschool dandelion can be shaken by the vicissitudes of adult life, faltering in the face of overpowering misfortune. My grandfather used to tell me, paraphrasing Carl Sandburg, that life is like an onion: you peel back the layers, one by one, and sometimes, you cry.

The third and final insight, derivative of the stories our now grown preschoolers told, is that *lives are intrinsically unpredictable.* Even in the span of thirty postnatal years, circumstances and lives can unaccountably change. Kids become challenged, not by lab stressors that we dream up to tweak their stress biology, but by real adversities—fathers dying, temptations beckoning, social pressures emerging, families moving, and failures occurring. The as yet incomplete stories of these eight young lives haunt us with questions of exactly why and how all the witnessed changes happen. Are the events and troubles that young lives absorb just random assaults from a universe of chance and a world torn open by its inherent chaos? Or is there in some sense, in *any* sense, a destiny enfolded into each young life, like seeds in a pod? Do orchid children arise from some mostly accidental convergence of gene sequence and environmental exposure, or is the orchid *born* an orchid, all but fated to a life of enduring sympathy, for better or for worse? Are our dandelions robust and implacable even as they float, with a growing, organic awareness, in the dark, warm water-world of fetal life?

All of our science—of child development and the inexorable emergence of the human brain—is designed to search for and detect the uniformities and patterns that will serve and fulfill the predictability of outcomes. We seek, and often find, powerful connections linking who a child is in her early years to who she becomes as her life evolves. Even where unanticipated events jar a child loose from the path on which he once traveled, there are consistent, definable regularities in development that render such departures and their consequences understandable, with an internal logic of their own. But superimposed on this sequence of predictable developmental regularities is a grid of chaos and unpredictability from which no life altogether escapes.

There are events within individual lives—events both tragic and kind—that can disrupt the progression of development and dislodge us from the logical, predictable road on which we were once accustomed to travel. These events are not randomly or equally assigned, by either person or time. Rather, some lives are disproportionately affected by such events, and they seem to occur in clusters, instead of randomly over time. So while a child's accurate assignment to the categories of orchid or dandelion can explain many of the developmental events and outcomes that come to pass in that child's life, there will always remain an element of disorder, of those unpredictable encounters with chance events that can either vitalize or derail the child's ongoing journey. Our role as parents, teachers, health care providers, and friends is to understand keenly the nature of each child—his or her location on the scale of orchid to dandelion—and to abet and model the most positive and life-giving responses to the events that may befall them.

10

The Sins of the Fathers, the Means of Grace

The Lord, a God merciful and gracious, slow to anger, and abounding in steadfast love and faithfulness . . . will by no means clear the guilty, visiting the iniquity of fathers on the children and the children's children, to the third and the fourth generation.

—Exodus 34:6–7

We bless you, Lord, for our creation, preservation and the blessings of this life . . . For the means of grace and the hope of glory.

—Liturgy of the Anglican Church

But what if our best efforts "to understand keenly the nature of each child" are hobbled or even crippled by an insufficiency of the resources that we bring forward, as parents, teachers, or doctors, from our own childhoods and histories? There are times when all of us stand in abject, slack-jawed terror before the staggering responsibility we bear for a new generation's needs and hopes. And yet our human capacities for parenting, teaching, or healing are powerfully dependent upon and affected by our psychological and socioemotional strengths and failings, which are rooted in the dim, distant realities of our own beginnings.

A patient's family once sat before me on a winter evening, years ago, looking wounded and hopeless, with an adolescent son whose life had reached a dangerous stalemate of addiction and disorder. A truly brilliant young man, whose future abounded with opportunity, he had lost his way and wandered into the darkly pooled oblivions of cocaine, cannabis, and depression. He now seemed bound for a long, languid abandonment of learning and ambition, and his family had brought him to me in the hope that some reclamation of his life chances might be found.

He sat, studiously unkempt and clothed entirely in black, with his face to the floor. His voice was slurred and muffled, his right arm was illustrated with circumferential and especially odious tattoos, and his contempt for his family was all but proclaimed in neon on the public billboard of his fifteen-year-old life. His two siblings, one younger and one older, glanced sideways around the room, nervously gauging the twin perils of violent familial anger and marital dissolution, while masking their justifiable anxiety with a storm of fidgets and twitches. In a tone that conveyed at once disgust and despair, the boy's father loudly demanded, "Anthony [not his real name], sit up and participate, for God's sake! We're trying to help you!"

The other four family members stiffened in their respective chairs, as Anthony shifted dully, drilling his father with a murderous stare. The aggrieved mom, urging equanimity and calm, said, "Okay now, let's all just take a deep breath here and talk about this. We're just trying to figure this out together."

"Don't undermine my authority with our son," her husband darkly admonished in response.

As I soon learned, this was a family in which the father and son had become grievously and cruelly combative. Anthony, whether biologically an orchid or not, was a self-evidently sensitive and fragile kid. He had become increasingly engaged in a kind of gothic antisociality involving sexual risk-taking, minor criminality, acts of unprovoked disrespect for adult authority and property, immersion in a drug-centered culture of all-night rave parties, and many physical signals of an unanchored moral life. His dad, angered and disappointed by the boy's increasingly ominous life choices, loudly declared his disbelief that one of *his children* could adopt a life of such shameful irresponsibility and ingratitude. No one—children, wife, neighbors, nor I—was long confused about where this father stood on issues of youthful perversity or debauchery.

But the father was also deeply and perceptibly anguished, envisioning as he did a sad, dead-end future for a son with abundant talent and rich creative possibilities. The father's angry condemnations had all but eclipsed from view his love for the boy, which he held in his heart like an inaccessible treasure. The anger had cowed and intimidated Anthony, who responded to his dad with retreat and ever-deepening commitment to a life of marginality and rebellion. Meanwhile, the parents' marriage was gradually eroding, as the mom's more moderating voice struggled to be heard above the din of her husband's disapproval and rancor. The other children were by no means unscathed as this daily battle played itself out in the family's home. The older boy, sensing his parents' agony and the now frightening tenuousness of their marriage, simply checked out—immersing himself in his own private life and trying earnestly to ignore the conflict that raged around him. The younger daughter, bewildered by her family's disarray, became conspicuously allied to her mother's cause and indignant at her dad's "unfair judging" of her brother's "lifestyle."

To be sure, Anthony's experimentation with drugs and delinquency was a legitimate cause for parental alarm. Many mothers and fathers, witnessing signs of a child's deviance from a life of purpose and virtue, have been similarly troubled. But this father's response had moved well beyond the parameters of rightful concern; he was drowning an entire family in a sea of anger and rebuke. However obsessive or intemperate his reaction to his son had become, as his own childhood came haltingly into view in our meetings together, I began to understand something of the provenance of this father's wrath toward his most sensitive and tender child.

His own father, Anthony's grandfather, coming of age in the teeth of a righteous but brutal world war, had become an embittered and abusive alcoholic. He disciplined his children with belt and brawn, convinced upon hazy religious grounds that this was how decency and honor became rooted within the "character" of a child. There had been, in that childhood family of Anthony's dad, high and unassailable standards of conduct, but little love and a collective life in which emotion was seldom considered and tenderness never revealed. The grandfather's principled demands for adherence to rules, unleashed by nightly visitations to the bottle, gave way to sad, cyclical rituals of abuse, rebuke, and remorse. The children were derided for their failings, ridiculed for mistakes and misdemeanors, and beaten for transgressions of their father's unbending law. These were the experiences of trauma and undefended harm that Anthony's father had carried unwittingly forward into the crucible of his own family's life, into the hidden, rigid structures that defined its shape and substance. Given these powerful experiences of early life, it was small wonder that coercion and condemnation became the unthinking responses to his own son's departure from upright behavior. As Anthony's special sensitivity to his father's judgment produced ever greater reactive withdrawals from the dad's unchallengeable values, the escalating paternal censure began a self-perpetuating cycle of alienation, distance, and retribution.

The dire situation of this family was painfully familiar to me.

Mary and Mom

My own mom and sister bore a telling and material resemblance to the multigenerational conflicts unearthed in my patient Anthony's unhappy family life. I have only conjecture—not a single, verifiable truth—about what dark substance poisoned the long-simmering stew that was my orchid sister's and mother's relationship, one to the other. I can only speculate, now sixty years hence from that fire's first kindling, what it was that went wrong, how an earnestly caring mother and a fragile daughter became tragically estranged and arrived at a stalemate of enmity and isolation. This brother-son's best, reflective guess about the source of that tragedy is offered here not as a lurid tabloid depiction of one family's long sorrow. Instead, my hope is for an instructive story of how experiences of harm in one generation can be handed down to another, however unintentionally and without malice. It also is an as-yet-unfinished story of how that chain of intergenerational trauma can be broken by a discovered alchemy of love, grace, and hope.

Certainly Anthony's present family and my own were not replicas of each other, but they shared certain features and processes that landed them on the same thorny ground. Growing up in a relentlessly competitive Depression-era family, my mom was raised by two powerfully intellectual and accomplished parents, both summa cum laude 1913 graduates of the University of Wisconsin. Her father held as well a PhD in geology from the University of Chicago. Her mother was one of four sisters and two brothers raised on a small Wisconsin farm, each becoming a Phi Beta Kappa graduate of UW. Like her husband, she was a scholarly force of nature who became a formidable and productive intellect in her own right. So committed had my mom's parents been to a life of shared inquiry and learning that their 1915 summer honeymoon was spent together exploring the Colorado Rockies on foot, accompanied only by a pack mule, so that my geologist grandfather could study, close up, the geophysical origins of those dramatic mountains. They walked that rugged Precambrian landscape for three uninterrupted months, with little more than rock picks, a canvas tent, and two saddlebags full of food and supplies. Though they were likely viewed as goofy, or even pathetic, by their families and friends, such a honeymoon always sounded to me like an epically romantic and auspicious beginning to married life—thus proving consanguinity with my grandparents' oddly cerebral lineage.

Nonetheless, it was an emblematic start for a long, successful partnership and marriage, which eventually produced four daughters and a son—all reared in an atmosphere of unbridled curiosity, unrelenting intellectual ferment, and firm expectations for high educational success. They lived in the sleepy southern town of Ardmore, Oklahoma, an early Santa Fe railroad stop with a population of around ten thousand souls in the early 1900s. As is sometimes true of devotedly academic families, however, my mom also grew up in an emotionally tethered environment. Neither anger nor pleasure, deep sadness nor great joy were often disclosed, let alone examined, celebrated, or explored. She was an artistic child, second in the order of birth, whose neediness for expression of feelings and whim was likely never given the room it required to flourish. Instead, I can only guess that her early emotional life was often mired in a coolly analytic and constraining family culture. Almost certainly, there was no preconceived intention on the part of my grandparents to stifle the expression of strong feelings; it was simply a by-product of who they were, individually and together, in that time and that place.

Such smothering of feelings and emotional expression resulted eventually, as it had in Anthony's dad, in my mom's defensive retreat into an isolated, often chilling affective emptiness. I can remember only one time in my childhood when I saw her come utterly undone. I was perhaps six or seven years old, and we were visiting my grandparents in my mom's Ardmore childhood home. She had brought with her for my grandfather, her dad, a special gift for Father's Day, an expression of her real and heartfelt admiration for him. The gift (I think it was a shirt) was presented, perhaps in hindsight with some faint hesitation, at the conclusion of a long midday family dinner, and he opened and examined it in a stony, perfunctory manner. Seemingly untouched by its significance and meaning, he abruptly stood up from the head of the table and erupted into a loud rage against the frivolity of expending "good money" on such a cultural artifice as "Father's Day." Without question, the value he was expressing—his allegiance to an austere frugality, forged in the exigencies of the Great Depression—was genuine, hard-earned, and well-intended. But he missed entirely the coy, devoted message that the gift had meant to convey. It was stunning for both me and my sister, Mary, to behold such wrath in response to a simple expression of love. And my mom dissolved into tears.

She was capable of deep feelings of all kinds, but she had learned well her family's proscription on the expression, perhaps even the experience, of strong emotion and sentiment. Our mom was also one of four tightly spaced, relentlessly competitive daughters, and she had acquired in her childhood home an enduring and at times moderately venomous suspicion of her own gender. She did have a few close female friends, and even with her sisters there was a playful if latently combative fondness. But her mom, my grandmother, did little, it seemed, to abate her daughters' adversarial leanings, having been herself raised in a pack of fervently competitive sisters. Nor did the presence of my mom's disabled older brother—a true genius who had acquired a severely withered leg in one of the polio epidemics early in the century—do much to quiet the sisterly fray. Thus her default response to new women entering her orbit was a slowly smoldering, narrow-eyed suspicion (perhaps on occasion deserved) of animus and untrustworthiness. My mom loved newborns and babies, who were largely helpless and utterly dependent upon her, but when babies, especially girl babies, grew into children, with wills, desires, and autonomy, the inevitable conflict became emotionally unmanageable. These two primal legacies of her childhood—an incapacity for negotiating the unfamiliar terrain of strong emotion and a reflexive distrust of other females—preordained my mom's inability to mother well and convincingly love a small, sentient, and breakable daughter.

Because of these realities, Mary eventually found herself in a difficult, if not impossible, family setting. It was a problematic and volatile pairing of an injured mother and her orchid daughter, and a kind of twinned contempt rose up between them. The result was a subtle but pernicious opposition that arose early and only grew as Mary morphed into a lovely but threatening adolescent girl. She became a quite beautiful young woman as she turned the corner into puberty at eleven or twelve, and her retreat into anorexia became a desperate preconscious attempt to return to the relative safety of her infancy. She stopped attending school, was recurrently hospitalized, and became dangerously emaciated. As Mary moved steadily toward this even deeper, more skeletal illness and dysfunction, our mom struggled, with little success, to curtail her own insistent demands for Mary to eat. I remember tense, bewildering dinner table interludes in which Mary and my mom would sit in prolonged, steamy showdowns over a plate of uneaten food. Meanwhile, my dad, a warm and much-loved college administrator, descended into a depression from which he never fully recovered, and I made a swift and probably unfortunate (albeit protective) retreat into the alternate realities of high school, sports, and friends.

As my understanding of the perplexities of life has deepened with time and familiarity, I have become ever more aware of the ways in which trauma and care can be passed among generations, as surely and reliably as genes move from parents to children to grandchildren. Maltreated kids grow up and, more often than we might hope or expect, abuse their own children; a grandparent's memories of violence and oppression can reappear in the vulnerabilities of his or her grandchildren; and, as written in the ancient Torah, the iniquities of the fathers are "visited upon the third and fourth generations" yet to come. Indeed, the intergenerational transmission of trauma is becoming a substantial scientific reality within contemporary research. We are now exploring how such transmission happens, at the level of parenting behavior, in the psychobiological processes involved in parent-child interactions, and even in the possibly epigenetic conveyance of generational risk. What is increasingly apparent is that not only risk and harm, but also protection and goodness, are heritable aspects of experience that move with striking regularity from one generation to the next. What we know, even now, has important implications for the care, rearing, and sheltering of both orchid and dandelion children.

I often lament, of course, that the doctors who examined and treated Mary knew so little then about the now emerging science of intergenerational harm. For most of us, there is no avoiding the trauma that torments us or the family inheritances into which we are born. But we are also born with great, often staggering resilience sequestered inside of us—if only we are shown how to unlock it. Even that resilience, it seems, can be passed from generation to generation. But if both trauma and caring, both psychological injury and unrevealed resilience can be passed from generation to generation, how does that passage happen? By what biobehavioral mechanism could my grandparents' emotional fetters be passed on to my mom, and from my mom to my sister? Doesn't such intergenerational transmission fly in the face of what we know is the glacial pace of evolutionary change? How could biological risk move in such short order from the psychological constraints of one generation to the mental disorders of the next? Nearly two and a half centuries ago, an obscure French naturalist was also pondering these very questions.

The Eyes of Bats and the Necks of Giraffes

Jean-Baptiste Lamarck was a late-eighteenth-century French biologist whose work on evolution was one of the seminal precursors to Charles Darwin's evolutionary theory, as presented in Darwin's 1859 work *On the Origin of Species.* Like Darwin, Lamarck had become convinced that life forms were not static, but rather evolved over time, becoming more complex and adaptive over the course of generations. In 1800, he delivered a lecture at the Muséum National d'Histoire Naturelle in Paris, in which he outlined his developing ideas on evolution. He set forth two important principles. The first was that the environment drives physical alterations in animal species by causing changes in behavior, which in turn result in the use or disuse of certain anatomical structures, causing them to enlarge or shrink in both form and function. The second principle was that all such experience-based changes become heritable and can be passed on to succeeding generations. Lamarck thus famously speculated that there may be an inheritance of acquired, generational experiences and characteristics.

Examples he used were the vestigial eyes of bats, which live principally in total darkness, and the long necks of giraffes, which survive by stretching to reach and nibble the ever-higher foliage of tall African trees. Although bats are in fact sighted, their eyes are diminutive and poorly developed, and they navigate and feed using a radarlike echolocation system. Lamarck's inferred belief was that the eye's value had diminished and the radar system's grown with each passing generation's exposure to dark environments. Similarly, the neck-extending experiences of one generation of giraffes, Lamarck believed, were heritably passed on to their progeny, who enjoyed the benefits of progressively lengthening necks. The prolonged stretching of the parent giraffes' necks became anatomically enshrined in their offspring's longer, more practical cervical spines.

Although Lamarck was by no means the first to make such assertions—similar observations and conjectures extended back into the Greek philosophical tradition—his theory became the target of increasingly caustic criticism with the ideological rise of Darwinian evolutionary theory. Charles Darwin, who was born in 1809, the same year that Lamarck published his formative *Philosophie Zoologique,* argued that evolution occurred not by the handing down of acquired generational experience, but rather by the opportunistic retention (i.e., natural selection) of chance variation in anatomical and functional forms. Thus the echolocation feeding system of bats arose at random (by what we now attribute to constantly and naturally occurring genetic mutations) and was preserved in subsequent generations, not by some heritable transfer of experiences within dark environments, but rather by the increased likelihood that individuals with primitive sonar capabilities would thrive, and by thriving, reproduce. In the same way, Darwin held that giraffes do not transmit their serviceably hyperextended necks to their offspring by some magical inheritance of feeding experience. Rather, primordial giraffes had shorter necks, and their offspring who by accidents of morphological variation could reach the topmost leaves disproportionately thrived, reproduced, and passed on their longer-necked, gene-based anatomies to the next generation of giraffes.

In the early twentieth century, Lamarck's theory became—not without some reason—something of a discredited whipping boy in the biological sciences community, with the ascension of Darwinian evolution as a scientific article of faith. Remarkably, however, Lamarck's long-abandoned "magical" ideas have returned, in these fast-paced early years of the twenty-first century, by way of both recent epidemiologic observations and emerging epigenetic science. Such renewal of interest prompted one evolutionary website to produce a lead article with the headline "Lamarck, Wake Up, You're Wanted in the Conference Room!"

One example of the scientific observations that have revived the fortunes of Lamarckian evolutionary theory is the story of the Dutch famine (or "Hunger Winter," as it was locally named) in the most desperately oppressive days of World War II. Following the Allied invasion of continental Europe on D-Day (June 6, 1944), conditions imposed by the occupying German forces grew increasingly harsh. An embattled government of the Netherlands issued a call for a railway strike as an act of resistance to the Nazi occupation, and the Reich retaliated in the winter months of 1944–45 by banning the transport of all coal and food into the country's west. Trains and trucking lines were stopped, deliveries by boat ceased as ports and waterways were destroyed or blockaded, and a famine affecting 4.5 million individuals descended upon the Dutch people. Deaths attributable to malnutrition quickly grew in incidence, with as many as 18,000 to 22,000 fatalities occurring over the course of the five-month siege.

Not unexpectedly, the children of women who were pregnant during the famine were born smaller in birth weight, length, and head circumference than children in utero before or following the German blockade. What was *not* anticipated, however, was the discovery that affected children and *their* children (the grandchildren of the hunger-exposed Dutch parents) later showed unusually high rates of obesity, metabolic disorders such as diabetes, and chronic cardiovascular disease, as well as schizophrenia and other severe neuropsychiatric conditions. Here was a suggestion that somehow the nutritional jeopardy of malnourished Dutch women in 1944–45 had been passed down to two subsequent generations, in the form of disrupted metabolic processes, greater risks for chronic physical diseases, and more frequent, serious psychiatric disorders.

The story of the Dutch famine and its aftermath is also consistent with several other, parallel sets of research findings. First, David Barker's work on the developmental origins of health and disease, mentioned in chapter 9, compared the geographical distribution of infant mortality between 1921 and 1925 in England and Wales with death rates from heart disease in adults five decades later. Based on visible similarities in the mapping of these measures across time (that is, the same areas with high infant mortality in the 1920s developed high heart disease rates in the 1970s), he proposed that fetal undernutrition, resulting in fetal growth retardation and low birth weight, might be implicated decades later in life in the development of coronary heart disease. Barker's work and that of other scientists has strongly suggested that nutritional deficiencies in pregnancy play a role in the "fetal programming" of an offspring's liability to heart disease, stroke, and high blood pressure.

Research on the health liabilities of children born to survivors of the Holocaust similarly gives hints that the psychological and physical traumas of one generation are heritable, by some means, into the next. Thus the children of Holocaust survivors, conceived well after the end of World War II and never exposed, even in utero, to the inhuman, lethal conditions of the German camps, nonetheless bear its traumas. Such individuals clearly show excessive rates of both mental health disorders (anxiety, depression, and post-traumatic stress disorder, or PTSD) and chronic physical conditions (diabetes, elevated blood lipids, and high blood pressure). In a parallel study of more recent and constrained generational trauma (evacuating the World Trade Center buildings following the 9/11 attacks), the one-year-old babies of women who survived the attacks but subsequently developed PTSD showed underactivated cortisol systems, a stress hormone marker of future psychiatric risk. Here again, exposure to a life-threatening, traumatic event seems to have been inherited in some way by fetuses who were in utero at the time of the terrorist strikes. Finally, more recent evidence has begun to emerge, in both humans and experimental animals, showing intergenerational effects on *positive* health—for example, exercise in one generation having protective effects on the metabolic and cardiovascular health of the next, or enriched maternal environments giving rise to positive health benefits among progeny. We seem to have more in common with Lamarck's bats and giraffes than science previously realized.

What remains a mystery of profound and material importance, however, is the question of *how* such "intergenerational inheritance" of harm and protection actually happens. *How* are the horrific, injurious experiences of the fathers (and mothers) "visited upon the children and the children's children"? *How* might the supportive social environments of one generation convey positive health benefits to the next? There are many *modalities of inheritance* from our parents and grandparents. Kids can materially inherit both poverty and wealth from their families of origin. All children bear the genetic endowments of their parents—half of our genomes from our fathers, half from our mothers, a fourth from each of our four grandparents. We look and act, to some degree, like our forebears, because we inherit both their money (or lack thereof) and their DNA. We also inherit, at least for a time, our parents' environments, since we are generally in need of their presence, protection, and provision for our early needs. And we inherit, through modeling, behavioral predispositions that will influence how we parent our own offspring. All such inheritances involve the conveyance of resources from one generation to the next—through genes, the modeling of behavior, environmental signals, and even socioeconomic position. All are forms of information that we pass on to our children, grandchildren, and potentially to the progeny that lie even beyond.

Hidden Inheritance

Notice, however, that none of these mechanisms of inheritance are what Jean-Baptiste Lamarck had in mind. Rather, he proposed an unintentional, biological transmission of acquired, experienced-based information from one generation to the next. The modeling of parenting behavior doesn't count as Lamarckian, for example, because it doesn't employ an environmentally driven change in a physical, anatomic characteristic. Children learn about how to take care of their own children by watching and experiencing how their parents took care of them. They can learn to parent differently than their own parents (say, by reading a book like this one), but it doesn't involve a change in the length of their necks or the acuity of their eyes. Neither does the transfer of genetic (that is, DNA sequence) information meet Lamarckian rules of evidence. Inheritance of DNA is biological and passive, but the actual DNA sequences carried by sperm and egg are unaffected by a father's or mother's lifetime experiences. There is growing evidence, however, that *epigenetic changes*, brought on by a parent's lifetime exposures, might actually be a pathway of intergenerational inheritance—at least in animals, but perhaps also in humans. This is complex, so let's see how Lamarck's two-hundred-year-old work dovetails with today's cutting-edge research on epigenetics.

Recall our earlier discussion of epigenetics from chapters 5 and 6. An individual's lifetime experiences place a latticework of chemical tags or "marks" on that person's genome, as a way of regulating levels of individual gene expression and thus changing important biological functions in response to adaptive demands. Certain experiences can altogether silence a particular gene, while others can boost its expression. Recall (from chapter 5) that this regulation of gene expression is like an audio equalizer that alters the tone and frequency balance of an unchanging tune by modifying the sound that individual piano keys produce. Epigenetic marks, which change the expression of a single protein product from an unchanging DNA sequence, are placed on genes to register and record our past experiences. What scientists are now learning is that these same marks, which control the decoding of our genes (and thus the functioning of our bodies), may sometimes be passed from one generation to another—grandparent to parent to child. Though human evidence for this intergenerational transmission is still scant and observational, there is rather substantial evidence for such epigenetic inheritance in mammalian animals.

Intergenerational transmission of acquired grandparental and parental characteristics can take place in two ways, both of which involve epigenetic processes. First, the parenting behaviors and experiences of mothers and fathers can themselves produce neurobiological changes that shape and guide the behavior and biology of their young. One example of this, discussed in chapter 6, is the work showing how naturally occurring differences in a rat mother's licking and grooming of her pups produce reliable differences in the pups' cortisol system reactivity (i.e., how they respond to stress), in their levels of anxious and depressed behavior, and in the character of their own parenting behavior in adulthood. Another example may be the differences in eating behavior and/or metabolism identified among Dutch children who were in utero during the Hunger Winter of 1944–45. Something about how such children were parented in the aftermath of that event may have changed crucial aspects of their appetitive behavior. Such differences in biology and behavior stem from the *indirect, experiential* transmission of an offspring's exposures to its mother's parenting behavior or environmental stressors early in the pup's or child's life. We are the clay our parents sculpt, who are in turn clay themselves, shaped by life before we entered the world. But this claylike malleability also penetrates into the cellular heart of our genes, which are remarkably open to inheriting surprising sensitivities.

A second means of intergenerational inheritance is the transfer of the parents' epigenetic record of experiences into the "germline" (i.e., the sperm and/or the egg) that gives rise to the fetus. The lifetime experiences of a chicken (unremarkable though they may generally be, at least to us) are built into the egg that one day becomes the chick. This *direct, germline transmission* involves a retention of at least some of the parental epigenetic marks in the process of making sperm or egg. One example of this second form of intergenerational inheritance is a mouse experiment in which animals were trained to experience fear whenever presented with a specific recognizable odor. Using conditioning experiments in which mild foot shock was delivered while in the presence of that odor, young mice learned a heightened, orchid-like sensitivity to the scent, even when it was not accompanied by a shock. This heightened sensitivity was derived from both an increase in the size of the brain areas responsible for smell and by an increase in the expression of an odor receptor molecule produced by a specific mouse gene. Remarkably, even the next two generations of mice were similarly sensitized to the same smell, showed the same fear responses, the same increase in the olfactory region of the brain, and the same activation of the odor receptor gene—despite never having been previously exposed to either the smell or the shock! The researchers were also able to show that epigenetic marks retained in the sperm of the original male mice were responsible for the transmission of sensitization to the subsequent generations. It was as if the sensitivity of a grandchild to loud noises might be traceable to her grandfather's wartime bombardment seventy years before.

Notice that both of these intergenerational inheritance pathways—indirect, experiential transmission and direct, germline transmission—involve processes that are epigenetic in nature. In the rat pups with minimally attendant moms, it was an epigenetic methylation of DNA, triggered by the experience of minimal licking and grooming, that resulted in greater cortisol system reactivity and the increased behavioral signs of anxiety and depression. And in the fear-conditioned mice, it was epigenetic change in the male germline (the fathers' sperm) that resulted in an amplified sensitivity of the second and third generations to the fear-linked smelly signal. Thus epigenetic processes appear to be at least one common denominator within both experience-dependent and germline transfer of parental traits and exposures.

We now know that in the embryonic development of mammals, including humans, these epigenetic marks are almost completely erased at two stages: first, in the production of gametes (the sperm or the egg), and second, after fertilization, when sperm has joined egg and formed a zygote with a full complement of paternal and maternal genetic material. These erasures of epigenetic marks produce a kind of clean slate, the purpose of which may be to disallow the passage of risks and susceptibilities acquired by parents (from, for example, smoking, exposures to air pollution, or severe stress) on to their offspring. In at least some species, it appears that the embryonic erasure of the epigenome can be incomplete and that some remnant epigenetic signatures can indeed be passed from one generation to the next. Such epigenetic inheritance could also presumably serve a complementary evolutionary purpose, by ensuring the transfer of adaptive epigenetic marks to offspring. Though there is not yet clear evidence of epigenetic inheritance in humans, there is also no definitive evidence of its absence.

What is not in question, however, is the reality that both harmful and protective experiences of parents and grandparents can be transferred, in some manner, to their progeny. After enduring two full centuries of moldering ignominy and humiliation, Jean-Baptiste Lamarck and his ideas have been unexpectedly resurrected by the emerging science of epigenetics. And the implications of this science both for the developmental successes and failures of orchid children and for the emergence of the orchid and dandelion phenotypes could not be more profound. Not only are there contrasting implications of such intergenerational inheritance for orchid and dandelion children, but that inheritance could also play a role in the actual developmental formation of these children.

If the experiences of harm and protection in one generation can be passed down to another, which and how many of those experiences are transmitted must powerfully influence the health and development of orchid children. But even the inheritance of so depraved a trauma as the suffering of the Dutch famine did not produce universal jeopardy in the children of survivors. Many of the children most severely affected may have had orchid-like susceptibilities, and those least compromised may have had the constitutions of dandelions. Although parental experiences of nurturance and support in their own childhoods can happily protect even their progeny, experiences of harm and maltreatment may powerfully undermine the orchid children of a new generation. Furthermore, since orchid and dandelion phenotypes are themselves the developmental products of genes and environments—both of which are heritable from an infant's parents—epigenetic processes may also plausibly guide the determination of which type of sensibility, dandelion or orchid, a given child will acquire.

The Means of Grace and the Hope of Glory

What then are we to make of this dramatic new scientific revelation, that not only the genes of our parents and grandparents, but their experiences and life histories as well, may influence who we are and who we become? What do we do with the emerging knowledge that the experiences forming our children's character and guiding their development are not simply those we provide for them now, in the present moment, but those as well that were once provided for us? In the case of the three-generation legacy that culminated in the birth of my sister, Mary, I believe there was simply a perfect, if unintended, storm of multigenerational harm. I suspect that both the genetic material and the experiential trauma that Mary was handed from the generations that preceded her interactively allowed her quite florid orchid sensibilities to unfold and to establish a substantial likelihood that her mental health would be one day compromised.

My sister, my brother, and I all loved our mom and dad. They were among the most generously giving people I have known in my lifetime, and I am convinced that throughout her life as a mother of three and grandmother of five, our mom made the very best effort within her grasp to be the most caring parent she was able to be. The same was certainly true of our dad. But there was an intergenerational inheritance of harm that came unwittingly into play in the unfolding of Mary's life. Though my dandelion brother and I survived that perfect storm of multigenerational injury, for Mary it was too much, for too long.

For the most part, parents love and yearn for the very best of life for their children. This is a platitudinous but demonstrable truth, played out in the meager, modest, or sumptuous homes of families around the world, and also in the lives of those children I have been privileged to meet and work with, week after week, in my aptly named "practice" of developmental pediatrics. There are exceptions, to be sure, when a child is caught in the fierce tempests of a deranged or demonic caregiver, or when malevolence toward a child becomes a starkly instrumental means of retribution within the grown-up world's warring ways. But far and away the abiding reality is that most parents' hearts around the world are filled with all the love, care, and protection for their children that those parents can muster from the circumstances and experiences of their lives. Even my patient Anthony's dad was able, in the end, to find that deep, freeing reservoir of love for his troubled, wayward son, who in turn grew up to become not a tattoo artist or a miscreant but a veterinarian. Imagine that.

What can we do when all we can mobilize is sadly insufficient to the enormous, exacting tasks of parenting? Where do we turn when we are simply unable to protect an orchid teen gone wrong or a dandelion toddler encountering the tortuous and despairing meanness of the world? We all do the best we can, as my own mother did with the too shallow vessel of her own emotional strength, but there are times when even our best falls well short of the need. What then?

I have come to suspect that a belief in some sheltering "higher power" is far more prevalent in our frail, earthly lives than the dictums of an "educated," "enlightened," or intellectually "serious" life might normally abide. Whether in the form of some Great Spirit, a diaphanous, sacred web of human connection, a menagerie of deities, or a personal, creator God, reliance at some level upon a grace and wisdom larger than and beyond our own is the unmentionable shelter to which many of us often turn, and must turn, when the very best parenting we can render to a child is insufficient. Even scientists, professors, and physicians, mired as we are in this era of lofty scientific naturalism, hunger for something our science seems never to satisfy—our longing for a greater, filling presence and a goodness that lies beyond and above the material constraints of finite lives and rocky soil. "Mystery is a great embarrassment to the modern mind," wrote Flannery O'Connor. For me, that sheltering, sometimes (alas) embarrassing mystery took the form of an itinerant first-century Nazarene, that ineffable god-man of the Gospel, the "heart that broke for all the broken-hearted."

It is to this kind of presence, in whatever peculiar form it takes for each of us, that we often turn when what we need most desperately to do becomes that least readily or simply done. Garrison Keillor once quipped that a parent's life is eighteen years of ceaseless prayer. It is an observation that errs only in its promise of an eighteen-year end. Whatever form that hope or heart or highness has taken for you, it is important for you to know of the comfort and steadfast love that millions of weary parents have found in discovering that they are not even close to alone. Even in the most anguished and lonely hours of delivering and raising a child, we are not alone. And even amid the terror of passing on an epigenetic signature of harm to a new and tender generation, there is the hope that we also pass on, by some mystery of grace, an ancestral legacy of kindness, comfort, and resilience.

One evening in Ardmore, later in that same June visit when that same grandfather made my mom cry over her Father's Day gift, he was left as the designated babysitter while all the aunts, uncles, and parents went out to a family dinner in town. My grandfather was left solely in charge of a sleeping litter of a dozen young cousins—all bedded down, tucked in, with lights out. And all were actually asleep—all except me, who was characteristically embroiled in a squall of worry about my parents' safety, out in a strange town, at night, facing who knew what peril.

Though more of a dandelion child than my sleeping sister, I actually lived far closer to the land of orchids than would my brother, Jim, a true and stalwart dandelion yet to come. I worried about why I wasn't asleep, surrounded by this batch of audibly sleeping cousins. So I lay agonizing about when the aunts and uncles would finally come home, about why I worried so much, and even about why I worried at times about worrying. Looking back on it now, it is one last reminder of an essential point: orchids and dandelions aren't a binary division cutting humanity into two categories. The two flowers are powerful metaphors, or a vivid shorthand, for what is actually a spectrum. Just because physiologically I reside more on the dandelion end of the spectrum doesn't mean that I don't possess orchid sensitivities, like my overactive talent for worry. (This sensitivity, like most, can be either a blessing or a curse, depending upon circumstances.) Likewise, my sister had traits associated with dandelions, like her modest resilience. After all, she survived multiple illnesses and hardships over decades, and still found sources of joy. But all of this was far off and unimaginable on that long-ago night, while I lay awake in dark, quiet Ardmore.

Finally, unable to contain any longer my wide-eyed anxieties, I crept from my bed, slowly down the shadowy, creaky stairway, and peeked warily around the corner of the mid-stair landing. There was my grandfather, reading quietly, fully awake, brightly illuminated by the living room lights. Then he suddenly, appallingly, turned his head and looked up directly into my shadowed eyes, and I fled in breathless terror back to my bed and lay, boardlike, awaiting the awful wrath. Moments later, I heard him slowly ascending the staircase, accelerating my heart to the cadence of hummingbird wings. But he came into the darkened room, sat quietly beside me on the bed, spoke a few soft, reassuring words, and rubbed my back until sleep at last overtook me.

The world can be a scary, dark, and lonely place—whether you are young and frightened or aged and tired, whether akin to a sturdy dandelion or to a tender orchid. There are moments and encounters in every life when the dread and terror of the world rise up, and there are places on the map of every life where "Here be dragons" should be prominently scrawled in seventeenth-century calligraphy. There are winged shadows of iniquity and cruelty that we all hand down, generation to broken generation, grandparent to sleepless child. But there are also moments of grace, when unexpected goodness arrives, from some deep, unseen reserve of love, and makes it possible for us to rest and sleep and trust that all will finally be well.

Conclusion

Helping All Children Thrive

In every child who is born, under no matter what circumstances, and of no matter what parents, the potentiality of the human race is born again: and in him, too, once more, and of each of us, our terrific responsibility towards human life; towards the utmost idea of goodness, of the horror of error, and of God.

—James Agee and Walker Evans, *Let Us Now Praise Famous Men*

There are memories that survive the redactions of time by virtue of their radiant, multicolored intensities. There are others that follow us into the fog of life's last decades for reasons impossible to discern—mundane, undistinguished fragments of experience with little to recommend them as "memorable" or worthy of retention, let alone within a mind challenged by ascending age and dwindling acuity. And yet our elegant, finely attuned brains were surely not designed—whether by evolution, the tinkering of a creator God, or both—as repositories for the unremarkable or hard drives for all the errant data ever personally acquired. So our "remembrance of things past"—especially *ordinary* things, from the *distant* past—must cling to some long-hidden wellspring of richer meaning, some deeper, brighter core of treasured substance. For reasons of which I am likely only partially aware, my memories of falling asleep at my grandparents' house are such prized relics—as seemingly stale and commonplace as scraps of time can be, but as vivid and clear as the shape of the moon that rose last night above the ocean's edge, here on an island off the coast of Washington where I write.

My grandparents raised their five children, the second of whom was my mom, in that rambling three-story house with a wraparound front porch, on a hot, flowered, densely green corner in Ardmore. Every summer, my family would make a two-week pilgrimage there by car, through the southwestern deserts and into the stolid, wet heat of the plains in which our grandparents' home was forever nestled. It was a trip replete with adventure and anticipation—of endless podunk motels with names like the Desert Sands Lodge or the Pink Adobe Inn; of miniature swimming pools full of pint-size to jumbo guests, the escapees of sweaty car rides; of the swarms of tarantulas and wild rabbits, dead and alive, that populated and littered those vast cross-country highways we once traveled. There were the departures before dawn, when my sister and I would be bundled into the backseat of an open-windowed 1950 green Plymouth coupe, to finish the night in cocooned oblivion and awake finally to the fierce desert sun climbing hazily above a dusty, distant east, like the reddening heat of an oven set to broil.

However onerous those long, hot days of travel might have been to a school-age boy and his younger sister (and eventually their even younger brother, Jim), the arrival in Ardmore was rapturous. Our grandparents' home was air-conditioned down to a deliciously icy temperature, and the neighborhood that surrounded it was a carnival of shenanigans, unexpected adventures, and forays into unfamiliar worlds. In the simple innocence of Ardmore in the 1950s, a moment in time and space that will never return, Mary and I could walk alone without so much as a thought of endangerment or worry—to the gas station, for grape sodas that cost a nickel, or for a chewy, well-named Sugar Daddy. We could trek to the public library, along streets alive with noisy cicadas and iridescent bugs the size of toy Volkswagens. We'd borrow stacks of books, all that we could carry home, and consume them in long, hypnotic afternoons on our grandparents' porch or in the backyard hammock.

We roamed that big house together, from the dank, musty basement to the sunny, peak-roofed attic, filled with crannied hiding places and wall-to-wall beds for visiting grandchildren. We discovered broken but repairable radios, cast-off Ouija boards, photographs of bearded nineteenth-century ancestors, discarded antique cameras, and ancient stereographs with 3-D pictures of Egyptian pyramids surrounded by exotic, gray-fezed Arabs. We marveled at our grandparents' two-piece old-fashioned telephones, like large black daffodils with a corded side-arm you held up to your ear. It had no dial tone, but rather the voice of a drawling lady somewhere in a windowless Ardmore office with a spinning, squeaky overhead fan. She knew everyone and connected you by hand to the fellow citizen to whom you were wanting to talk—even if he or she were, for the moment, at someone else's house! She knew everyone and where everyone was. We found a seemingly bottomless jar of homemade molasses cookies, which mysteriously refilled each time it was emptied. And we reveled in the wonder and novelty of abiding for a time each summer in this living museum of a house, amid the enchanted, comforting remains of our mother's youth.

But the sweetest of all such summer memories was the simple nightly act of falling asleep beside my sister, in our matching twin beds, the window air conditioner buzzing on against the hot, damp, cricketed nights. The beds were high and immense compared to those in which we slept at home, and we grappled into them, foot over hand, like peril-ous ascents into a lofty, snowy-white summit. There was also a little bev-eled glass window above the closed bedroom door, kept always ajar so we could just detect, over the air conditioner's monotonous drone, the dis-tant downstairs talk and chortling laughter of our parents, grandparents, uncles, and aunts. It was a moment set unexpectedly apart in our young, simple lives. With our heads buried deep in crisp, frosty feather pillows, we lay silently awake for a time in the Oklahoma dark, inventorying the day's events, wondering what odysseys tomorrow might bring, both of us listening to the other's steady, metered breaths. And in those fading moments of each sweltering summer day, there was a timeless quiet in which we knew only what we needed to know: that we were at home in the world, cradled in our grandparents' vast white beds, that another blistering, intrepid day would surely follow, and that we were safe and loved. We simply belonged, in some powerful, unspoken way, to that family and that house.

However prosaic and unexceptional those Ardmore nights were, as I fell into sleep at my orchid sister's side, there was an unforgettable peace that came upon me, and perhaps upon her, against which the sad events that were to follow in my family's life have been forever measured. My sister's deep sensitivity to the hidden and often dark architecture of human feeling was one that, at another time or within another child's family, might have become a treasured asset. It was Mary's aching young tenderness to the world that might have afforded her the responsive intuitions of a beloved teacher, the empathic heart of a talented therapist, or the animate wisdom of a great theologian or pastor. It could have made of her one whose living presence became an unforgettable sign of human charity and singularity. She bore, to be sure, the unmistakable marks of the orchid child—heightened susceptibility to sensory and emotional overload; an awkward, muted shyness in new social settings; and a delicate potential for the best or worst of life attainments. Her great sensitivity was both her rarest gift and her ponderous burden. It was that facet of her humanity that might have opened a door to a life of uncommon brilliance and rich achievement. But it was the very same facet that guided her eventual descent into an anguished territory from which there was, in the end, no return.

Each human life is a pearl of inestimable value. At our core, every one of us born into this bright, troubled world is a being of radiant complexity and unspeakable worth. We are all, as the psalmist had it, "fearfully and wonderfully made." Whether we ascend some vaunted ladder of fortune or abide within a hidden life, whether we achieve great things or small, whether we are clever, average, or dull, whether pleasing to the eye or possessed of a countenance only a mother could love, we are each of us so great a miracle of creation as to make all the vagaries of station, stature, and strength like the window dressings for a masterpiece. And yet...

And yet there are lives, like that of my sister, Mary, that possess within them such enormous, silent possibility for both misery and joy, foundering and flourishing, that there falls perhaps upon all of us a shared obligation to intervene, a collective responsibility to assure protection and safety in the lives of the vulnerable. There is so much at stake in the life of an orchid child that it becomes incumbent upon us all—parents, doctors, teachers, coaches, and friends—to maximize and unmask the great potential that each such child possesses. How do we accomplish this, individually or collectively, in the lives of children, who are our societies' greatest promises? Two final stories illustrate some of the ways in which both orchids and dandelions can blossom and thrive.

Seismology and Sensitivity

At 5:04 in the afternoon on Tuesday, October 17, 1989, I was standing in the UCSF bookstore, perusing shelves for a volume on childhood trauma. Suddenly, the solid, concrete, and presumably immovable floor began to undulate, like ocean swells beneath a boat at sea. Whole rows of books began to fall loudly to the floor, people glanced at each other with wide, fearful eyes, and the lights in the store blinked completely black. An emergency light flashed on. Another patron and I backed reflexively into the frame of a doorway and watched with disbelief as the entire store shook, swayed, and groaned in a kind of awful sinusoidal dance, for perhaps fifteen interminable seconds.

We had all just experienced the first shocks of the Loma Prieta earthquake, a 6.9 Richter scale event centered in the mountains ten miles northeast of Santa Cruz. The quake is remembered as the one that interrupted a 1989 World Series game in Candlestick Park and as the largest disruption of the San Andreas Fault since the catastrophic 1906 quake that decimated and ignited turn-of-the-century San Francisco. As a California native, earthquakes were nothing new to me. I can remember many nights in my childhood home, standing in the doorframe of my bedroom, my sister and parents across the hall in their own, waiting out the shaking as the earth and house beneath us returned to their solid, stable states. Not a big deal. This one, on the other hand, was an experience of an altogether different breed, in both magnitude and result.

I left the bookstore and walked along a still tremulous Parnassus

Avenue sidewalk toward the shuttle van that was scheduled to take me and a dozen other UCSF faculty and staff across the bridge to our East Bay homes. As we sat in the van waiting to leave, however, emergency radio broadcasts began to sketch out revelations of what had in fact just happened. An upper segment of the San Francisco–Oakland Bay Bridge had shaken loose and crashed onto the bridge's lower deck, surely killing people and bringing traffic to a panicked and permanent stop in both directions. Eastbound drivers were abandoning their cars and running full tilt back toward the San Francisco shore. A freeway structure in Oakland had collapsed in a fatal jumble of concrete, steel reinforcement rods, and crushed cars. And broken gas lines had sparked multiple fires in San Francisco's Marina District. Lives had been lost, and a pediatric surgeon was attempting to amputate a child's leg in a desperate effort to free her from the Oakland freeway wreckage. Moment by moment, it was becoming clear that a genuine catastrophe had occurred and that I wouldn't be sleeping at home that night.

I gathered my backpack and jacket and stumbled up the hill to find a pay telephone where I could attempt a call to my wife and kids (1989 was, remember, well before the age of cell phones). After several notifications that "all circuits are busy now . . . ," I was able, with immense relief, to reach Jill, who assured me that she and our children were safe, and that our house, a full twenty-five miles to the east, had shaken mightily in the quake but survived largely intact. I let her know that I wouldn't be getting home.

I next made my way to the Moffitt Hospital emergency room to volunteer for assistance if pediatric casualties were anticipated to be appearing. There were sirens sounding all over the city and, looking north, an ominous cloud of dark smoke had begun to rise. By now the sun was setting over the Pacific, and I could see darkened neighborhoods where power outages had occurred. At mid-evening, I left the hospital and walked many of those dark blocks to a colleague's home, where I found a whole assortment of fellow refugees holed up for the night until they could find a way home the following day. Like a family of Londoners during the 1940–41 Blitz, we sat around a kitchen table in the dark, periodically startled by aftershocks, watching the ominous glow of fires in the distant Marina, and listening to the radio reports of the many casualties and the vast destruction of property all over the Bay Area, from Santa Cruz to Marin County. When all statistics had been summed, the Loma Prieta earthquake was responsible for 63 deaths and 3,757 injuries.

As it happened, the October quake occurred, on another, more personal note, precisely midway through the data collection period in a research project we had launched to study how the stress of starting school affected children's susceptibilities to respiratory illnesses during the fall months of a new school year. At first we grieved that an historic natural calamity had occurred in the midst of a study of children's experiences of psychological adversity. How could we possibly redeem so powerful and horrific an intrusion into an otherwise carefully planned and tightly controlled study? Then, upon further reflection, we realized that many important and descriptive pieces of information had already been ascertained on study children by the time the quake occurred, and we had another full period of data collection that was yet to follow. Quite unexpectedly, the Loma Prieta temblor transformed itself from a study's ruin to an opportunistic natural experiment.

Examining immune system reactivity (i.e., changes in immune cell functions and counts) from just before to just after the children began school in September, we found that those with lymphocytes that were highly responsive to the challenge of starting school had significant increases in respiratory infection rates following the earthquake. We were thus able to show that immune responses to a minor, normal stressor (starting school) were linkable to colds and viral illness rates following a major adverse event (the earthquake). This was one of the first studies to show that children's immune systems were reactive to stressful events and that such reactivity had observable consequences for infectious illnesses, like runny noses, pneumonias, and ear infections.

We also mailed each of the study children a box of crayons and a pad of paper and asked them to "draw the earthquake" and provide a caption. We got back beautiful, big portrayals of the earthquake from almost every child. But the drawings were strikingly variable in content, color, and mood. Many of the children sent back pictures that were bright, cheery, and reassuring—showing homes with minor damage, happy families, and smiling yellow suns. The more orchid-like children, however, depicted scenes of grave destruction, sketched in blacks and grays, and people with clear facial expressions of fear and sadness, some with visible injuries. An example of each is shown in the pictures below.

Any guesses which children were sickest in the post-disaster weeks? Those who presented us with the most dire, distressed illustrations of the earthquake event stayed relatively healthy in the weeks following the earthquake, while the children whose drawings were optimistic and cheery sustained substantially more respiratory infections and illnesses. What could this anomalous observation possibly have meant? I believe it meant that it was healthy and protective for children to create honest, even brutal depictions of a no-doubt-about-it disaster—destruction, fire, fear, injuries, and all. The telling of fearful tales and experiences, whether in language or in art, is a human proclivity with an ancient past. We tell about things that scare us, because it makes them gradually less scary; about sadness, because it makes the sadness diminish a little each time we do. Our long-gone forebears surely sat, themselves, on dark

Two children's depictions of the Loma Prieta earthquake and its aftermath. In the drawing on the left, the colors used were largely black and dark; the parent's transcription of the child's caption read, "It is a broken house with a broken chimney and a huge crack in the earth (the black) and two smaller cracks." The drawing on the right was rendered in pink and shows several smiling people under a table; the caption read, "These are the babies under the dining room table playing tent. Mommy was in the kitchen cleaning up the spilled cheese. . . . The little round things the kids are holding are rice cakes."

winter nights around hearths and fires and told each other of narrow escapes, frightful adversaries, and how they almost didn't make it. And even then, there must have been not just comfort but protection in the telling.

So it is with orchid children. Those of our kids who experience the events of their lives—those both thrilling and frightful—in Technicolor brilliance and brilliant relief have much shelter to derive from the expression of fears and pain. An eight-year-old orchid paints a frighteningly realistic scene of a massive earthquake or a threatening schoolyard bully. A four-year-old tearfully recounts his worry that his mom, running late, might not show up today after preschool. An orchid boy of sixteen years plays a violin sonata with such moving sadness that it brings tears to his listeners' eyes. Although the expression of emotion, in writing, language, or music, is likely therapeutic to us all, small orchids especially can find consolation and healing in the simple expression of difficult or painful feelings to another human being. Telling, in this sense, is protecting, and our orchid children, with their extravagant capacities for emotional receptivity and empathy, are those perhaps most likely to garner that protection from just saying or showing "what happened."

Getting the Lead Out

A four-year-old child we'll call Julio whom I long ago cared for as a pediatrician was brought to my clinic out of concerns for his aggressive and disruptive behavior in preschool. He was described by his teachers as "dangerously impulsive" and was known for pushing, yelling, and hitting anytime he was frustrated by another child or denied something he wanted. These behaviors, initially only sporadic when he started preschool at age three, had become progressively more prevalent and severe, and the staff had begun seriously contemplating his expulsion. His single mom, who managed to eke out a living for her two young children on the wages of a part-time job, lived in low-income housing in an old, dilapidated apartment complex amid one of San Francisco's most blighted neighborhoods. She had herself witnessed Julio's aggressive behavior with other children, sometimes toward even his younger, two-year-old sister.

Initial routine laboratory tests revealed that Julio was anemic, and his behavior in the clinic exam room suggested an unusual level of hyperactivity for a four-year-old child. A screening developmental assessment indicated that the boy was lagging behind in acquisition of cognitive and social skills, like sustained attention and a capacity for cooperative play with peers. Upon questioning, his mom noted that their apartment building stood immediately adjacent to an old, abandoned gasoline station that had gone unreclaimed and undeveloped for many years.

With this constellation of physical and historical findings, I ordered a blood lead test on Julio, which returned with a value of 28 micrograms per deciliter, a level nearly three times that designated as "acceptable" by the Centers for Disease Control and Prevention. With the assistance of a pediatric toxicologist, Julio was treated using chelation therapy, in which a medicine given by mouth over several days effectively removed the excess lead from his body. Though no immediate change in his disruptive behavior ensued, several years later, when I was last in contact with his family, he was learning in school, and his behavior had become sufficiently controlled to avert any subsequent threats of expulsion.

Long before the 2014 sad events in Flint, Michigan, refocused national attention on lead exposure as a cause of mental disability among children, we knew that reducing the harmful effects of lead on brain development and mental disability was an essential public health mandate. Lead toxicity can cause declines in children's IQs, impair their ability to pay attention in school, and produce an impulsivity that places them at risk for injury, drug abuse, and inappropriate behavior. The children of Flint became exposed through an unfortunate, possibly criminal decision to switch the city water supply, resulting in more lead leaching from pipes into homes. But children, especially those living in disadvantaged circumstances, can be exposed to lead through a variety of pathways, including eating chips of old, lead-based paint, breathing fumes from lead-based gasoline, living next to abandoned battery factories, or getting lead-tainted household dust in their mouths or on their hands.

We have known for a long time about the insidious health effects of lead. Ancient Greeks knew of the metal's deadly consequences but still built tanks, plumbing, and kitchenware containing it. Benjamin Franklin cautioned against the "mischievous effect from lead" among printers who were routinely exposed to it. And contemporary U.S. society regulates lead exposure. From the 1960s to 1991, the federally defined toxic blood lead level in children decreased from 60 micrograms per deciliter to the current value of less than 10 micrograms per deciliter—a dramatic reduction in the threshold for clinical action. This resulted in the identification and treatment of tens of thousands of U.S. children with damaging exposures to lead.

What drove that policy change was in part the recognition that some children carry a gene variant that alters the production of heme, an essential component of blood hemoglobin. Being a carrier of that variant is linked to higher blood lead concentrations for a given level of lead exposure. These children, who can make up as much as 20 percent of the population, have a special, heightened sensitivity to the toxic effects of lead and thus incur higher levels of neurological damage from exposures. Thus recognition and protection of the society's most lead-sensitive children resulted, in effect, in a greater protection against lead for *all of our children*.

Protection from Trauma

It would not be illogical to argue that, just as we have done for lead, we should put in place another set of universal protections for the orchid children of our communities. These are the children who, we now know, have inordinate susceptibilities not to lead, but to the health effects of family stressors and economic adversities, of harsh parenting, of impoverished neighborhoods and exposures to violence, and of maltreatment, neglect, and abuse. Diminishing the exposures of these children with special sensitivities to *social* environmental "toxins" might not only protect them from the pernicious effects of unsupportive or abusive childrearing settings, but could also make our societies safer, better, and healthier for all children. Even more compelling, we now understand that this same subgroup of orchid kids, most sensitive to the developmental and health effects of poverty, violence, and despair, are the same group that is most likely to dramatically benefit from exposures to supportive, nurturant, and encouraging social contexts. Given what we now know of these great reversals of fortune among highly sensitive children, should we not ask whether the world and our nation can afford *not* to provide a new level of safety and protection to orchid children?

What then could we actually do, collectively as parents and siblings, teachers and clinicians, scientists and makers of social policy? How might we best respond, as families and societies, to the recognition of individuals (especially children) who are exceptionally responsive to both the virulence of our society's worst social conditions and the health- and life-giving effects of its best? Might we take even more seriously our obligation to support and sustain young families, especially those in great need? Though often mired in the political realities of our day and time, the policies we could choose to enact have known beneficial effects on the economic well-being of young families, the chances that a marriage will survive, and the establishment of close parent-child bonds, right from the beginning of life. Such policies might include, for example, paid parental leave, universal health care for children, support for preschool education, ensuring a minimal level of income for young families, and bolstering support for schools.

Might we also train parents, teachers, and physicians in how to better create caring, supportive environments for children's learning, growing, and health? We could provide a basic level of training to all new parents, to ensure that they know what to expect, how to cope, and where to get help. We could require a basic level of graduate education for teachers in preschool settings and instruct primary and secondary school teachers in the basics of fostering socioemotional development, not just teaching cognitive skills. We could even take the audacious step of training the doctors who care for our children in trauma-informed clinical medicine and the basic sciences of child development.

Could we not shift our national resources toward a richer scientific understanding of early life, of exposures to adversity and their consequences? We could direct a far greater portion of our collective research dollars toward new knowledge of how early life shapes health, well-being, and productivity across the life span. We could even create powerful multidisciplinary alliances focused on human development. We may one day reach a level of knowledge where the mechanisms of individual susceptibility could guide us toward social and biological interventions at a whole variety of levels, from school-based programs to protective diets and healing medicines. But maybe it is a sufficient and worthy beginning, for now, to simply recognize and acknowledge the extraordinary and consequential sensitivities of a small subset of our children and citizens. That subset is small in proportion but vast in absolute numbers, and there is reason to believe that changing those lives for the better, especially in early life, could reap disproportionately magnificent societal and economic rewards.

The Fundamental Errors

We thus arrive, here in these final pages, at the most basic and core message this book has aspired to convey. The way the scientific community has collectively thought about the variation in children's susceptibility to trauma and adversity has contained within it two fundamental and profound mistakes. One is a category error, and the other an error of proportions.

The *first fundamental error* is the following. Recognizing inconstancies in the health and developmental effects of early childhood adversity, we have assumed that the most informative account lay in the distinction between those children who are *vulnerable* to such adversity and those who are *resilient*. We know that some children seem able to thrive and flourish despite otherwise harmful exposures to early stressors—an observation on which everyone agrees. But we then leap to the assumption that while most children are vulnerable to the effects of adversity, there are some—special, "resilient" children—whose vulnerability is blunted or missing, rendering them immune or invincible to the troubling consequences of trauma and stress.

Several faulty inferences come from this assumption. We imagine, for example, that this special group of resilient children is somehow preternaturally strong and unbreakable—able to withstand almost any assault, any blow that their lives can deliver. But it is demonstrably the case that *there are no unbreakable children;* rather, any child can be harmed and undone if the stressors are sufficiently pervasive, pernicious, and severe. We need only think of Jewish children during the Holocaust of World War II, where virtually no child survived unsullied by the brutality of the Third Reich, the perils of the camps, and the horrific losses of loved family and dear friends. There were undoubtedly differences in the harm done to those millions of Jewish and Romani children sent to the camps, but no child escaped unscathed by the inhumanity and murder to which they were subjected. We can even think, too, of Robert Coles's remarkable story of Ruby Bridges, the six-year-old black girl who participated with courage and dignity in the integration of the New Orleans school district in 1960. Ruby disclosed to Coles that she quietly prayed for the racist crowds as they taunted and abused her each day while she entered school. She was surely as resilient as any child we might ever find, but her experiences were almost certainly not without impact or effect on her psyche and spirit. What Ruby Bridges ultimately made with the effects of that childhood trauma, however, was an adult lifetime of devoted and honored service on behalf of U.S. civil rights, the promotion of tolerance, and the valuing of differences.

What we can sometimes mistakenly infer from the stories of Holocaust survivors, Ruby Bridges, and others like them is that the solution for children growing up in poverty, abuse, and adversity is to make them all like Ruby or Anne Frank—find out what made them so strong and infuse *that* into vulnerable children, rendering them resilient as well. It so easily becomes a conclusion that there is something wrong with or missing from the vulnerable child himself or herself. We are prone to make those who failed to survive responsible for their own defeat, rather than condemning the often horrific circumstances that they have faced. No child is unbreakable, and given conditions sufficiently hopeless and cruel, virtually all children will falter and fall.

Yet another mistake provoked by the assumption that differences in childhood adversity effects are attributable to vulnerable and resilient children is the misimpression that the "vulnerable" are susceptible only to negative environments and are indifferent to positive conditions. But what our research has shown repeatedly is that *sensitive, susceptible children have more powerful, influential responses to both negative, stressful circumstances and to positive, caring, and supportive conditions.* The good news of this work is that the very orchid children most likely to suffer and wilt when subjected to bad environments are the same children most likely to flourish, succeed, and prosper in settings of nurturance and care. This is indeed magnificent news for those children, their parents, their teachers, and their friends! The kids about whom we worry most—as parents, teachers, and friends—are the most responsive to and have the most to gain from social conditions that support and encourage them. Many of my own patients, who are among the most orchidly of our orchids, are the best of my examples; many have grown up to become young women and men of extraordinary generosity and accomplishment. They have become magnificent moms and dads; physicians and nurses who care daily for sick and traumatized children on the wards of local hospitals; gifted teachers who, year by year, dramatically affect the lives of the children they teach; and friends and neighbors who have become the consciences and souls of their communities. They are living attestations that highly sensitive, orchid children often become remarkable adults. Such children are indeed most likely to stumble from misfortune, but they are also most likely to prosper from the world's kindness and goodwill.

Most elementally, the vulnerability/resilience assumption commits what philosopher Gilbert Ryle called a *category error*—the logical fallacy of thinking something is one kind of thing, when it is really another. It is like inferring that body and mind must be two different kinds of realities: one existing in three-dimensional space and subject to physical/mechanical laws (i.e., physical, neurological processes) and the other not spatially located and unfettered by such laws (i.e., products of mind, like rationality and thought). In considering the problem of health effects that follow early childhood trauma, we mistakenly presume that those children who suffer most under conditions of trauma are members of the category "vulnerable," while those who survive unscathed are of the category "resilient." Our research of the past thirty years instead suggests that the more apt and cogent contrast is between children of *exceptional and typical sensitivity to the nature of their social worlds*. Children who do poorly under conditions of early adversity are not simply vulnerable—they are instead, like orchids, keenly more sensitive and susceptible to the influences of both noxious and nurturant environments. That is a conceptual difference of crucial importance. What it means is that highly sensitive, orchid children, when protected from aversive contexts and placed in supportive, loving milieus, do not simply achieve normative health and well-being, as the "vulnerable" ones might if removed from the adversity. Rather, they become exceptional in their positive health, their robust development, and their sometimes superlative achievements.

The *second fundamental error* we have typically made is the assumption that so-called resilient children are rare, isolated occurrences within a sea of childhood vulnerability. This is a mistake in proportionality, in how we think about the number and proportion of those deemed resilient. Pondering those truly remarkable children like Ruby Bridges, we easily imagine that resistance to adversity and the capacity to survive are rare commodities within populations of children. We assume that these scarce specimens of "resilience"—exceptions to the rules of adversity-related risk and morbidity—hold a mysterious key to survival, an antidote to the poison of trauma. Our research, on the other hand, suggests that just the opposite is true: that most children have a substantial reservoir of resilience and hardiness, a relative resistance to the extremes of the social world, which allows them to survive and advance under all but the most pernicious of social conditions.

Recall that around 80 percent of the young kids we tested in our laboratory over the years showed few or no biological compromises during their encounters with moderately stressful challenges and events. The vast majority of children were relatively insensitive to, and only modestly perturbed by, the artificial adversities to which we exposed them. The same appears to be true in the real world: most children, when confronted with modest, relatively normative stressors that occur in real social environments, manage to weather the storms of life with an easy composure. All but the most sensitive children will accommodate, over time, to trials of family moves, parental arguments, intimidations at school, or the death of a pet. Resilience is common, not rare.

That said, however, it is also true that in many areas of the world, including North America, way too many children are subjected to adversities that lie well beyond the "normative stressors" with which the children in our studies mostly contended. Millions of young children around the globe face powerful, pervasive harm, in the forms of poverty, war, family dissolution, subordination and bullying, exposure to violence in both homes and communities, parental mental illness or addiction, and physical, psychological, or sexual maltreatment. These are all, in specific areas of the world, highly prevalent adversities by which even biologically protected, dandelion children are injured and undermined.

So the good news is that *vulnerability is really sensitivity,* which carries with it a capacity for a remarkable reversal of fortune within positive, supportive environments. Because of this, our tender orchid children, who often struggle and stumble, can triumph and thrive in ways we can scarcely imagine; and resilient children are common, not rare, and cope adeptly with the mundane, typical stressors that life sometimes brings. The bad news is that orchid children can be undone by their exposures to atypical, non-normative adversity and that such adversity is far too endemic in the world.

My Sister, My Self

It is one thing to surmise the implicit broad social consequences of recognizing and responding to the differential sensitivities of dandelions and orchids, their disparate susceptibilities to the character and supportiveness of the social world. But it is another thing altogether to contemplate the intimate, all too personal implications of this novel and convicting perspective. What began for me as an enthralling scientific journey—a captivating intellectual puzzle—came round in the end to where it probably began: within the intricate and confounding complexities of my own early life, within the family into whose arms I was once delivered. It has been said that every photograph is a self-portrait.

Every puzzle we choose to solve, every career we decide to follow, comes finally down to who we are and where we began.

My sister Mary's life was not by any means devoid of joy or meaning. Even in the midst of paranoid and delusional thinking, she was a caring mom to her beloved only child. She made a fine and beautiful home, full of small treasures. She went to movies and read books. She delighted in the poetry of Seamus Heaney and the novels of William Faulkner. She had good and steadfast friends, some for more than forty years, and was friendly with her neighbors. Though her relationship with food was sometimes prickly and mercurial, she loved a good meal, served in a fine restaurant.

But she had within her a beautiful and dreadful frailty that we scarcely knew. Where I was troubled and dismayed by my parents' combat, she was immobilized—frozen and folded into a small girl's dystonic fear. Where I returned to sleep after discovering sadly my father's dreadful tears, long past midnight, she must have lain awake for hours, battling demons that would one day infest her mind and heart. Where I was sometimes distressed by the pubertal complexities of life in a middle school, she was undone by the rancorous, coercive exchanges that so regularly filled those mean, grassy schoolyards. Where I found solace in the arms of a blue-eyed girl, she found, in the embrace of those who held her, only abandonment and grief.

Mary's adult life was neither barren nor joyless, but eventually she must have tired of the battle she regularly joined, with the voices that haunted her and the emotions that so often enveloped her like storm-driven Pacific waves. She fought for her disabled daughter's schooling and moved a thousand miles to the best public special education program she could find. She wrote long, elegant letters in an era of 140-character vacuities and championed the dignity and rights of those without homes or loved ones. She subjected herself to one mind-blurring medication after another, for years, before concluding that none would ever remove her most basic and damaging affliction. By the end, she had emptied herself of all hope and aspiration, and just before her fifty-third birthday, she swallowed an overdose of those pills and died of respiratory failure a few weeks later.

Which ones of us are responsible for the care and protection of those in our midst who are most vulnerable? Was I, in some failed dereliction of brotherly duty, my sister's keeper? Did I give up too soon? Could I, as the elder of the two brothers she eventually lost, have somehow softened the blows that the world delivered and saved her from the fate that overcame her? Might a different family or a different brother have worked the magic that can change a pallid, wilting orchid into a flowering vision of beauty? Do those of us with mostly dandelions flowing in our blood bear some deep responsibility to the orchids at whose sides we grow and sleep and live? As an orchid child, Mary in her life and mind bore a brilliance and possibility that my own mind could only imagine, but to which my work and research eventually pointed. She might have led a charmed and celebrated life, replete with great goals and greater deeds. She might have been an orchid who blossomed into a flower of exceptional and rare attainment.

At the broader, more global level of the world's moral responsibilities and duties toward the children who are the orchids of all humankind, the very survival of our species depends, at least in part, upon how we choose to acknowledge and protect those who are most vulnerable and susceptible within our world. It is the infants, toddlers, schoolchildren, and teens who are the keepers of our collective future. They are the promise of generations yet to come, the innocents into whose hands we are poised to deliver a tattered and sorry but also magnificent world. May heaven help us if we fail to provide the redemptive care and steadfast love that renders the weakest strong, the most fragile hearty, the least the best. And may heaven reward us if we manage so to do.

This book and journey now end as they began: with that hope of redemption. To one degree or another, we are all one of those that our research revealed—orchids or dandelions, the sentient or the unaware, people who differ, sometimes sharply, in their sensitivities and tendernesses to the world. Might the hidden beauty lying unseen in the scientific recognition of orchid children be a revelation that there is no human frailty beyond such redemption? That even the most inimical of human traits and shortfalls is redeemable and perhaps even protective within the right settings and conditions of life? Might it further be, as our research is now asking, that such redemption lies in particular profiles of epigenetic, molecular marks that lie upon our genomes, marks that are the physical traces—the embodied vestiges—of the interactions between our natures and our nurture, between genomes and "parent-omes," between our inner constitutions and our outer worlds? And finally, might such an excruciating and beautiful truth offer at least a partial, provisional account of how two red-haired children—reared in the same family, exposed to the same earnest, caring, but baffled parenting, and surely as genetically matched as siblings are allowed to be— diverged so tragically and unjustly: one to a life of almost embarrassing opportunity and abundance; the other to a troubled lifetime of disorder, devolution, and descent? And might one have discovered in such a story not only the sadness that was surely there, but something at once true, beautiful, and possibly hopeful?

Coda

An Eden Rendered Whole, the Orchid and the Dandelion

How do you accomplish,
Said the orchid to the dandelion,
This extravagant survival,
This penchant to prevail?
Abiding as ably in the cracks of roads
As in the fertile fields.
Blooming with quiet glory
Amid both stone and ground,
Who gave the dandy lion a name
And good fortune without bound?
You, unperturbed by frosty cold and desiccating drought,
Ne'er distressed by snow nor sleet;
Unbowed by scythes or heat.
The hurried, harsh winds of storm or child's breath
Serve only to launch and spread
Your gossamer white globe
Of seed and wing and thread.
You come undone in a mist of spores,
Live on in scores of births,
Disperse yourself in splendid soaring
To the shores of a yellowed earth.

I can do no other,
Said the dandelion in return,
For I am built of sturdy stuff,
Unmoved by fire and burn.
A fortress against tempests,
A shield against life's swords,
I weather on as I was made,
Unbound by kismet's cords.
But how do you, fair orchid, bear this life so raw,
Its festive griefs and awful joys
And your being's gifted flaw?
How do you move a gardener's care
From nurture to bright beauty,
Change rank ground to exquisite flower
And make loveliness your duty?
You are wondrous tender
As I must hardy dwell,
As prone are you to injure
As I to live on well.
Lament for me, dear orchid,
Cocooned in stolid stillness,
Unmoved by dread and bliss,
Scant touched by life's great poles
Of summit and abyss.

You are each as loved and crucial,
Said the sun that both require,
As air and land, as light and shade,
as the aged and the youthful.
Each for the other given,
As "either" and as "or."
Each the other's counterpart,
With its opposite made more.
A fimbriated floral treasure
And a sublimely stalwart soul,

You together shape a garden,
An Eden rendered whole.
Take the other's hand,
Said the earth on which both rest,
And sanctify the distant goodness
With which you both are blessed.

W. Thomas Boyce
Berkeley, California
2017

Postscript

What They Asked

In the time since the publication of *The Orchid and the Dandelion* in January 2019, I have traveled thousands of miles; made scores of book presentations, readings, and lectures; and done a dozen or more radio interviews and podcasts across the height and breadth of North America and beyond. Audiences have ranged from novice parents to aging grandparents, schoolteachers to psychologists, physicians to physicists, dandelions to orchids—all enthralled, to one degree or another, by the sensible, and apparently compelling, metaphor describing human differences in our sensitivities to the social and physical world. Listeners and readers in remarkably diverse groups both small and large came with a single commonality: they all had intriguing, insightful questions about the origins, consequences, and approaches to those sensitivities—their children's, their students', their own. I have been pleased and encouraged by my readers' (and listeners') serious engagement with the science and stories of orchid and dandelion lives. I have been sometimes flummoxed by the subtleties and complexities of their questions—questions that the book either overlooked, failed to answer, or answered only in part. Here is a sampling of those questions, along with my best attempt at answers:

Is there a shorthand way for parents (or teachers) to remind themselves what their orchid children need most?

The book's chapter 8 captures, in narrative form, a set of six parenting strategies that my colleagues and I have noted, in clinical settings, to foster and sustain the healthy development of families' most sensitive, orchid-like children. Those six strategies conveniently form the mnemonic O-R-C-H-I-D, which can bring to mind the following:

O: One's own true self. In Alice Miller's book *The Drama of the Gifted Child*, she notes that a commonality among many of her adult patients with serious mental health disorders was a childhood that disallowed, in some manner, the identification and flourishing of the individual's *own true self*—that essential core that makes each of us who we are, that drives our values, passions, and worldviews. Miller's insight was that the sensitive, "gifted" child, in his or her efforts to fulfill the parents' hopes and desires, loses a full sense of self and moves into adulthood defined by others' needs and with a trailing emotional emptiness. Children need to discover who they are and what they can become.

R: Routines and predictability. Family routines—eating dinner together, bedtime rituals, designated homework time, game or movie night, or weekly religious services—are protective and beneficial for all children but especially for children with orchid sensibilities. There is now a half century's worth of research supporting the efficacy of family routines in reducing household chaos, upholding children's sense of stability and support, decreasing common illnesses and infections, and fostering good mental health. Such routines and rituals seem likely to benefit all children and perhaps their parents and caregivers as well, but the sense of permanence and reliability that routines impart appears especially good for orchid children, with their vigilant sensitivities to life's structure and dependability. Back in the 1980s we studied a group of pregnant adolescent girls and found that these young moms' sense of permanence, predictability, and continuity was significantly predictive of both maternal and newborn outcomes of pregnancy. Routines and rituals, far from rendering life boring or monotonous, seem to have tangibly protective effects on the young people and families who pursue them.

C: *Caritas*, **the Latin word for compassion or steadfast love.** All children deeply need their parents' love and affection. Indeed, they depend upon that love from their grandparents, caregivers, communities, and siblings as well. But orchid children are especially in need of their caregivers' constant, reliable presence and love. Sometimes that love is revealed with hugs and words. Other times, it is a provision for needs—for a good and healthy meal, an attention to toothbrushing, or a constant and predictable bedtime. Still other times, a parent's love is best demonstrated by the containment and censure of a child's behavior. A caring parent might well say, "I love you too much to let you act any way you want." Whether in the recognizable forms of reassuring words, physical affection, or dependable discipline, that steadfast love is what all orchid children crave and need.

H: **Human differences.** Some families find it convenient or simpler to blur and obscure the usually obvious differences between their children. One-size-fits-all parenting is certainly easier, and it conforms to the cultural value of "treating all of our kids the same." But such parenting risks overlooking and ignoring important individual differences in children's needs and abilities. As *The Orchid and the Dandelion* argues in its core message, kids—even those from a single sibship, conceived and born of the same parents—are strikingly different in their temperaments, their cognitive and behavioral capacities, their sensitivities to the environment, and their parenting and caregiving needs. As chapter 6 points out, no two children are actually raised in "the same family," anyway. Differences in birth order, gender, personality, and other factors render an individual child's experience of the family different, to say nothing of the events, illnesses, and changes of circumstance that alter parenting over the course of individual childhoods. So all of these factors conspire to make the *experienced* family different for each child. And kids do best, especially orchid kids, in families where the differences between children are celebrated, not hidden; recognized, not masked.

I: **Imaginative play.** Many parents, never having been told anything different, regard their children's play as trivial, childish, or unimportant. It is in fact *anything but* unimportant. The play that children pursue, whether alone, with other children, or with adult caregivers, has a crucial role in their development and well-being. It is in the midst of play that children learn who they are as individuals, acquire the social skills needed to navigate complex peer groups, and encounter the need to compromise with friends' demands and wills. It is during fantasy that they ignite their own creativity and discover the joy of collaborative imagination. Play is also one of the ways by which children recover and heal from traumas and difficulties. It is thus no coincidence that therapists for children use play and fantasy as one important modality for building a child's ability to endure and overcome adversity and stress. Parents who encourage their children's play, allow time for play to take place, and protect it from the distractions of screens and digital media are actively promoting healthy development and a child's engagement with social relationships.

This protection of time for play seems especially important, living as we do in a time of cultural bias, especially in middle-class families, toward the arrangement of frenetic, nonstop activity to fill a child's day. I have often encountered, in my clinic, well-to-do children whose every extracurricular moment is scheduled with language lessons, soccer practice, swim lessons, and computer courses. One child I remember had a personal taxi driver who was contracted by the parents to move the child from activity to activity every day after school. But while parental arrangement of such breathless scheduling is no doubt well intended, children need free time as much as, if not more than, any of us. Such time allows for not only the essential experiences of imaginative play but also for reflection, reading, catch-up sleep, creative activities, and time with friends. The movement toward so-called "free-range parenting," where children's unsupervised time is protected, is one sign of parents' intuitive return to the value of unstructured, unmanaged time for their kids.

D: Danger. One of the most challenging and potentially consequential decisions that the parent of an orchid child must recurrently face is when responding to the child's expression of fear or perceived endangerment in the face of a novel or challenging situation. An example that I often use is the setting in which an orchid child is invited to a birthday party at which he or she will know the birthday kid but few other invitees. A parent in this situation must choose between two dichotomous positions: either honor the child's concern and fearfulness, allowing the party to be skipped; or nudge the child forward into an uncomfortable but ultimately adaptive lesson in courage.

When and how did you realize that your research was concentric with a major misfortune in your biological family's life?

I am a sailor. And when I'm out on the blue-green waters of San Francisco Bay or Puget Sound, I am keenly attuned to the surface conditions that govern the course and speed of my boat: the wind direction and velocity, the intensity of the surface chop, the timing of tides that flow in and out of those bodies of water. But there are also deeper, more powerful currents that flow around and through the earth's oceans, and the great French theologian and sociologist Jacques Ellul said that there are the equivalents of these deep, oceanic currents at work within individual human lives. The trajectories of our lives are affected, of course, by the day-to-day, month-to-month experiences that we have in normal, daily existence, but they are also moved by much deeper, less visible "currents" that guide the overall direction and course of our lives.

One such oceanic current in my own life has been my work, for over forty years, as a pediatrician-scientist with a great interest in how stress and adversity affect the health and developmental biology of children. It began when I was a young resident physician, noticing how some children had far more than their "fair share" of health problems. As I came to know those children's families better, I realized how frequent and intense their experiences of adversity, stress, psychological pain, financial insecurity, racism, and subordination had been. The sickest of the kids I cared for were those with families most full of misfortune and trauma. So I came to believe that a compelling research question would be to ask: Why are children from challenging, stressful environments showing more biomedical illnesses (e.g., respiratory infections), psychological and behavioral disorders (e.g., depression and anxiety), and chronic diseases (e.g., asthma)? That original, beginning question became a kind of North Star for me, orienting and motivating what became a lifetime of research.

But there was another even more personal and powerful oceanic current in my life, one that had its origins at an even earlier age. This deeper, more primordial force is captured by the snapshot on the facing page, showing two young children at a California beach—me at about age seven on the right and my sister, Mary, age five. In the first ten or so years of our lives together, Mary and I were truly the best of friends, each the other's favorite go-to playmate, alike in temperament, curiosity, and imagination. But as that first decade ended and we moved heedlessly into puberty and adolescence, Mary's and my life took a profound departure. Mine became a life of what I characterize in the book as one of almost embarrassing good fortune: a gratifying and productive professional career; a stable, forty-five-year marriage; two thriving adult children and 4.75 (as of this writing) spectacular grandsons. Mary's life, on the other hand, became one of disappointment and affliction. She developed a chronic biomedical disorder at age eleven, followed by the appearance of increasingly troubled and troubling psychiatric symptoms and a diagnosis of schizophrenia by age twenty. As a graduate student at Harvard, she sustained an accidental pregnancy and later delivered a birth-asphyxiated, ultimately disabled child. Following years of multiple psychiatric hospitalizations, she took her own life at age fifty-three with an overdose of pills.

The truth is that I failed to see the seemingly obvious connection between these two deeply powerful currents in my life—a research career focused on childhood adversity and a sensitive, orchid-like sister with a profound psychological disturbance—until perhaps a dozen years ago. A good psychoanalyst would no doubt have a field day with my long psychological blindness to this connection. But connected they indeed were. My pediatric fascination with the adversities that some children sustain; my experience of the important, troubling conflicts in my biological family's early life; and my sister's psychological undoing were all entwined by a common reality of a young girl's trauma and her special sensitivity to anguish and fear.

You said that orchid children often have special sensory sensitivities. Isn't that true of autistic kids, as well, and if so, is an orchid child on the autism spectrum?

It is true, but typical orchid children do not have autism spectrum disorder (ASD). Children on the autism spectrum frequently have exaggerated aversions to tactile, auditory, taste, or visual stimuli. But it's important to understand that the orchid/dandelion phenotypes discussed in the book are not, as ASD is, a psychiatric disorder described in the *Diagnostic and Statistical Manual of Mental Disorders* (*DSM-5*).

There are many features of a child's temperament or behavior that resemble diagnoses found in DSM-5 but are not disorders. A predisposition to melancholy, for example, may be a component of major depressive disorder, but it can also be present in a person who is not clinically depressed. Fastidious attention to detail is a characteristic of many people, without rising to the level found in obsessive-compulsive disorder. Even within *DSM-5* there are areas of symptomatic overlap, where the same feature can be found in two different (or multiple) psychopathological conditions. So it is not particularly surprising that an orchid child's special sensitivity to loud noise can be a shared feature of a child with ASD. In fact, there are multiple aspects of ASD (e.g., preferring to play alone, difficulty talking about feelings, or speech delays) that can be shared with typically developing children.

What do you tell an orchid child about his or her own sensitivity and reactivity?

This is an important question, especially given an orchid child's heightened sensitivity to social differences and judgments. Most orchid children, by the time they start school, are at least partially aware that they are somehow different from other children, even from their siblings. Parents often wonder how much these differences should be revealed to or discussed with their child. Orchid children may be aware, for example, that their feelings and sensitivities are more intense than those of other children. They may recognize that sources of their own discomfort (e.g., socks wrinkled inside shoes or being excluded from other children's play) may generate emotions more negative and urgent than those of other children. Or such children may feel less courageous than other children when facing novel or somehow threatening situations.

Under such circumstances, I think a parent's best strategy is to restrict their observations and shared thoughts to those that are responsive to the orchid child's own specific questions. This is a good approach to many parenting dilemmas over children's questions: answer only those that are asked, and answer when they arise. There is no need to sit a six-year-old orchid preemptively down and explain how he or she is different from other kids: more sensitive, more fragile, more tender. On the other hand, if the child expresses dismay at their relative oversensitivity to what another child thinks about her or how another child responds, judges, or treats her (e.g., "Why doesn't Gabby like me anymore?" or "How come Sam is more brave than I am?"), then having an age-appropriate talk about those questions or observations is a generally helpful and supportive thing to do. Such a conversation might be framed, for example, as a discussion of strengths and weaknesses:

> You know how all kids, and even adults, have some things about them that are strengths and other things that seem like weaknesses? Like your brother, Jamal: He is a really good artist, but he doesn't sing very well, does he? He can run fast, but he's still learning how to throw a ball. Well, you're like that, too. You have a wonderfully creative imagination; that means you can dream up great games and amazing stories. But you're also really sensitive when your feelings or another child's feelings are hurt. That makes you sometimes easily hurt, but it also makes you a good friend and a good big brother. So your tender feelings aren't just a strength or just a weakness: they're both!

One nicely presented aid to such a talk with a young child is a book by Canadian children's author Jean Little entitled *Jess Was the Brave One*. It tells the story of two sisters, Claire and Jess. Jess is always the brave one, climbing trees, never crying at the doctor's office, undaunted by thunderstorms. But Claire surprises herself one day: when Jess's teddy bear has been taken by some older boys, she comes to the rescue and recovers Jess's bear with a cunning story. It's a nice illustration of differences between children and how they express themselves.

My orchid child takes so much more time than my other children. What do I do about that?

There is no question that the rearing of an orchid child can be more time-intensive and fraught than a parent's care for a more dandelion-like child. With their greater permeability and susceptibility to the world around them, orchid children are more reliant on parents to buffer the impact of adversities at home or school, to hear out the high emotions that are inevitably felt, and to provide the structure and dependability that such children need. But dandelion children need their parent(s), too, and there is only so much time in a day that a parent has to give, especially working parents who return home with little of themselves left to share. In the end, parents must give the love and attention they have, mindful that it's important to all children and remembering that their orchid child will inevitably require, at times, even more parental care and even greater reminders of the steadfast love that will see them through. Remember the *H* for human differences in the *O-R-C-H-I-D* mnemonic: strictly egalitarian parenting is a cultural myth; it is simply not possible. So we give what we can when it is needed, knowing that different kids require different parents; sharing the burden where we can; and believing that abiding, self-evident love is every child's greatest need.

You mentioned that there are critical periods in children's exposures to trauma and adversity. What are those, and how do they occur?

Critical periods are windows of time in the course of a child's development when the brain is most open and susceptible to the expected influences of environmental experience. An example is amblyopia, or lazy eye. For a child born with misaligned eyes (strabismus) or a congenital cataract, the affected eye must be corrected (by patching, surgery, or other treatments) by age seven to eight years or the eye becomes functionally blind, even though it is structurally normal. Another example is the acquisition of language: in order for a child to speak a new language without an accent, that child must acquire the language before the end of the first decade of life. So a child moving to, say, France at age eight will generally learn flawless French, while after a move at age twelve the child can become fluent but will always speak in accented French.

There also appears to be a critical period in a young child's exposures to trauma and adversity. In the Bucharest Early Intervention Project (see note, but this is also discussed in chapter 6), for example, investigators found that children growing up in Romanian orphanages, where the ratio of caregivers to young children was 1 to 15, developed a variety of cognitive and socioemotional deficits as a consequence of their early deprivation. On the other hand, institutionalized children who were transferred to in-home foster care by age twenty months were able to avoid the deficits and had the same developmental trajectories as children placed in foster care at birth. So there appeared to be a critical period for deprivation-related developmental delays. We now know that such critical periods open and close due to molecular processes in the developing brain, and scientists are studying whether certain critical periods might be reopened using pharmacological approaches. There are also likely critical periods, early in life, when children track into the development of either an orchid or dandelion pattern of responsivity.

Given how much experience affects development in the first few years of life, shouldn't we be paying preschool and kindergarten teachers more?

Absolutely. Harvard economist Raj Chetty has calculated (as economists do) how much societal cost savings would be derived from twenty children in a kindergarten class having an outstanding, highly trained teacher for their first, formative year of primary school. The savings would come from the later reductions in adolescent pregnancies, criminality, unemployment, premature educational curtailment, and other impediments to social productivity that are known correlates of poor or ineffective early education. The number was $320,000 per year! How many kindergarten teachers do you know making $320,000 per year? And, in fact, our investments in teacher salaries ironically run precisely counter to what we now know about brain plasticity and learning over the years of primary and secondary education. The figure shown illustrates this irony. It displays, for each educational level from preschool to university, how much teachers are generally paid (shown in gray) and the developing brain's capacity for learning through experience (shown in black). While brain plasticity diminishes dramatically over the first few years of life, teacher's salaries generally increase. Our apportioning of educational funds runs opposite of what we now know about learning and brain capacity. This is further discussed in chapter 7.

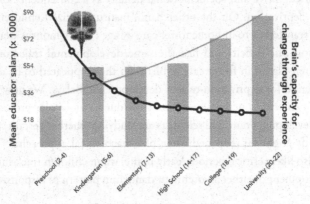

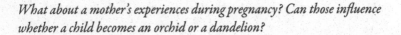

Educational Level (Ages in Years)

What about a mother's experiences during pregnancy? Can those influence whether a child becomes an orchid or a dandelion?

There is now a steadily growing body of evidence that the experiences and stressors encountered by a pregnant mom can affect the development and well-being of her fetus following birth. Knowing what we do about the transfer of stress hormones and other substances across the placenta, this is not surprising. There is even evidence, in animal models, that trauma-related epigenetic marks in the mom's eggs or the dad's sperm can be passed on to the fetus—an actual transgenerational inheritance of adversity exposures. (Such evidence of epigenetic transfer is not yet as clear, however, in humans.) We also know that maternal depression during the perinatal period or a pregnant mom's experiences of major trauma—like the Holocaust, the Ontario Ice Storm, the Dutch Hunger Winter, or periods of geographic famine—can have profound effects on the developing baby, effects that often continue into adult life. Prenatal adversity is also a known correlate of premature birth, which can affect a fetus's chance of survival and the development of neonatal complications. Although it is currently not known whether prenatal maternal exposures can influence a fetus's orchid or dandelion phenotype, there is some evidence (for the reasons explained in the book's endnote from page 53) that a higher-than-average proportion of births will be orchid babies at the extremes of adversity exposure levels—that is, under very high-stress conditions and very low-stress, supportive conditions. For all of these reasons, it is widely believed that minimizing a pregnant woman's exposures to trauma and stressors will be best for both mom and baby.

Wouldn't these categories of orchid and dandelion children be mostly applicable to middle-class kids and families? Aren't differences in sensitivity just overwhelmed in disadvantaged communities by the harsh adversities some of those children sustain?

It is certainly true that children growing up in impoverished, disadvantaged communities sustain far more adverse childhood exposures— more parental mental health problems and addictions, more violence in the home and neighborhood, more chaos and noise, and often more racism and bullying. But children from low socioeconomic, indigent communities also show substantial variation in their sensitivity to the social and physical world, and orchid children from such communities show the same proclivity toward poorer health and disturbed development when confronted with adverse events. The celebrated filmmaker

Roger Weisberg, in fact, produced a film about such children, entitled *Broken Places* (see https://brokenplacesfilm.com). In it, he tracks the lives of several children he has known and filmed from troubled communities in New York City, showing how the futures of such children, as they move from childhood into adult lives, are powerfully influenced by their orchid or dandelion characteristics. This varying susceptibility to the environment appears equally salient to health and development in both middle-class kids and those from more deprived communities.

At the end of the day, why do you think your life and your sister's life turned out so differently?

In all likelihood, my own life path and that of my sister Mary dramatically diverged as a consequence of many factors. One was undoubtedly our so-called "unshared" experiences in our family of origin. As previously noted, and in chapter 6, I explain how "no two children are raised in the same family." While Mary and I were both present and aware during our parents' marital conflicts and periods of psychological crisis, Mary's and my actual experiences of those times were almost certainly different. Though such moments surely affected us both, I suspect that for her they were substantially more aversive and lasting. Secondly, there were inevitable differences in our experiences based on gender and birth order. I was a firstborn boy; she was a female middle child. During my first two-plus formative years, I had the advantage of my parents' first enamored encounters with a growing, breathing child that they had made together. Mary's first years were likely spent, to some degree, in her older brother's shadow. Third, even matched as we were in so many ways, Mary and I were genetically different creatures, recipients, as we all are, of chance elements from our parents' genetic assets and liabilities. Finally, and perhaps most tellingly, we acquired predictably different epigenetic profiles that were the interactive products of both our genotypic differences and the dissimilarities in our experiences of our family. These epigenetic disparities plausibly resulted in the reality that

I became a dandelion and she an orchid. My life was blessed with good fortune; hers was blighted by misfortune and affliction.

What are the implications of your work for the situation at the United States southern border, where thousands of immigrant children are being separated from their parents?

Part of the reason that the current federal policy of separating immigrant children from their parents at the southern border has been deemed so hateful and malevolent is the reality that children—especially those uprooted from home and community—depend critically upon their parents and families for love and protection. Depriving children of their parents' love and shelter is an act of unprecedented, historical barbarism by the government of one of the previously most benevolent nations on earth. All children are biologically more susceptible to the destructive effects of toxic stress. As defined by the National Scientific Council on the Developing Child, toxic stress is an exposure to psychological adversity that results in a heightened and sustained activation of the two stress response systems in the human brain. As the book describes, there is great variation in children's individual biological reactivity to toxic stressors, leading, in some especially orchid-like children, to profound effects on health and development. But at the broader level of human populations, it is *all of our children* who comprise the most sensitive and susceptible orchids within every nation-state. Science shows that exposures to both psychological and physical "toxins" are more consequential among children. They are more likely, for example, to develop malignancies following exposures to nuclear radiation, to bear inordinate psychological harm due to family or community violence, and to sustain the greatest risk of serious respiratory disease in conditions of poverty. As a pediatrician it is impossible for me to believe that immigrant children separated from their families will not bear some unmistakable psychological scars from their experiences of America.

But separation from immigrant parents is only the most visible and current of the U.S. administration's assaults on children in 2019. Threatening child health insurance coverage, removing federal offices focused on children's health protection, lifting controls on toxic air pollution, impeding regulations to prevent toxic exposures, and using Immigration and Customs Enforcement (ICE) agents to generate fear and anxiety in immigrant communities—are all federal policies with disproportionate and deleterious biological impacts on children. The very survival of our species depends, at least in part, upon the degree to which we acknowledge and defend those who are most vulnerable and susceptible within our communities and world. *It is children* who are the orchids of our greenhouse, the keepers of our collective future, the promise of generations yet to come. And we fail to protect them from a cynical and rapacious government at our great, collective peril.

What can parents of an orchid child do to support and sustain themselves?

This is another really important question. It is often not easy being the parent of an orchid child; dandelions are thankfully far easier. Orchid children often have over-reactive emotional responses to certain events and conditions, and these can be difficult for parents to address. Especially during the early adolescent years, an orchid child can run into difficulty with peers, can develop problems with anxiety or depression, or can sometimes stray into friendships or activities that are destructive for positive development. It can be discouraging and lonely supporting a child through such deep and dangerous waters. Adolescence, like very early childhood, is a critical period of development, when adult identity begins to take shape, educational aspirations are set or abandoned, and the influence of peers and friends is formative. During such times, it is important not only for the parent to be closely vigilant and encouraging to the child but also for the parent to find support and care for himself or herself. In two-parent families, this support can often come from the other parent; it is one of the times when the advantages of two parents are vividly obvious and when the exigencies of being a single parent are most palpable and profound. Whether one or two adults are available in the home, it is always important for a parent to find support and concern outside their relationship to the orchid child. This could take the form of other parents, a parenting support group, a therapist or pediatrician, a religious leader, or a close friend. Just as steadfast love is a critical element in the raising of orchid (and all) children, caring for oneself is an essential asset for orchid parenting.

Acknowledgments

So much of human life and work rests on hidden but elemental foundations of alliance, mentoring, and friendship. The work and experiences recounted here were carried forward on the backs, imaginations, and goodwill of friends and colleagues generous enough to bear its weight alongside me. Among these are the following irreplaceable people and institutions, to each of whom and which I convey my immense and lasting gratitude.

My professional life and work has been honored, beginning to end, by the transformative affirmation of a small number of lifelong mentors. The unforeseen gifts of encouragement from John Cassel, Sir Michael Rutter, and Leonard Syme propelled me into a life of scholarship and research that I had in those early, formative years only scarcely imagined. Art Ammann, T. Berry Brazelton, Robert Coles, and Bob Haggerty became exemplars of how physician-scientists could contribute meaningfully to the enterprise of biomedical science, while concurrently testifying to the real, human tragedies and triumphs that populate the lives of the children we study.

Nancy Adler, Marilyn Essex, Chuck Nelson, Jack Shonkoff, and Marla Sokolowski gave me the consummate gift of becoming not only my most cherished and revered colleagues, without whom none of my work could have been achieved, but my friends and accomplices as well. They are the lifetime academic partners who proffered me their wisdom, passion, and abiding brilliance. Abbey Alkon, Nicki Bush, Margaret Chesney, Pam DenBesten, Bruce Ellis, John Featherstone, Jan Genevro, Young Shin Kim, Mike Kobor, Max Michael, Jelena Obradović, Jodi Quas, Craig Ramey, Danielle Roubinov, Juliet Stamperdahl, Steve Suomi, Melanie Thomas, and Allen Wilcox likewise entrusted me with long, loyal, and treasured collegiality within the studies and projects I have chronicled in this book.

There are special places in my heart for the late Clyde Hertzman, for Ron Barr, and for the people of the Human Early Learning Partnership at the University of British Columbia, who discerned, at precisely the right moment in my career, the implications of differential susceptibility for children's health and development and gave me utter freedom to shine light on its effects. Similarly, the astonishingly smart and creative memberships of the several research networks to which I have been honored to be a part—the Child and Brain Development Program of the Canadian Institute for Advanced Research, the JPB Research Network on Toxic Stress, the NIH-sponsored Network on Inequality, Complexity and Health, and the MacArthur Foundation Research Network on Psychopathology and Development—together breathed new life into my search for the origins and consequences of human adversities. Special thanks go to the leaders of these groups—Alan Bernstein, Chaviva Hošek, George Kaplan, David Kupfer, Fraser Mustard, and Hermi Woodward—without whose commitments to the genius of multidisciplinarity much insight would have been lost. The Robert Wood Johnson Foundation gave me an opening glimpse into the joy and intrigue of research; the WT Grant Foundation gave me a first, indispensable research grant; and the National Institute of Child Health and Human Development and the National Institute of Mental Health offered sustained investments in my work, moving it forward in unprecedented ways.

I am indebted, as well, to the Departments of Pediatrics and Psychiatry at the School of Medicine, University of California, San Francisco, to the School of Public Health at the University of California, Berkeley, and to their deans and chairs—the late Patricia Buffler, Donna Ferriero, the late Mel Grumbach, Abe Rudolph, Larry Shapiro, Steve Shortell, and Matt State. These institutions and leaders not only trained me as a pediatrician-scientist and then invited me back, but taught me as well to think beyond the individual child to the populations in which the world's children reside. The Lisa and John Pritzker family of San Francisco generously endowed the UCSF chair from which I am now so honored to work. And Nina Green and Tanya Erb, of UC Berkeley and the University of British Columbia, lent administrative support and friendship, giving me the room to work.

There are also friends whose enthusiasm for the ideas and writing of *The Orchid and the Dandelion* fostered my growing conviction that there was something worthy of sharing, among them Karen and Russ Cook, Julie and Craig Gay, Gretchen Grant, Kim and Teddi Hamilton, Mark Labberton, Bill Satariano, Lew Sprunger, John Swartzberg, Tom and Barbara Tompkins, and Bruce, Sara, Dave, and Holly Williams. Kim Hamilton, Phyllis Lorenz, and Elysa Marco also offered much valued early readings of and suggestions for the manuscript.

Vicky Wilson, senior editor and vice president at Alfred A. Knopf, provided, in addition to her insightful early reviews of the manuscript, critical editorial oversight for the structural and rhetorical approaches of the finished book. Doug Abrams, the founder and impassioned force behind Idea Architects, a literary agency with no lesser objective than to "create a wiser, healthier, and more just world," played a truly guiding role in the genesis of *The Orchid and the Dandelion*—one that would be difficult to overstate. Over a 2015 lunch initiated by Doug, I presented him with a competent preliminary outline for a scientifically sound but probably lifeless book on my work. Through his warm, persistent encouragement and gentle commentary, the inanimate outline became the hopefully far more engaging *story* of *The Orchid and the Dandelion*. Without Doug's deep editorial wisdom, along with that of Idea Architect collaborative writer Aaron Shulman, there would have been no book worthy of my readers' collective time. Doug's and Aaron's help allowed an inveterate writer of stuffy science to become as well (and nearly without pain) a writer of stories.

I want to thank my families—both my past family of origin and my present one—for the indelible and merciful roles they have played in both my life and this book. My dad and mom were caring and loving parents who taught me the undying lesson of how to work hard, with a soft heart. Like all of us, they did the very best they could with the parenting skills and insights they had accrued over lifetimes of trying. My brother, Jim, and sister, Mary, as my readers have now witnessed, have also been endearing and admired presences in my life, though Mary's story remains an unintended but only partly healed wound for us all. May she rest in the peace that I believe lies beyond this troublous but thoroughly benevolent life.

Finally, I am grateful beyond words for my beloved Jill, Andrew, and Amy, who fill the cracked vessel of my soul with love, faith, and human kindness. They are those to whom, by grace, my life has been forever bound, even before I met and loved them.

Glossary

ALLELES: Alternative forms of a single gene; allelic variation refers to the total variability in a gene's DNA sequence.

ALLOSTATIC LOAD: The physiological "cost" of maintaining the body's biological stability.

AUTONOMIC NERVOUS SYSTEM (ANS): A peripheral component of the nervous system with two branches, the sympathetic branch that accelerates fight-or-flight reactivity, and a parasympathetic branch that brakes reactivity. Together, these two branches control physiological responses to stress that include dry mouth, increased blood pressure and heart rate, changes in blood sugar levels, and immune system regulation.

BEHAVIOR GENETICS: The field of psychology whose objective was to parse the origins of behavior into those components attributable to genes versus those attributable to environmental dimensions, like parenting. Estimating the heritability of a behavioral trait was often accomplished through studies of identical and fraternal twins.

CELL DIFFERENTIATION: The process by which stem (undifferentiated) cells become tissue-specific cells, like liver, brain, or lung cells. Though all cells have precisely the same genetic makeup, the differential expression of those genes allows the emergence of dramatically different cell types.

DIFFERENTIAL SUSCEPTIBILITY: A special, relatively intense sensitivity to the nature and character of the experienced social world; most importantly, a sensitivity to both the toxic and supportive aspects of social environmental conditions.

DNA SEQUENCE: The ordered series of nucleotides of DNA (deoxyribonucleic acid), the hereditary material of the genome in humans and most other organisms.

EPIGENETICS: The science of how environmental exposures can modify gene expression, without altering the DNA sequence of the gene itself. The Greek prefix *epi,* meaning "upon" or "above," connotes how the epigenome, a lattice of chemical "marks" or tags, literally lies upon the genome and controls the expression or silencing of DNA during life.

EPIGENOME: The total complement of epigenetic marks that guide cell differentiation and experience-dependent differences in gene expression.

EPISTASIS: A circumstance in which the effect of one gene is interactively dependent upon a concurrent effect of another, thus a gene-gene interaction.

ETIOLOGY: Cause, as in "the etiology of a disease."

GENE-ENVIRONMENT INTERACTION: A synergy, where genes and environments, biology and experiences converge to have a combined, nonadditive effect on a behavioral or developmental outcome.

HOMEOSTASIS: The process of achieving biological stability through physiological or behavioral changes.

HYPOTHALAMIC-PITUITARY-ADRENOCORTICAL (HPA) AXIS: The hormonal system, comprising the hypothalamus in the brain, the pituitary gland, and the adrenal glands (just above the kidneys), which together produce and release the powerful hormone cortisol. Cortisol has major effects on the cardiovascular, immune, and metabolic systems of the body.

MORBIDITY: A general medical term for illness, injury, or disorder, both physical and mental.

NEOPHOBIA: A fear of or discomfort with the new: new settings, new people, new tastes, or new challenges.

NEURON: A nervous system cell, found either in the brain or the periphery.

NEUROTRANSMITTERS: The chemical "messengers" that bridge the tiny gap between neurons, resulting in activation of the downstream neuron and the communication of information.

NUCLEOTIDES: The four organic molecules constituting the building blocks of DNA: adenine, guanine, cytosine, and thymine.

PHENOTYPE: The set of observable, visible characteristics—such as eye color, height, personality, and behavior—that describe an individual person or organism.

SYNAPSE: The tiny gaps between the "arms" of two neurons, which function as points of connection and convey information from one neuron to another.

Notes

Introduction

xiv Though we had intermittently fussed and stewed: The latest count, since you've asked, is four grandsons. One more and we'll have a basketball team.

xvii As I map out the defining features: In the closing lines of *Middlemarch*, George Eliot (née Mary Ann Evans) wrote of her heroine Dorothea Brooke, "Her finely touched spirit had still its fine issues, though they were not widely visible. Her full nature, like that river of which Cyrus broke the strength, spent itself in channels which had no great name on the earth. But the effect of her being on those around her was incalculably diffusive: for the growing good of the world is partly dependent on unhistoric acts; and that things are not so ill with you and me as they might have been, is half owing to the number who lived faithfully a hidden life, and rest in unvisited tombs."

1 A Tale of Two Children

15 "He was a skinny, vivid little boy": William Golding, *Lord of the Flies* (New York: Putnam, 1954), 24.

15 They can be, as family therapist Salvador Minuchin taught: S. Minuchin et al., "A Conceptual Model of Psychosomatic Illness in Children: Family Organization and Family Therapy," *Archives of General Psychiatry* 32, no. 8 (1975): 1031–38.

16 The strength and health of both orchids and dandelions: J. P. Shonkoff, W. T. Boyce, and B. S. McEwen, "Neuroscience, Molecular Biology, and the Childhood Roots of Health Disparities: Building a New Framework for Health Promotion and Disease Prevention," *Journal of the American Medical Association* 301, no. 21 (2009): 2252–59.

16 But orchids' *differential susceptibility:* B. J. Ellis et al., "Differential Susceptibility to the Environment: An Evolutionary-Neurodevelopmental Theory," *Development and Psychopathology* 23, no. 1 (2011): 7–28.

2 The Noise and the Music

25 René Dubos, the famed American microbiologist: R. J. Dubos, *Man Adapting* (New Haven, CT: Yale University Press, 1965).

25 "a remarkably similar set of social circumstances": J. Cassel, "The Contribution of the Social Environment to Host Resistance," *American Journal of Epidemiology* 104 (1976): 107–23.

26 Following in the tradition of Walter Cannon's early studies: H. Selye, *Stress: The Physiology and Pathology of Exposure to Stress* (Montreal: Acta Medical Publishers, 1950); L. E. Hinkle and H. G. Wolff, "The Nature of Man's Adaptation to His Total Environment and the Relation of This to Illness," *Archives of Internal Medicine* 99 (1957): 442–60.

26 There were also those, like Robert Ader: R. Ader, N. Cohen, and D. Felten, "Psychoneuroimmunology: Interactions Between the Nervous System and the Immune System," *Lancet* 345 (1995): 99–103.

27 We found and reported, in a 1977 paper: W. T. Boyce et al., "Influence of Life Events and Family Routines on Childhood Respiratory Tract Illness," *Pediatrics* 60 (1977): 609–15.

29 For a given level of family stress: Here is an example of the kind of data derived from our early studies of stress and illness. The scatterplot on the facing page shows the level of experienced family stress among a group of three- to five-year-old children, predicting the severity scores for parent- and teacher-reported behavior problems. The plot reveals the great variability in an otherwise highly significant, linear relation, which was unlikely to be attributable to chance alone.

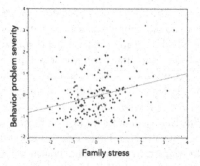

31 Thus, even before the systematic and elegant studies of resilience: N. Gar-mezy, A. S. Masten, and A. Tellegen, "The Study of Stress and Competence in Children: A Building Block for Developmental Psychopathology," *Child Development* 55 (1984): 97–111.

31 Previous studies, primarily in adults: "Psychopathology" refers to recog-nizable, criteria-meeting mental disorders, as described and codified in the *Diagnostic and Statistical Manual 5* (*DSM-5*) on psychiatric diagnosis. Many such disorders do not fully emerge until adolescence or young adult-hood, and their first, partially expressed forms are often referred to as "pre-syndromal psychopathology."

32 ACTH causes the adrenals: C. E. Hostinar, R. M. Sullivan, and M. R. Gun-nar, "Psychobiological Mechanisms Underlying the Social Buffering of the Hypothalamic-Pituitary-Adrenocortical Axis: A Review of Animal Models and Human Studies Across Development," *Psychological Bulletin* 140, no. 1 (2014): 256–82.

33 Children who are acutely or chronically responding: R. M. Sapolsky, *Why Zebras Don't Get Ulcers,* 3rd ed. (New York: Henry Holt, 2004).

33 All of these physiological stress responses: For the more biologically inclined, the first stress response system is also called the corticotropin-releasing hormone (CRH) system and is driven by two hypothalamic nuclei, the paraventricular and arcuate nuclei, that secrete various neurotrans-mitters and hormones, including CRH, which triggers or alters multiple pituitary functions. One of these is the expression of adrenocorticotropic hormone (ACTH), which causes the adrenals to release cortisol, a power-ful endocrine hormone that is released by stress and exerts multiple effects on the cardiovascular, immune, and metabolic systems. Such effects include regulation of blood pressure, glucose and insulin control, and suppression of various components of cellular and humoral immunity. Together, the hypothalamic nuclei, the anterior pituitary gland, and the adrenal cortex

comprise the hypothalamic-pituitary-adrenocortical (HPA) axis, which is keenly responsive to experiences of psychosocial stress and exerts profound effects on whole-body regulatory and metabolic processes.

The second stress response system is centered in a brain stem nucleus called the locus coeruleus. The locus coeruleus–norepinephrine (LC-NE) system is also activated in conditions of stress, and, via adrenergic neurons (brain cells secreting the signaling molecule norepinephrine), connects with the hypothalamus to unleash the fight-or-flight responses of the autonomic nervous system (ANS). These responses reflect the relative balance of arousal in its sympathetic (or activation) branch and parasympathetic (or deactivation) branch. The CRH and LC-NE systems engage in extensive cross-communication, with CRH also activating the LC-NE circuitry and ANS having regulatory influence on CRH system reactivity. Both systems have powerful monitoring and regulatory effects on multiple peripheral physiological processes, including glucose levels in the blood; blood pressure, heart rate, and other cardiovascular functions; and the balancing of immunological responses to microorganisms and foreign substances, such as pollens or vaccines. Children who are acutely or chronically responsive to stressful environments tend to have higher blood sugars and risk for Type II diabetes, higher blood pressure and risk for coronary and cerebrovascular disease, and shifts in immune functioning.

33 Neuroscientist Bruce McEwen has suggested: B. McEwen, "The Brain on Stress: How the Social Environment Gets Under the Skin," *Proceedings of the National Academy of Sciences USA* 109, Suppl. 2 (2012): 17180–85.

3 Lemon Juice, Fire Alarms, and an Unanticipated Discovery

42 The research assistant said she had forgotten something: The tired versus gleaming toy dilemma is a modification of the so-called marshmallow test conceived by Stanford professor Walter Mischel many years ago to assess self-regulatory skills in young children. See W. Mischel, E. B. Ebbesen, and A. R. Zeiss, "Cognitive and Attentional Mechanisms in Delay of Gratification," *Journal of Personality and Social Psychology* 21 (1972): 204–18.

48 These highly sensitive, orchid-like children: W. T. Boyce et al., "Psychobiologic Reactivity to Stress and Childhood Respiratory Illnesses: Results of Two Prospective Studies," *Psychosomatic Medicine* 57 (1995): 411–22.

49 Jerome Kagan, a professor of developmental psychology: J. Kagan, J. S. Reznick, and N. Snidman, "Biological Bases of Childhood Shyness," *Science* 240 (1988): 167–71.

49 According to the early work of Alexander Thomas and Stella Chess:

S. Chess and A. Thomas, *Temperament in Clinical Practice* (New York: Guilford Press, 1986).

50 What Belsky found: J. Belsky, K. Hsieh, and K. Crnic, "Mothering, Fathering, and Infant Negativity as Antecedents of Boys' Externalizing Problems and Inhibition at Age 3: Differential Susceptibility to Rearing Influence?," *Development and Psychopathology* 10 (1998): 301–19.

50 His interpretation of this and later findings: J. Belsky, S. L. Friedman, and K. H. Hsieh, "Testing a Core Emotion-Regulation Prediction: Does Early Attentional Persistence Moderate the Effect of Infant Negative Emotionality on Later Development?," *Child Development* 72, no. 1 (2001): 123–33.

52 He was even then on a path: For a more scholarly rendition of Bruce Ellis's work, see his book with David Bjorklund: B. J. Ellis and D. F. Bjorklund, *The Origins of the Social Mind: Evolutionary Psychology and Child Development* (New York: Guilford Press, 2014).

52 The core tenets of that fledgling theory: W. T. Boyce and B. J. Ellis, "Biological Sensitivity to Context: I. An Evolutionary-Developmental Theory of the Origins and Functions of Stress Reactivity," *Development and Psychopathology* 17, no. 2 (2005): 271–301; B. J. Ellis, M. J. Essex, and W. T. Boyce, "Biological Sensitivity to Context: II. Empirical Explorations of an Evolutionary-Developmental Hypothesis," *Development and Psychopathology* 17, no. 2 (2005): 303–28.

53 So we proposed that the expected relation:

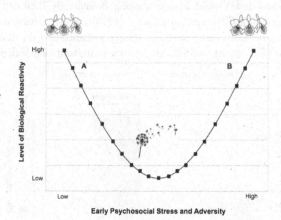

This graph shows the theoretical shape of the relation between early psychosocial stress and adversity and the anticipated level of biological reactivity in offspring. Evolutionary biology has shown how, in so-called conditional adaptations, fetuses and infants unconsciously appraise their physical and social environments and make biological and physiological adjustments that can maximize their adaptive successes in those environments. There is now some evidence that children born into moderately stressful settings (the midline of the graph) disproportionately become dandelions with low biological reactivity. On the other hand, children born to extremely low-stress homes (point A) and extremely high-stress homes (point B) disproportionately become orchids. Children at point A become orchids because they can derive more "goodness" from their environments, while those at point B become orchids to maximize vigilance for threats.

54 Buckeye butterflies develop: S. F. Gilbert and D. Epel, *Ecological Developmental Biology: Integrating Epigenetics, Medicine, and Evolution* (Sunderland, MA: Sinauer Associates, 2009).

54 Perhaps the best-known example of a conditional adaptation: J. Belsky, L. Steinberg, and P. Draper, "Childhood Experience, Interpersonal Development, and Reproductive Strategy: An Evolutionary Theory of Socialization," *Child Development* 62 (1991): 647–70.

55 Jay Belsky has correspondingly suggested: J. Belsky, "Variation in Susceptibility to Environmental Influence: An Evolutionary Argument," *Psychological Inquiry* 8, no. 3 (1997): 182–86.

58 We found that there had been a fivefold increase: W. T. Boyce et al., "Crowding Stress and Violent Injuries Among Behaviorally Inhibited Rhesus Macaques," *Health Psychology* 17, no. 3 (1998): 285–89. This graph shows the number and severity scores for injuries sustained by a rhesus macaque troop before, during, and following a required stressful six-month period of

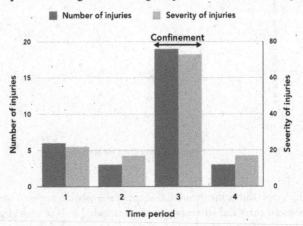

group confinement. As shown, the confinement resulted in a fivefold increase in both the rate and severity of violent injuries.

4 An Orchestration of Orchids and Dandelions

60 A team of scientists in London: J. Belsky, K. Hsieh, and K. Crnic, "Mothering, Fathering, and Infant Negativity as Antecedents of Boys' Externalizing Problems and Inhibition at Age 3: Differential Susceptibility to Rearing Influence?," *Development and Psychopathology* 10 (1998): 301–19.

60 Investigators at the University of Pittsburgh: S. B. Manuck, A. E. Craig, J. D. Flory, I. Halder I, and R. E. Ferrell, "Reported Early Family Environment Covaries with Menarcheal Age as a Function of Polymorphic Variation in Estrogen Receptor-Alpha," *Development and Psychopathology* 23, no. 1 (2011): 69–83.

60 In Jerusalem, another group: A. Knafo, S. Israel, and R. P. Ebstein, "Heritability of Children's Prosocial Behavior and Differential Susceptibility to Parenting by Variation in the Dopamine Receptor D4 Gene," *Development and Psychopathology* 23, no. 1 (2011): 53–67.

63 The average monkey: Normal core body temperature for a human is 37°C or 98.6°F, whereas that of a rhesus monkey is just slightly warmer, at 37.3°C or 99.1°F.

65 Although at first glance the human brain: Readers with a particular interest in brain asymmetry are referred to a remarkable book by psychiatrist Iain McGilchrist: *The Master and His Emissary: The Divided Brain and the Making of the Western World* (New Haven, CT: Yale University Press, 2009).

65 We know, for example, that the brain: N. A. Fox, "If It's Not Left, It's Right: Electroencephalograph Asymmetry and the Development of Emotion," *American Psychologist* 46, no. 8 (1991): 863–72; R. J. Davidson and K. Hugdahl, *Brain Asymmetry* (Cambridge, MA: MIT Press, 1995).

66 We began to see a warmer right eardrum: W. T. Boyce et al., "Tympanic Temperature Asymmetry and Stress Behavior in Rhesus Macaques and Children," *Archives of Pediatric and Adolescent Medicine* 150 (1996): 518–23.

68 Thus, orchid children, like their nonhuman primate orchid counterparts: W. T. Boyce et al., "Temperament, Tympanum, and Temperature: Four Provisional Studies of the Biobehavioral Correlates of Tympanic Membrane Temperature Asymmetries," *Child Development* 73, no. 3 (2002): 718–33.

72 On the other hand, the dandelion-like kids: W. T. Boyce et al., "Autonomic

Reactivity and Psychopathology in Middle Childhood," *British Journal of Psychiatry* 179 (2001): 144–50.

73 Here was an even more powerful demonstration: M. J. Essex et al., "Biological Sensitivity to Context Moderates the Effects of the Early Teacher-Child Relationship on the Development of Mental Health by Adolescence," *Development and Psychopathology* 23, no. 1 (2011): 149–61.

75 Might the parental relationships of these orchids and dandelions: Those readers with some level of botanical knowledge may rightfully protest that orchids do not, in fact, grow in soil. So to clarify: although a few, terrestrial orchids do grow in soil, most tropical orchids are epiphytes, meaning that they grow in the air rather than in soil. This and subsequent allusions to the "soil" in which orchid children grow are thus instruments of metaphorical license, for which the author begs the reader's indulgence.

76 For reasons that are only partially understood: The average age for menarche has declined over the past hundred years from about seventeen years to about twelve years. Over the past forty years, girls have gotten their first menstrual periods an average of a few months earlier, but have started breast budding as much as one to two years earlier. Most experts attribute these secular trends to decreased rates of disease and increased nutrition. Those with more interest in this phenomenon could read *The Falling Age of Puberty in U.S. Girls,* by Sandra Steingraber (http://gaylesulik.com/wp-content/uploads/2010/07/falling-age-of-puberty.pdf).

76 Using stress reactivity data:

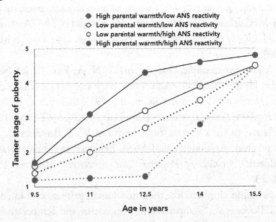

This graph shows trajectories of pubertal development (measured by Tanner stages 1–5) over time by level of parental support and fight-or-flight reactivity (measured by autonomic nervous system [ANS] responses). Orchid youth with high reactivity showed either the fastest or slowest pace of pubertal development depending upon the level of parental warmth and support. B. J. Ellis et al., "Quality of Early Family Relationships and the Timing and Tempo of Puberty: Effects Depend on Biological Sensitivity to Context," *Development and Psychopathology* 23, no. 1 (2011): 85–99.

77 Thus what might appear to be a meaningful association: Those with an appetite for further explication of the slings and arrows of interpreting scientific research may enjoy M. Michael, W. T. Boyce, and A. J. Wilcox, *Biomedical Bestiary: An Epidemiologic Guide to Flaws and Fallacies in the Medical Literature* (Boston: Little, Brown, 1984).

80 The orchids remembered nearly everything: J. A. Quas, A. Bauer, and W. T. Boyce, "Physiological Reactivity, Social Support, and Memory in Early Childhood," *Child Development* 75, no. 3 (2004): 797–14.

5 Where Do Orchids (and Dandelions) Come From?

82 Children with this shorter allele: C. A. Nelson, N. A. Fox, and C. Zeanah, *Romania's Abandoned Children* (Cambridge, MA: Harvard University Press, 2014); K. L. Humphreys et al., "Serotonin Transporter Genotype (5HTTLPR) Moderates the Longitudinal Impact of Atypical Attachment on Externalizing Behavior," *Journal of Developmental and Behavioral Pediatrics* 36, no. 6 (2015): 409–16.

82 Similarly, a team of Dutch researchers: M. J. Bakermans-Kranenburg and M. H. van Ijzendoorn, "Differential Susceptibility to Rearing Environment Depending on Dopamine-Related Genes: New Evidence and a Meta-analysis," *Development and Psychopathology* 23, no. 1 (2011): 39–52.

85 Careful epidemiologic work: N. Razaz et al., "Five-Minute Apgar Score as a Marker for Developmental Vulnerability at 5 Years of Age," *Archives of Disease in Childhood. Fetal and Neonatal Edition* 101, no. 2 (2016): F114–F120.

86 Babies entering the world: Five-year-old children with lower Apgar scores at birth had substantially higher levels of developmental vulnerability, over the entire 10-point range, as estimated by their kindergarten teachers. For each developmental domain on the Early Development Instrument, there was a graded association with Apgar scores, with lower scores consistently predicting greater vulnerability. Ibid.

87 You can think of this view of human behavior: It was Charles Darwin's cousin, the British natural historian Francis Galton, who first used the phrase "nature versus nurture"—the forced polarity that has finally yielded to the recognition of the epigenome, where nature and nurture converge.

90 And it is only religious faith: S. Kierkegaard, *Either/Or*, trans. S. L. Ross and

G. L. Stengren (New York: Harper & Row, 1986 [originally published in 1843]).

6 No Two Children Are Raised in the Same Family

112 I happened upon what is now a dog-eared and famous paper: R. Plomin and D. Daniels, "Why Are Children in the Same Family so Different from One Another?," *Behavioral and Brain Sciences* 10 (1987): 1–16.

114 The most celebrated and widely known research: Readers hungry for a deeper understanding of the work of Meaney and Szyf on the epigenetics of parental behavior are referred to the following resources: J. D. Sweatt et al., *Epigenetic Regulation in the Nervous System: Basic Mechanisms and Clinical Impact* (London: Elsevier, 2013); M. J. Meaney, "Epigenetics and the Biological Definition of Gene × Environment Interactions," *Child Development* 81 (2010): 41–79; M. Szyf, P. McGowan, and M. J. Meaney, "The Social Environment and the Epigenome," *Environmental and Molecular Mutagenesis* 49 (2008): 46–60; I. C. Weaver et al., "Epigenetic Programming by Maternal Behavior," *Nature Neuroscience* 7 (2004) 847–54.

115 For scientists who have studied both human and nonhuman: Though we as humans are astonishingly homologous with other mammalian species in genes, biology, and behavior, it is also important to recognize and acknowledge the vast differences in the capacities, creativity, and imaginative and adaptive successes of *Homo sapiens*. We differ genetically from chimps in just over 1 percent of our genomes, but what a remarkable 1 percent it is!

117 The effect is a wholesale alteration:

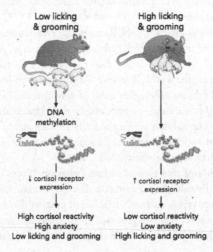

This figure shows how the cortisol system's reactivity to stress, susceptibility to anxiety, and style of parenting behavior are affected by maternal licking and grooming over the first few days of postnatal life. The glucocorticoid (cortisol) receptor (GR) gene, unmethylated at birth, becomes methylated in the offspring of low licking moms, resulting in higher stress responsivity, more anxiety, and a predisposition to become less attentive parents. M. J. Meaney and M. Szyf, "Maternal Care as a Model for Experience-Dependent Chromatin Plasticity?," *Trends in Neurosciences* 28, no. 9 (2005): 456–63.

117 The other biological agent: The biology of oxytocin has a long and fascinating history that is nicely presented in the works of Sarah Hrdy: S. B. Hrdy, *Mother Nature: Maternal Instincts and How They Shape the Human Species* (New York: Ballantine, 1999); and Meg Olmert: M. D. Olmert, *Made for Each Other: The Biology of the Human-Animal Bond* (Cambridge, MA: Da Capo, 2009). For a more scientific view of the still emerging oxytocin story, see C. S. Carter, "Oxytocin Pathways and the Evolution of Human Behavior," *Annual Review of Psychology* 65 (2014): 17–39.

117 As with the effects of licking and grooming: A. K. Beery et al., "Natural Variation in Maternal Care and Cross-Tissue Patterns of Oxytocin Receptor Gene Methylation in Rats," *Hormones and Behavior* 77 (2016): 42–52.

118 The Bucharest Early Intervention Project: C. A. Nelson, *Romania's Abandoned Children* (Cambridge, MA: Harvard University Press, 2014).

124 Both low and high licking: P. Pan et al., "Within- and Between-Litter Maternal Care Alter Behavior and Gene Regulation in Female Offspring," *Behavioral Neuroscience* 128, no. 6 (2014): 736–48.

7 The Kindness and Cruelty of Children

128 Lan was what psychologist Elaine Aron: E. N. Aron, *The Highly Sensitive Child* (New York: Broadway Books, 2002).

128 Neuroscientists have in fact shown: N. I. Eisenberger, M. D. Lieberman, and K. D. Williams, "Does Rejection Hurt? An FMRI Study of Social Exclusion," *Science* 302, no. 5643 (2003): 290–92.

129 a kind of "ouch" zone in the brain: See "'Ouch Zone' in the Brain Identified," University of Oxford News & Events, March 10, 2015, www.ox.ac.uk/news/2015-03-10-ouch-zone-brain-identified.

129 Although it is sometimes relegated: J. B. Richmond, "Child Development: A Basic Science for Pediatrics," *Pediatrics* 39, no. 5 (1967): 649–58.

130 One group of scientists used computer animations: L. Thomsen et al., "Big

and Mighty: Preverbal Infants Mentally Represent Social Dominance," *Science* 331, no. 6016 (2011): 477–80.

133 The animals at the top of the pack: Readers may also enjoy Frans de Waal's *Chimpanzee Politics: Power and Sex Among Apes* (Baltimore: Johns Hopkins University Press, 2007), which explores in greater detail the origins and architectures of monkey hierarchies, and Christopher Boehm's *Hierarchy in the Forest: The Evolution of Egalitarian Behavior* (Cambridge, MA: Harvard University Press, 1999).

133 The dominant animals eventually became sick: R. M. Sapolsky and L. J. Share, "A Pacific Culture Among Wild Baboons: Its Emergence and Transmission," *PLoS Biology* 2, no. 4 (2004): E106.

134 In the years since, the formerly number three clan: A. M. Dettmer, R. A. Woodward, and S. J. Suomi, "Reproductive Consequences of a Matrilineal Overthrow in Rhesus Monkeys," *American Journal of Primatology* 77, no. 3 (2015): 346–52.

134 Across the animal kingdom: C. Boehm, *Hierarchy in the Forest: The Evolution of Egalitarian Behavior* (Cambridge, MA: Harvard University Press, 1999).

134 Such "biological embedding" of low social status: C. Hertzman and W. T. Boyce, "How Experience Gets Under the Skin to Create Gradients in Developmental Health," *Annual Review of Public Health* 31 (2010): 329–47.

135 As Sapolsky has pointed out: R. M. Sapolsky, "The Influence of Social Hierarchy on Primate Health," *Science* 308, no. 5722 (2005): 648–52.

136 Just as troops of monkeys: There is some evidence that hunter-gatherer bands among indigenous people, even in the contemporary world, show more egalitarian practices and social structures—thought to be reminiscent of hominid groups in prehistorical times. See K. E. Pickett and R. G. Wilkinson, *The Spirit Level: Why Greater Equality Makes Societies Stronger* (New York: Bloomsbury, 2009).

138 Marmot's work shows: M. Marmot, *The Health Gap: The Challenge of an Unequal World* (London: Bloomsbury, 2015).

138 It is not simply poverty that drives health inequities: The graph on the facing page shows the number of chronic health conditions of childhood by family socioeconomic status (SES). There is a continuous, graded association between the family's socioeconomic position and children's levels of ear disease, asthma, injuries, physical inactivity, and all limiting health conditions. Redrawn from E. Chen, K. A. Matthews, and W. T. Boyce, "Socioeconomic Differences in Children's Health: How and Why Do These Relationships Change with Age?," *Psychological Bulletin* 128, no. 2 (2002): 295–329.

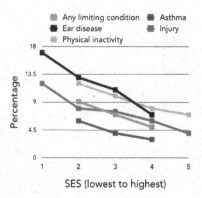

138 In fact, Richard Wilkinson and Kate Pickett: Pickett and Wilkinson, *The Spirit Level.*
139 As Nancy Adler and her colleagues: A. Singh-Manoux, M. G. Marmot, and N. E. Adler, "Does Subjective Social Status Predict Health and Change in Health Status Better Than Objective Status?," *Psychosomatic Medicine* 67, no. 6 (2005): 855–61; MacArthur Foundation Research Network on Socioeconomic Status and Health, *Reaching for a Healthier Life: Facts on Socioeconomic Status and Health in the U.S.* (Chicago, John D. and Catherine T. MacArthur Foundation, 2007); E. Goodman, S. Maxwell, S. Malspeis, and N. Adler, "Developmental Trajectories of Subjective Social Status," *Pediatrics* 136, no. 3 (2015): e633–40.
140 One systematic review paper found: K. L. Tang et al., "Association Between Subjective Social Status and Cardiovascular Disease and Cardiovascular Risk Factors: A Systematic Review and Meta-analysis," *BMJ Open* 6, no. 3 (2016): e010137.
142 They were universally eager: For the original use of this movie viewer paradigm, see W. R. Charlesworth and P. J. La Frenière, "Dominance, Friendship, and Resource Utilization in Preschool Children's Groups," *Ethology and Sociobiology* 4 (1983): 175–86.
143 Being low on the movie viewer hierarchy:

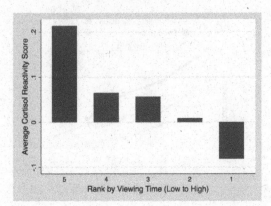

Above is a graph showing cortisol system stress reactivity by the movie viewer viewing-time rank in kindergarten children. The lowest-ranking children had the greatest cortisol reactivity to laboratory stressors, while the highest-ranking children had the lowest.

My Berkeley colleague Darlene Francis cleverly devised a comparable version of the movie viewer paradigm for quartets of rats. Instead of enticing videos, chocolate was melted into a glass candlestick and inserted into the side of cages housing four same-sex rats, and research assistants recorded the amount of time each rat got at licking the chocolate treat. The same clear hierarchy emerged: rats with lower licking times showed substantially greater corticosterone system (the rat version of cortisol) reactivity to a separate stressor than did those with the longest access to the chocolate.

149 In fact, the Stanford economist Raj Chetty: R. Chetty et al., "How Does Your Kindergarten Classroom Affect Your Earnings? Evidence from Project Star," *Quarterly Journal of Economics* 126, no. 4 (2011): 1593–1660.

150 As we discussed together what lay behind: G. W. Ladd, "Having Friends, Keeping Friends, Making Friends, and Being Liked by Peers in the Classroom: Predictors of Children's Early School Adjustment?," *Child Development* 61 (1990): 1081–1100; R. C. Pianta and B. K. Hamre, "Classroom Processes and Positive Youth Development: Conceptualizing, Measuring, and Improving the Capacity of Interactions Between Teachers and Students," *New Directions for Youth Development* 2009, no. 121 (2009): 33–46; D. Stipek, "Context Matters," *Elementary School Journal* 112, no. 4 (2012): 590–606.

150 This could occur if the teacher: V. G. Paley, *You Can't Say You Can't Play* (Cambridge, MA: Harvard University Press, 1992).

150 The result of these classroom differences: W. T. Boyce et al., "Social Strati-

fication, Classroom 'Climate' and the Behavioral Adaptation of Kindergarten Children," *Proceedings of the National Academy of Sciences* 109, Suppl. 2 (2012): 17168–73.

150 Not altogether surprisingly: The opposite might be legitimately argued: that is, that depressive symptoms could relegate a child to the hierarchy basement, rather than subordinate roles causing the emergence of depressive symptoms. This is the interpretive dilemma of "reverse causality," which can beset social science research. But in the case of our Berkeley kindergarten study, the mental health symptoms, such as depression, were measured later, in the spring of the year, after the observational ascertainment of classroom social position. This ordered measurement of the variables (social position first, depression and other mental health symptoms second) makes it somewhat more likely subordination was causing depression, rather than the other way around. The only way of proving this beyond doubt would be to randomly assign children to dominant or subordinate social roles—an experiment that would be very difficult, if not impossible, to carry out.

153 "I am sick of this messy life": Https://parenting.blogs.nytimes.com/2009/03/12/parents-and-school-shootings/.

8 Sowing and Tilling the Gardens of Childhood

160 There was, in fact, a whole body of research: B. S. Dohrenwend and B. P. Dohrenwend, *Stressful Life Events: Their Nature and Effects* (New York: Wiley, 1974).

161 Barbara Fiese, a developmental psychologist: B. H. Fiese, H. G. Rhodes, and W. R. Beardslee, "Rapid Changes in American Family Life: Consequences for Child Health and Pediatric Practice," *Pediatrics* 132, no. 3 (2013): 552–59.

161 "I would like to debunk": W. T. Boyce, "Life After Residency: Setting Priorities in Pediatric Professional Life," *American Journal of Diseases of Children* 144 (1990): 858–60.

163 In response to the sociocultural "mommy wars": M. A. Milkie, K. M. Nomaguchi, and K. E. Denny, "Does the Amount of Time Mothers Spend with Children or Adolescents Matter?," *Journal of Marriage and Family* 77, no. 2 (2015): 355–72.

164 Nonetheless, many studies find: L. M. Berger and S. S. McLanahan, "Income, Relationship Quality, and Parenting: Associations with Child Development in Two-Parent Families," *Journal of Marriage and Family* 77, no. 4 (2015): 996–1015.

164 We also know that child development: R. L. Repetti, S. R. Taylor, and T. E. Seeman, "Risky Families: Family Social Environments and the Mental and Physical Health of Offspring," *Psychological Bulletin* 128, no. 2 (2002): 330–66.

164 There is also substantial evidence: M. E. Lamb, *The Role of the Father in Child Development,* 3rd ed. (New York: Wiley, 1997).

167 Alice Miller's work: A. Miller, *The Drama of the Gifted Child: The Search for the True Self* (New York: Basic Books, 1997).

169 This is at least part of the reason: The internet and popular media have been abuzz of late with exhortations for parents to remove risk-obsessed obstacles to children's natural play and to return to past generations' comfort with risky playgrounds and "wild" recreation. Children raised in this new regime of freedom are apparently referred to as "free-range kids." See, for example, Hanna Rosin, "The Overprotected Kid: A Preoccupation with Safety Has Stripped Childhood of Independence, Risk Taking, and Discovery—Without Making It Safer. A New Kind of Playground Points to a Better Solution," *Atlantic,* April 2014; Amy Joyce, "Are We Protecting Kids or Ruining Families?," *Washington Post,* July 22, 2014; Tim Elmore, "Three Huge Mistakes We Make Leading Kids . . . and How to Correct Them," GrowingLeaders.com; and Eleanor Harding, "Parents in England Are Among the Most Overprotective: Fears over Traffic Mean Children in Germany, Finland, Norway, Sweden and Denmark All Have Greater Freedom," *Daily Mail,* August 10, 2015. This return to a less fettered childhood and its consequences for positive child development has become a focus of serious scholarship by epidemiologists and psychologists; see M. Brussoni et al., "Risky Play and Children's Safety: Balancing Priorities for Optimal Child Development," *International Journal of Environmental Research and Public Health* 9 (2012): 3134–48; and K. Clarke, P. Cooper, and C. Creswell, "The Parental Overprotection Scale: Associations with Child and Parental Anxiety," *Journal of Affective Disorders* 151 (2013): 618–24.

9 The Arc of Life for Orchids and Dandelions

171 All parents yearn: M. Oliver, *New and Selected Poems* (Boston: Beacon, 1992).

172 This area of study was launched: D. J. Barker and C. Osmond, "Infant Mortality, Childhood Nutrition, and Ischaemic Heart Disease in England and Wales," *Lancet* 1, no. 8489 (1986): 1077–81.

172 Ethologist Konrad Lorenz: See "Konrad Lorenz Experiment with Geese," YouTube, www.youtube.com/watch?v=2UIU9XH-mUI.

172 And three major research reports: J. P. Shonkoff and D. A. Phillips, eds., *From Neurons to Neighborhoods: The Science of Early Child Development* (Washington, DC: National Academies Press, 2000); M. Marmot, *Fair Society, Healthy Lives (The Marmot Review)* (Institute of Health Equity, February 2010); M. Boivin and C. Hertzman, eds., *Early Childhood Development: Adverse Experiences and Developmental Health* (Ottawa: Royal Society of Canada, 2012).

197 Rather, some lives are disproportionately affected: In the early research (1950s and '60s) on stressful life events and their relation to human health, investigators such as Lawrence Hinkle and Harold Wolff meticulously recorded the month-by-month, year-by-year occurrences of such events within individual lives. See, for example, L. E. Hinkle and H. G. Wolff, "The Nature of Man's Adaptation to His Total Environment and the Relation of This to Illness," *Archives of Internal Medicine* 99 (1957): 442–60. What Hinkle and Wolff discovered was that adverse events clustered within biographical time, tending to occur in temporal groups rather than randomly over the course of an individual life. Some, but not all, of this clustering could be attributed to the ways in which one stressful event can lead to another. Divorce, for example, is often attended by a residential move. But the observation of such clustering, though repeatedly recorded by stressful events researchers, has never been fully explained.

10 The Sins of the Fathers, the Means of Grace

207 In the early twentieth century: The Lamarckian scientific exploits of one Paul Kammerer, an early-twentieth-century Austrian biologist, are intriguingly recounted in Arthur Koestler's book *The Case of the Midwife Toad* (New York: Random House, 1971). By changing the temperature of toads' aquatic environments, Kammerer claimed to have switched their breeding venues from land to water and thereby fostered the cross-generational development of "nuptial pads" on their legs to facilitate aquatic encounters.

207 "Lamarck, Wake Up": Denyse O'Leary, "Epigenetic Change: Lamarck, Wake Up, You're Wanted in the Conference Room!," *Evolution News & Science Today*, August 25, 2015, www.evolutionnews.org/2015/08/epigenetic_chan/.

208 Here was a suggestion that: E. Susser, H. W. Hoek, and A. Brown, "Neurodevelopmental Disorders After Prenatal Famine: The Story of the Dutch

Famine Study," *American Journal of Epidemiology* 147, no. 3 (1998): 213–16; U. G. Kyle and C. Pichard, "The Dutch Famine of 1944–1945: A Pathophysiological Model of Long-Term Consequences of Wasting Disease," *Current Opinion in Clinical Nutrition and Metabolic Care* 9, no. 4 (2006): 388–94.

208 First, David Barker's work on the developmental origins: D. J. Barker and C. Osmond, "Infant Mortality, Childhood Nutrition, and Ischaemic Heart Disease in England and Wales," *Lancet* 327, no. 8489 (1986): 1077–81.

208 Such individuals clearly show excessive rates: M. E. Bowers and R. Yehuda, "Intergenerational Transmission of Stress in Humans," *Neuropsychopharmacology* 41, no. 1 (2016): 232–44.

209 Here again, exposure to a life-threatening, traumatic event: R. Yehuda et al., "Transgenerational Effects of Posttraumatic Stress Disorder in Babies of Mothers Exposed to the World Trade Center Attacks During Pregnancy," *Journal of Clinical Endocrinology and Metabolism* 90, no. 7 (2005): 4115–18.

209 Finally, more recent evidence: L. Taouk and J. Schulkin, "Transgenerational Transmission of Pregestational and Prenatal Experience: Maternal Adversity, Enrichment, and Underlying Epigenetic and Environmental Mechanisms," *Journal of Developmental Origins of Health and Disease* 7, no. 6 (2016): 588–601; T. Garland Jr., M. D. Cadney, and R. A. Waterland, "Early-Life Effects on Adult Physical Activity: Concepts, Relevance, and Experimental Approaches," *Physiological and Biochemical Zoology* 90, no. 1 (2017): 1–14.

211 One example of this second form: B. G. Dias and K. J. Ressler, "Parental Olfactory Experience Influences Behavior and Neural Structure in Subsequent Generations," *Nature Neuroscience* 17, no. 1 (2014): 89–96.

213 In at least some species: For a fuller account of evidence for and mechanisms of intergenerational (i.e., two-generational) and transgenerational (i.e., three-generational) epigenetic inheritance, readers are referred to: (a) S. D. van Otterdijk and K. B. Michels, "Transgenerational Epigenetic Inheritance in Mammals: How Good Is the Evidence?," *FASEB Journal* 30, no. 7 (2016): 2457–65; or (b) T. Klengel, B. G. Dias, and K. J. Ressler, "Models of Intergenerational and Transgenerational Transmission of Risk for Psychopathology in Mice," *Neuropsychopharmacology* 41, no. 1 (2016): 219–31. It is important to note that even when epigenetic processes are involved in the "programming" of offspring phenotypes, this does not necessitate transgenerational epigenetic inheritance. The groundbreaking work of Meaney and colleagues, for example (described in chapter 6), showed that epigenetic marks on the cortisol receptor gene governed cor-

tisol reactivity in rat pups and that such marks were regulated by the level of their mothers' licking and grooming. This does not imply, however, that such epigenetic marks were embryonically transferred from mothers to pups. The low or high licking and grooming behaviors were transferred from one generation to a second and third, but the transfer was likely behavioral in mechanism, rather than one of germline inheritance.

215 "Mystery is a great embarrassment": Flannery O'Connor, "The Teaching of Literature," in *Mystery and Manners: Occasional Prose* (New York: Farrar, Straus and Giroux, 1969), 124.

215 For me, that sheltering, sometimes (alas) embarrassing mystery: M. Guite, "Ascension" (sonnet), https://malcolmguite.wordpress.com/2011/06/02/ascension-day-sonnet/.

Conclusion: Helping All Children Thrive

218 And yet our elegant, finely attuned brains: It is interesting to note, however, that there are people with a rare capacity for exceptional, "autobiographical" memory—who can recall, for example, what they had for lunch twenty years ago on a Tuesday in November (see Gary Stix, "Exceptional Memory Explained: How Some People Remember What They Had for Lunch 20 Years Ago," *Scientific American*, November 16, 2011, http://blogs.scientific american.com/observations/group-with-exceptional-memory-remembers -what-was-for-lunch-20-years-ago/). To date, there is no evidence for obvious structural or neurobiological functional differences in their brains, nor is there evidence that such capacity serves some valuable role in their lives.

224 We were thus able to show: W. T. Boyce et al., "Immunologic Changes Occurring at Kindergarten Entry Predict Respiratory Illnesses Following the Loma Prieta Earthquake," *Journal of Developmental and Behavioral Pediatrics* 14, no. 5 (1993): 296–303.

226 And even then, there must have been: There is a substantial body of psychological evidence that the act of disclosing trauma and negative emotion ameliorates to some extent the health costs of having experienced threat and adversity. See, for example, J. W. Pennebaker and J. R. Susman, "Disclosure of Traumas and Psychosomatic Processes," *Social Science and Medicine* 26, no. 3 (1988): 327–32.

232 Most elementally, the vulnerability/resilience assumption: In his 1949 book *The Concept of Mind*, Gilbert Ryle suggested that to attribute the phenomena of mind and rationality to immaterial processes, as Cartesian mind-body dualism famously did, was to commit a category error—that is,

mistakenly attributing something of one category to another. In one of his examples, a child watching a military parade of battalions, batteries, and squadrons asks when the division is going to come. The child has regarded a division, in error, as of the same category as battalions, batteries, and squadrons, not understanding that these are all components of the division. G. Ryle, *The Concept of Mind* (San Francisco: Barnes & Noble, 1949).

Postscript: What They Asked

244 In Alice Miller's book: Alice Miller. *The Drama of the Gifted Child: The Search for the True Self* (New York: Basic Books, 1997).

244 There is now a half century's worth of research: Barbara H. Fiese, Thomas J. Tomcho, et al., "A review of 50 years of research on naturally occurring family routines and rituals: Cause for celebration?" *Journal of Family Psychology* 16, no. 4 (2002): 381–390. https://doi.org/10.1037/0893-3200.16.4.381.

244 Back in the 1980s we studied a group: W. Thomas Boyce, Catherine Schaefer, and Chris Uitti, "Permanence and change: Psychosocial Factors in the Outcomes of Adolescent Pregnancy," *Social Science & Medicine* 21, no. 11 (1985): 1279–1287.

251 One nicely presented aid to such a talk: Jean Little, *Jess Was the Brave One* (New York: Viking Kestrel Picture Books, 1992).

253 In the Bucharest Early Intervention Project: Charles A. Nelson, Nathan A. Fox, and Charles H. Zeanah, *Romania's Abandoned Children* (Cambridge, MA: Harvard University Press, 2014).

Index

Page numbers in *italics* refer to illustrations.

Permissions Acknowledgments